Geoff Dyer is the author of three novels: *Paris Trance*, *The Search*, *The Colour of Memory*; a critical study of John Berger, *Ways of Telling*; a collection of essays, *Anglo-English Attitudes*; and four genre-defying titles: *But Beautiful* (winner of the 1992 Somerset Maugham Prize, shortlisted for the *Mail on Sunday*/John Llewellyn Rhys Memorial Prize), *The Missing of the Somme*, *Out of Sheer Rage* (a finalist, in America, for a National Book Critics Circle Award) and *Yoga For People Who Can't Be Bothered to Do It*. He is also the editor of *John Berger: Selected Essays* and co-editor, with Margaret Sartor, of *What Was True: The Photographs and Notebooks of William Gedney*. Geoff Dyer is a recipient of a 2003 Lannan Literary Fellowship. He lives in London.

'A natural essayist' David Sexton, *Evening Standard*

'Geoff Dyer is a writer whom I would unhesitatingly recommend to anyone . . . Dyer's style – and the breadth of his intelligence – absorbs, impresses and simply entertains' *Time Out*

'For the sheer diversity of his passions, his career is already hard to beat' Simon Garfield, *Financial Times*

'A treasure box of delights' *Scotsman*

'A consummate stylist' *Birmingham Post*

'One of the most rewarding books to emerge from Britain in the last twelve months, "fiction" and "non-fiction" alike' *Modern Painters*

Anglo-English Attitudes

Essays, Reviews, Misadventures 1984–99

Geoff Dyer

An *Abacus* Book

First published in Great Britain by Abacus in 1999
This edition published in 2004

Collection copyright © Geoff Dyer 1999

The moral right of the author has been asserted.

A CIP catalogue record for this book
is available from the British Library.

ISBN 0 349 11195 2

Typeset in Berkeley by M Rules
Printed and bound in Great Britain
by Clays Ltd, St Ives plc

Lines from 'Egon Schiele' by Jeremy Reed (from *Nineties*, Cape 1990) and 'Las
Casas' by Michael Hofmann (from *Corona, Corona*, Faber 1993) are reproduced
by kind permission of the authors. Lines from 'September 1, 1939' by W. H.
Auden (from *The English Auden*) are reproduced by kind permission of Faber
and Faber Ltd.

Original publication details for each piece appear in
the acknowledgements on pp 363–364

Abacus
An imprint of
Time Warner Books UK
Brettenham House
Lancaster Place
London WC2E 7EN

www.TimeWarnerBooks.co.uk

This book is for Chris Mitchell
and for Charles De Ledesma

Contents

List of Illustrations   x

Introduction   1

Blues for Vincent   7
Ecce Homo   11
Violets of Pride   20

Jacques Henri Lartigue   27
Henri Cartier-Bresson   31
Robert Capa   39
If I Die in a Combat Zone   52
W. Eugene Smith   61
Robert Doisneau   65
Leaf Reed Land-er   69
William Gedney   74
Nan Goldin   95
Andres Serrano   100
Richard Misrach   105

Atkinson Grimshaw   115
The Life of Paul Gauguin   119

Pierre Bonnard   129
Edvard Munch   132
Egon Schiele   136

The Airfix Generation   141
Action Man   149
Unpacking My Library   156
Comics in a Man's Life   162

Albert Camus   171
The Life of Roland Barthes   189
Louis Althusser   195
The Life of Graham Greene   199
Milan Kundera   203
Jayne Anne Phillips   208
Richard Ford   211
Michael Ondaatje   219
Cormac McCarthy   223
Jay McInerney   232
Martin Amis   237

Pounding Print   241
Muhammad Ali   247

John Carey   251
Artificial Stupidity   257
Fred-Perry: Jameson and Anderson   261
The Absent Woman: Janet Malcolm   266

'My Favorite Things'   271
Nusrat Fateh Ali Khan   278
Rabih Abou-Khalil   282
Nils Petter Molvær   291

Ramamani 294

The Guidebook 297
Oradour-sur-Glane 304
Parting Shots 312

Def Leppard and the Anthropology
of Supermodernity 319
The Ghost and the Darkness: Safari Notes 326
The Wrong Stuff 338
Point Break 351

Cherry Street 359

Acknowledgments 363

Index of Names 367

List of Illustrations

p. 15   Chris Smith: 'Barry McGuigan: Las Vegas 1986'

p. 16   Antonello da Messina: 'Ecce Homo (detail)' (K&B News Foto, Florence/Bridgeman Art Library)

p. 17   Gentile Bellini: 'Pieta (detail)' (AKG London/Cameraphoto)

p. 49   Robert Capa: 'Near Nicosia, Sicily July 28, 1943' (Magnum)

p. 45   Henri Huet: 'War Zone C, Vietnam, 1965' (Associated Press)

p. 59   Henri Huet: 'Chu Lai, Vietnam, 1965: US Marine Corps chaplain John Monamara of Boston administers the last rites to dying war correspondent Dickey Chapelle' (Associated Press)

p. 70   Lee Friedlander: 'New York City, 1985' (courtesy of the photographer)

p. 85   William Gedney: 'Eastern Kentucky, 1972' (Special Collections Library, Duke University)

p. 91   William Gedney: 'India, 1969–71' (Special Collections Library, Duke University)

p. 92   William Gedney: 'Eastern Kentucky, 1966' (Special Collections Library, Duke University)

p. 116   Atkinson Grimshaw: 'Silver Moonlight', 1886 (Harrogate Museums and Art Gallery/Bridgeman Art Library)

p. 169   Andrea Pozzo: 'The Triumph of Saint Ignatius (detail)', 1694 (Alinari/Art Resource, NY)

p. 192   'Roland Barthes, Paris, 1963' (private collection)

p. 339   Peter Marlow: 'Author, Moscow, 1994' (Magnum)

One might reasonably ask: why tigers instead of leopards or jaguars? I can only answer that spots are not pleasing to me, while stripes are. If I were to write *leopard* instead of tiger the reader would immediately sense that I was lying.

Borges

Introduction

When writers have achieved a high enough profile they are sometimes prevailed upon to publish their 'occasional pieces' (i.e. their journalism). The author agrees, reluctantly, modestly – Martin Amis offered his first collection, *The Moronic Inferno*, 'with all generic humility' – because this kind of put-together is considered a pretty low form of book, barely a book at all.

My own case – and my own opinion of such collections – is a little different. For a start it was my publisher who was prevailed upon and I was the one doing the prevailing. Almost as soon as I began writing for magazines and newspapers I hoped one day to see my articles published in book form. If a piece was mauled by editors or subs I consoled myself with the thought that one day I would see it re-published exactly as intended, in a book. (With this option in mind I often sent off one version for immediate publication, and kept another, longer one for future use.) If we're being utterly frank, there were times when it was only the prospect of one day being able to publish my journalism that kept me writing 'proper' books: do a few more novels, I reasoned, and maybe my obscurity will be sufficiently lessened to permit publication of the book I really care about, a collection of my bits and pieces.

I especially wanted to publish such a book because I virtually never read the review pages of newspapers or magazines. If I see a piece by a writer I admire in a paper I very rarely read it; but as I look through catalogues of forthcoming books the ones that catch my eye are collections of exactly these pieces that I have neglected to read in their original context. Since I prefer to read other people's journalism in book form, it's not just vanity that makes me want to see my own presented that way too. When I broached the possibility – at first, hesitantly, hypothetically, around the third glass of wine, then, increasingly shamelessly, before we'd even ordered our starters – my editor asked if these pieces would be linked, if there might be some way of passing off these bits and bobs as a coherent book organised around a defining theme. Would it be possible, for example, to compile a book of my writings about photography? Or American writers?

Possible, yes, but, from my point of view, not at all desirable because it was, precisely, the unruly range of my concerns that I was keen to see represented in a single volume. I wanted the book to serve as proof of just how thoroughly my career (though I should add immediately that writing, for me, has always been a way of *not* having a career) had avoided any focus, specialism or continuity except that dictated by my desire to write about whatever I happened to be interested in at any given moment.

It seemed to me – or so I claimed at the four- or five-glass mark – that this variegation might even give the collection a kind of unity or coherence. The *more* varied the pieces, I argued, the more obviously they needed to be seen together as the work of one person – because the only thing they had in common was that they were *by* that person. If there was one thing I was proud of in my literary non-career it was the way that I had written so many different kinds of books; to assemble a collection of articles would be further proof of just how wayward my interests were. Such a collection would also show that I had remained faithful to the example of my mentor, John Berger. In *Ways of*

Telling, my dull little book about him, I claimed that Berger's ability to write on so many different subjects in so many different ways was an indication not only of his ability but also his *success* as a writer; over the years this was exactly the kind of success, of freedom, I tried to carve out for myself. Introducing his collection of articles on French writers and thinkers, *The Word from Paris*, John Sturrock counsels that literary journalists 'do well professionally to have a territory that is known to be theirs, and not to lay claim to a diffuse expertise qualifying them to write about anyone or anything.' If Sturrock's right – and he almost certainly is – then I feel very fortunate to have remained conspicuously in the wrong for so long.

A distinction is often made between writers' own work – which they do for themselves – and the stuff they do for money. The ideal, in this scenario, is to be able to devote all your time to your own writing. Again, my case is rather different. Most of the journalism I do is as much my own writing as, well, my own writing. Whereas Martin Amis talks about writing his *Moronic Inferno* pieces 'left-handed', tailoring them for the particular audience of whichever publication had commissioned him, all these pieces were written right-handed (metaphorically speaking, since I am naturally left-handed). That is to say, I have always written without any regard for a tacit target audience. Subject or mood always dictated the form and style of these pieces, not the publications for which they were intended. Often they weren't intended for anywhere; I wrote them and sent them off, on spec as they say, like short stories, hoping someone, eventually, would take them.

If something occurs that moves me deeply – the kind of experience that might provide inspiration for a poet – my instinct is not to weave it into the *he said/she said* of fiction but to articulate and analyse it in an essay. I feel at home in essays. They're what I most enjoy reading and writing. When I left university I thought being a writer meant you wrote novels; either that or you were a critic who wrote about writers' novels. A few years later, during what I still regard as my period of most intense intellectual development (aka, living on the dole in Brixton), I discovered Roland Barthes, Walter Benjamin, Nietzsche, Raymond Williams and, crucially, Berger, and realised there was another way of being a writer, one that I might aspire to. Like Aldous Huxley, then, I consider myself 'some kind of essayist sufficiently ingenious to get away with writing a very limited kind of fiction.' The life of the long-haul novelist, moreover, has never seemed as attractive to me as one which was made up of all sorts of different kinds of writing, including periods of fictioning. What could be nicer than one day to be doing a review of Althusser's autobiography and the next to be going off to Moscow to write about flying a MiG-29? Put like that, the pipe-smoking scribe with leather patches on his elbows might seem like a relic or fossil from a bygone era of literariness; on the other hand, this M & A (MiG-and-Althusser) style of freelancing represents the contemporary embodiment of a deeply traditional idea of the man of letters. Would it be immodest to claim that this book gives a glimpse of a not unrepresentative way of being a late-twentieth-century man of letters?

I was twenty when I read of Hazlitt's 'First Acquaintance with Poets' and knew immediately that I wanted to emulate this man who had 'loitered [his] life away, reading books, looking at pictures, going to plays, hearing, thinking, writing on what pleased [him] best.' What could be better (assuming, of course, that you substitute 'films' for 'plays')? A crucial part of such a life is that you loiter – with no intent of entering – outside of the academy, unhindered by specialisms (obviously) and the rigours of imposed method. As I grew older I came increasingly to feel that my working life should be virtually synonymous with living my life as I wanted, irrespective of whether I was doing any work. Effectively, as my American publisher put it, I had found a way of being paid for leading my life. I liked that a lot, naturally, and I liked the way that the hazards of this life led me from one passion to another. Increasingly at ease with the vagaries of my nature, I came to relish the way that getting interested in one thing led to my becoming very interested in something else – so interested, in fact, that I invariably lost interest in whatever it was that, a little while previously, had transfixed me utterly. Out of this relay of awakened and abandoned interests a haphazard kind of narrative hopefully emerges in the pages that follow.

Reviewing books, trying to have some say in the fate of writers and their work, is something I've never tired of. Because they were such important books I assumed initially that reviews of *Fugitive Pieces* by Anne Michaels, *The Sorrow of War* by Bao Ninh, *The Soccer War* by Ryszard Kapuściński, *Libra* by Don DeLillo, *Extinction* by Thomas Bernhard – to mention some obvious ones – would be included here. It quickly became clear that many of these pieces – especially those from the late 1980s – were too short to make the cut (a thousand words is the minimum condition of entry to this volume). Either that or they came to seem of value only in the context of that initial intervention in the critical marketplace. So they, and a great many others beside, have gone – including the piece from which this volume takes its title. 'Anglo-English Attitudes' is all that remains of an essay – published in the first *New Writing* anthology – in which I examined (or, it seems to me now, *failed* to examine) the consequences of the fact that, in contrast to writers who were Anglo-Indian, Anglo-Chinese or Anglo-Whatever, I was English through and through (my parents are English, so were my grandparents): Anglo-English, in fact.

Blues for Vincent

It must be four years ago that I first saw Zadkine's sculpture of Vincent and Theo Van Gogh in one of the museums in Amsterdam. Carved in angular-cubist style, the sculpture is of two men sitting, one with his arm around the other's shoulders. I think their heads are touching but I could easily be wrong (works of art that affect you deeply are seldom quite as you remember them). Unusually for a piece so thoroughly committed to the language of cubism the sculpture works on us very simply, directly addressing the humanity of its subjects where normally the cubist effect distorts and dislocates. Rarely has the hardness of stone been coaxed into such softness.

Zadkine wanted his sculpture to express the relationship of dependency and trust that existed between Vincent and his brother; in doing so he reveals all the tenderness of which men are capable of offering each other.

It is not immediately obvious which of Zadkine's figures is Vincent and which is Theo. Like all who relieve the suffering of others Theo – in a process that is the exact opposite of a blood transfusion – has taken some of Vincent's pain into himself. Soon, however, it becomes obvious that while the sky weighs heavily on both figures, one, Vincent, feels gravity as a force so terrible it can drag men beneath the earth. From this moment on you are held by the pathos and beauty of what Zadkine depicts: despair that is inconsolable, comfort that is endless. One figure says: *I can never feel better*; the other: *I will hold you until you are better.*

Last night, a few yards from where I am living, on Third Street, just off Avenue B, I saw a homeless guy the same age as I am (I guessed he was my age because he looked twice that age) grabbing his head and hurling himself at a storefront, falling to the floor screaming, lying still for a few seconds and then, exhausted but still in the grips of this frenzy, picking himself up and doing it again. An hour later he was unconscious on the sidewalk.

Each morning people are sprawled in the streets, so deeply comatose that even the indifferent kicks of cops fail to rouse them. Throughout the day the destitute and the addicted, the insane and the desperate, sit in pairs in doorways and on steps, heads bowed, hearing each other out or reaching out an arm while the other groans and shivers.

I see your face everywhere, wandering through it like rain and the drifting steam of streets. I wake at four in the morning and think of you doing ordinary things: hunting for your glasses that you can never find, taking the tube to work, buying wine at the supermarket.

Before I unlock the mailbox I can tell if there is a letter from you. I long for your letters and dread the announcements and decisions they might contain, spend whole days waiting for you to call.

I pick up the phone on the second ring, hear an American voice say:

'Hi, how ya doin'?'

'Fine.'

'What's happenin'?'

'Who is this?'

'I'm just somebody callin' up.'

'What about?'

'I'm just a guy hangin' out. So how ya doin'?'

'What?'

'Ah, I'm feelin' kind of low.'

'So I don't know you?'

'No.'

'I can't talk to you, man.'

'No . . .?' As if he had *eternity* on his hands.

At eight – one in the morning London time – I call you, the familiar English tones becoming bleak after six rings. In case you are just coming through the door I let it ring another ten times, hoping that when you return you will be able to tell I have called, furniture and walls preserving a message there was no answering machine to receive: I miss you, I want you, I love you. Then I just let it ring, the phone pressed to my head like a pistol.

Halfway through the closing set of a week-long stint at a club in Greenwich Village, David Murray announces 'Ballad for the Black Man'.

Murray started off as an energy player but in recent years he's been digging back into the tradition and now sounds like a whole history of the tenor saxophone: in his playing you can hear Ayler, Coltrane, Rollins, Webster . . .

In the same way, 'Ballad for the Black Man' contains the cry of all the spirituals and sorrow songs, all the blues there have ever been. Murray's solo lasts for ten minutes, climaxing with notes so high they disappear, as if a part of the song were not addressed to human ears at all. The blues is like that, not something you *play* but a way of calling out to the dead, to all the dead slaves of America.

The message of the blues is simple: as long as there are people on earth they will have need of this music. In a way, then, the blues is about its own survival. It's the shelter the black man has built, not only for himself but for anyone who needs it. Not just a shelter – a home. No suffering is so unendurable that it cannot find expression, no pain is so intense that it cannot be lessened – this is the promise at the heart of the blues. It cannot heal but it can hold us, can lay a hand around a brother's shoulder and say:

You will find a home, if not in her arms, then here, in these blues.

(for Fi)
1989

Ecce Homo

This summer I have spent many afternoons near the Louvre, in the Jardin des Tuileries, lying on the scorched grass, looking at the statues. I am not sure which mythical or biblical characters are depicted (though I guess that the one in chains might be Prometheus). My appreciation of the statues would be greatly improved, I am sure, by some kind of mythological guidebook or commentary but, even without one, the essential concerns of the statues are obvious: punishment and suffering, agony and ecstasy.

Tourists look up at the statues and photograph them. Sightless, the statues never return their gaze. In classical tragedy blindness is a frequent affliction and in Tuileries, too, some of the statues seem either to have been blinded or – and it amounts to the same thing – to have been condemned to the lidless torment of never shutting their eyes.

Those who sentenced the statues to their varied fates – the Gods? their sculptors? – have gone. Only the statues and the indifferent sky remain, *endure*. Always, in some way, the figures are resisting, or trying to rise. One – Prometheus? – strains against his chains, against gravity, toward the sky. This sense of strain is so great that the statues seem to be struggling to free themselves of the stone in which they are cast. The medium through which they strain to free themselves is the body in which they are imprisoned.

The statues are immersed so completely in their exertions that the rest of us, even those who jog past in shorts and trainers, seem engaged in a form of more or less active lolling. This is what gives the figures their enduring appeal.

In late August, with the sun blaring from a soundless sky, the World Athletics Championships begin. I have borrowed a TV and reception is poor; there is no aerial, just a coat hanger jabbed into the back of the set. The commentary is in French and I understand little of what is said. Still, grateful to have a TV at all, I peer through a molecular buzz of snow as athletes strain to defy gravity, to push back the limits of the physical. Lacking the context-forming commentary, I watch Carl Lewis break the 100 metres record. Katrin Krabbe wins both the women's sprints. In the final leg of the 400 metres relay, Kriss Akabusi charges past Antonio Pettigrew . . .

What with the poor picture quality and the French commentary I am often unsure of exactly what is happening (contrary extremes of passion – tears and laughter, rage and celebration – curiously resemble each other) and so, each morning, I buy an English paper to check what occurred the day before. The morning after the 100 metres final, it was reported that, in post-race interviews, Lewis had cried several times when mentioning his dead father. A few hours before the race Leroy Burrell, who came second, had received news that, following heart surgery, his father had come out of intensive care. Drawn two lanes to the left of Lewis, he did not have a clear view of his rival because he is blind in his left eye. The article is accompanied by a photograph of all eight runners as Lewis crossed the line, arms raised in triumph and vindication.

For every image of triumph like this, however, there is one of dejection, for the strength and power of athletes coexists with extraordinary fragility. Jackie Joyner-Kersee falls and sprains her ankle in the long jump, crashes to the floor in her sprint heat; Steve Cram strains a groin – not in training but while getting off a train. The athlete's body is a precipice and victory involves advancing close to – and even, for Ben Johnson or boxer Johnny Owen, beyond – its edge.

I don't know, but I suspect that the statues in Tuileries are not particularly outstanding pieces of sculpture. If this is the case then they reveal how, at certain moments in the tradition of any art, the expressive potential of the average can exceed that of the outstanding at earlier or later dates. Nowadays, for example, the human form cannot so readily be coaxed into such impressive attitudes; only an exceptional artist today could achieve the power routinely managed by the sculptors whose work is displayed in Tuileries. (In sport the opposite is true: most top athletes now surpass the record-breaking feats of thirty years ago.) Partly this is because of internal, art historical exhaustion; but it is also because the hunger that such sculptures sought to assuage is now satisfied by sport. More precisely, sport both answers and simultaneously exacerbates that need in such a way that it is incapable of being satisfied by carved or moulded stone. Most obviously, the increasingly sculpted bodies of athletes have now gone beyond the ideal that once could only be achieved in stone (the posing of boxer Chris Eubanks and the strength-sapping stillness and balance of gymnasts make this point literally). More broadly, in the age of mass media, only images of war and famine offer a starker revelation and depiction than sport of the human body in *extremis* as key moments are slowed down, expanded, replayed and, ultimately, frozen. This enables us to dissect visually athletes striving to burst free of the confines and limits of the body. In slow-motion and close-up the glimpses of straining sinews, swollen muscles, even that strange bobbing of the sprinter's lower lip, are revealed and preserved. What remains of the 100 metres final, or Akabusi's lunge for the line, is a succession of slowed or frozen moments, of photographs. Long after the event is over and the cameras have departed the athlete remains captured in passed time, like a statue.

The extent to which photographs like these duplicate attitudes found in sculpture is often startling; in the case of a picture of boxer Barry McGuigan we actually have to draw on the art historical past to explain why it works on us so powerfully.

The photo was taken by Chris Smith just before the last round of McGuigan's unsuccessful world featherweight title defence against Steve Cruz in Las Vegas in 1986. The effect of the photo is immediate and direct: there is pain turning into numbness, exhaustion – for any boxer physical exhaustion is always ontological exhaustion: he senses not just his energy but his *being* draining away – and a courage that, through years of training, is a matter of reflex. An active representative of our own compassion, the black trainer rubs the head of the white fighter (a reversal of the usual racial roles) as tenderly as a mother soothing her child. Perhaps he whispers encouragement but, at this distance from the everyday, words are meaningless.

What makes the photograph so haunting, though, is the way that it elides a number of common and closely related (so closely related they tend, in memory, like the statues in Tuileries, to blur into each other) Renaissance representations of Christ. Most obviously, McGuigan's glazed eyes are illuminated by the unfocused agony of the Passion (see, for example, Antonella da Messina's *Ecce Homo* on page 16) with the corner-post and top rope forming a cross just behind his head.

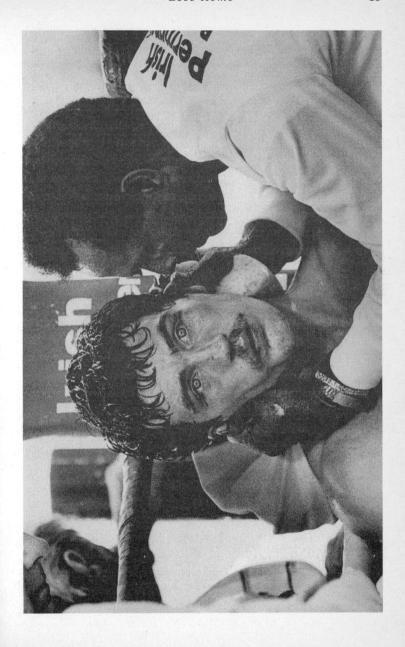

More generally, the arrangement of the figures in the photograph is uncannily reminiscent of any number of Pietàs or
Depositions in which the dead Christ is taken down from the
cross and mourned by the Virgin and others. Earlier I wrote that
the trainer's touch was as tender as any mother's; in Smith's

photo and in paintings by Giotto and Bellini (whose Christ, below, has the sinewy body of a featherweight) there is the same attempt to breathe life back into the battered body, to restore it to life. There is even a similarity between the simple accessories of the trainer – sponge, ointment, towel – and the traditional instruments of the passion (nails, sponges and so on).

Though Christ is dead when he is taken down from the cross, the Resurrection is often implicit in representations of the scene (in Bellini it is as if Christ is being helped to his feet). For McGuigan, the Resurrection of the last round – short-lived though it will be – is only seconds away, and in Smith's photo he shares with images of the Resurrected Christ the devastating look of someone who has gone beyond the physical limits of the body.

Smith's is not a great photograph *because* of these art historical parallels (like all great photographs there is something

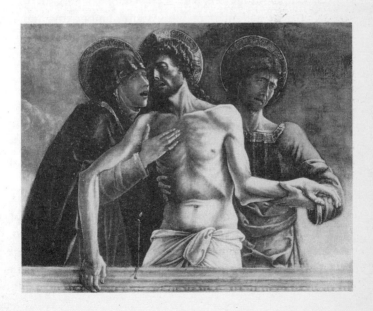

startlingly felicitous – lucky – about it). However, for 2,000 years the single most potent image in Western culture has been of a man, almost naked, in the extremes of exhaustion and pain – on the very brink of life and death – while others look on. With this in mind it is not surprising that the photograph *holds* us. Moreover, boxing, with its naked suffering and triumphs, lends itself to a vocabulary at once relentlessly violent and strangely religious: the vocabulary of the Bible (the Old Testament primarily), of tragedy. After the devastating Ali–Frazier fight in Manilla, one witness recalls finding Frazier lying in bed in semi-darkness:

> Only his heavy breathing disturbed the quiet as an old friend walked to within two feet. 'Who is it?' asked Joe Frazier, lifting himself to look around. 'Who is it? I can't see! Turn the lights on!' Another light was turned on, but Frazier still could not see. The scene cannot be forgotten; this good and gallant man lying there, embodying the remains of a will that had carried him so far – and now surely too far. His eyes were only slits, his face looked *as if it had been painted by Goya.* [My italics.]

Or by Holbein, specifically his *Body of the Dead Christ in the Tomb*, the painting that so disturbed Dostoyevsky: 'In the picture the face is terribly smashed with blows, tumefied, covered with terrible, swollen, and bloodstained bruises, the eyes open and squinting . . .'

Years later, Frazier looked back and elaborated further: 'I'm a hard man. I can look at you hard enough to make tears come out of your eyes. And I'm a proud man. I do whatever I got to do, whatever it is that's got to be done. That's the kind of man I am . . . I hit [Ali] punches, those punches, they'd of knocked a building down. And he took 'em.'

Looking back on the first Madison Square Garden fight of 1971, Ferdie Pacheco, Ali's doctor, observed: 'He [Ali] was going to get up if he was dead. If Frazier had killed him, he'd have gotten up.'*

Earlier I wrote of how photographs of sport replicate gestures from the art of the past. This is fascinating but it provides the means to go further and see how sport, serving the same needs as the myths and religious traditions utilised by sculpture and painting, offers its own culture of parable, tragedy and redemption – its own art; how sport affords the same potential for the expression of genius, passion and vision which our culture often considers the preserve of opera, sculpture, painting

There is a fair at the edge of the park. The air is full of screams from girls on the rides; the statues, meanwhile, maintain a stony silence. Summer is almost over. Many of the tourists have departed; tanned Parisians are returning from their holidays. I am reading on the grass. Nearby, some boys are annoying everyone by playing football. A mis-kick curls the ball towards one of the statues. Neck muscles tensed, it appears as if the stone figure is straining up to reach for the ball. There is a cheer as he heads clear and then play continues. I wish I had a camera to record that moment, to capture it.

1991

---

*All quotations about Ali and Frazier are from Thomas Hauser, *Muhammad Ali: His Life and Times*, 1991.

Violets of Pride

In April I returned to Gloucestershire for my Uncle Eric's funeral. He had killed himself in his car and then, from a combustion of gases, the car had burst into flames. The garage was destroyed and part of the house was also damaged by fire.

My uncle had built this house himself. During the day he worked as a bricklayer and then, in the evenings and at weekends, he worked on his own home. He had first tried to kill himself, my father explained after the funeral, soon after completing his house.

On the day of his funeral I took the first train from Paddington. Hurtling, slowly, towards Gloucestershire I read Ivor Gurney's *Collected Poems* with a mixture of admiration and frustration. Gurney was born in Gloucester in 1890 and wrote about the county obsessively. In poems written from the trenches during the First World War he exclaims again and again how – a source of comfort and torment – the landscape of northern France resembles Gloucestershire. Appropriately, his first volume of poetry, published in 1917, was entitled *Severn and Somme*.

My father met me at Stroud, dressed in his black suit. Near Painswick we stopped at a layby where I changed into a freshly laundered white shirt and black tie that he had brought with him.

My mother was waiting at Eric's house in Shurdington. Eric's wife – my father's sister, Dink – was there and so were his daughter, Anne, and his grandchildren. One side of the house, where the garage had been, was blackened by fire. Some of Eric's tools had been cleaned and set out by the door. There were five or six separate items but the only one I was able to name with confidence was the trowel.

We walked to the church which was just a few minutes up the lane. Other relatives were waiting there, many of whom I had not seen for ten years or more. No one had changed much, not even Auntie Lena who, since I last saw her, had won half a million pounds on the pools.

My grandfathers were farm labourers. Both sides of the family have given their lives to carrying and digging, to hard labour. We should have evolved stocky, broad backs but by some genetic fluke most of us have the build of House of Usher aristocrats. Like me, my father and his brother Jim are six foot two and thin as rakes. Eric himself was over six foot and his brother Marce, one of the bearers, is even taller, even thinner.

The coffin was carried from the hearse into the churchyard. We walked past the graves of my father's parents who died within six months of each other in 1956, two years before I was born. The writing on their grave is kept clean by my father's sister, Joan. She never married and still lives in the house where they all grew up together.

My father rarely speaks about my grandfather. It was only recently I learned that, in the Great War, he served with the Gloucesters, with Gurney's regiment.

During any crisis or difficulty my parents are the first people anyone in the family turns to. My father especially is the man everyone knows they can depend on. He is seventy-one and my mother is sixty-six but after Eric had been buried they helped his son, Ian, to clear away the black rubble of the old garage and build a new one. It was my father who found the note Eric had left scrawled on a piece of paper: 'I am sorry but I can't go on. God bless you all.' When Dink left to go to work he kissed her goodbye and then, later in the morning, made his way to the garage.

I sat by my father during the service. He has always hated everything to do with the church. When we rose to sing he held the hymn book at arm's length but refrained from looking at it. (Hymns in a man's life: he liked some of the tunes, he said later, but didn't go much on the words.) When we knelt to pray he did not even bow his head. I have never felt more proud of him than I did then, my eyes full of tears, our long legs crammed against the pew in front.

During the vicar's eulogy he explained how Eric had 'emigrated' from Guiting Power, a village ten miles away, before making Shurdington his home. He was 'a stone mason', the vicar explained. I thought of Jude, the stone mason who wants to be an Oxford student but ends up maintaining the walls that exclude him. Eric's monuments, the vicar was saying, could be seen in all the villages around Shurdington in the shape of the houses he built. His greatest monument was the house that had almost been destroyed by his death, the one he built for his family. Finally, the vicar said, he was a good man. It was a conventional phrase but the weight of those two words was enormous. He was good and he was a man. A man in the only sense of the word that matters, the one defined by a quiet passage in Lawrence: 'To be brave, to keep one's word, to be generous.'

The coffin was borne outside. Anne supported her mother as she tossed some earth on to the coffin.

We went back to Dink's house, where my mother had made tea and sandwiches. Soon the garden was full of tall people drinking and eating. The weather was perfect and from the

garden we could see the churchyard where Eric now lay. Blue
sky, a few slow clouds. Sheep nibbling the fields beyond the
brook. When I shook his wife's hand Ian introduced me as 'a
graduate of Oxford University'. Later, Marce, Eric's brother,
talked to me about the War, the Second that is. He had been with
Montgomery's Eighth Army in the North African campaign and
then in Italy. After he was demobbed – and he had never told
this to anyone before, he said – he was so revolted by the army,
by the things he had seen and done, that he took his uniform
and all his papers and burned them in Guiting woods.

For the rest of his life he had suffered from nightmares and
depression. But on that side of the family, my father explained
when we were back home, there was a history of depression. It
was then that he told me of Eric's earlier attempts at suicide.

The three of us – my mother, my father and me – ate our
lunch and talked about Eric's funeral. It was Ian who insisted
that his father was buried in the churchyard where, he felt, some
comfort could be found. I would like my parents to be buried in
Shurdington churchyard, too, but they have already arranged to
be cremated. Practical to the last, my father said he couldn't see
what difference it makes since once you're dead you don't know
anything about it.

Does it matter where you are buried?

The cemetery of Père-Lachaise – a sprawling city of the dead –
is only fifteen minutes walk from where I am living. I go there
from time to time when friends come to stay but don't have
strong feelings about it one way or the other – except to feel
sorry for those unfortunate enough to have relatives buried near
Jim Morrison. Oscar Wilde is buried there too but I have never
chanced upon his grave and have no impulse to seek it out.

After lunch I went up to my bedroom and sat at the desk
where I studied for my O and A levels. All my books are stored
here and whenever I go home I always spend an hour or two

browsing along the shelves. Wilfred Owen, born in Oswestry, near my mother's father's home, buried in Ors in France. Lawrence, born in Eastwood, Nottinghamshire, buried (for a while) in France, where his remains were exhumed, cremated and re-interred in New Mexico. And Raymond Williams, where is he buried? In Pandy or in Cambridge? None of my copies says, but in an old Pelican edition of *Culture and Society* I read: 'The tragedy of Lawrence, the working-class boy, is that he did not live to come home.'

Gurney, unlike Owen, made it home from the war. In June 1918 he threatened suicide and was discharged from the army with 'deferred shell-shock'. He returned to Gloucestershire in October of the same year but in 1922, after further suicide threats, he was confined to the asylum at Barnwood House. The last fifteen years of his life were spent at the City of London Mental Home.

Hatherley Brook runs past the bottom of our garden and passes within half a mile of Twigworth, where Gurney was buried, in 1937. The place-names that litter his letters and poems – even those written in France – are the place-names of my childhood and my family, my home: Crickley, Cranham, Birdlip, Cooper's Hill, Leckhampton, Cheltenham, Stroud . . .

My father drove me back there, to Stroud, to wait for the train to Swindon and on to London from where, a few days later, I would fly to France. Before setting out for the station my father had looked at our garden and said:

'Take away the birds and the flowers and there's not much beauty in the world . . .'

The train was late and looked like being even later. We didn't mind waiting, it was such a lovely day. I browsed through the bookshop and then chatted with my father in the car park.

After an hour BR gave up on the train and ordered taxis to take passengers on to Swindon. I shook hands with my father who, as always, gave me two five pound notes, one each from him and my mother.

We drove up over the Cotswolds towards Kemble. Through gaps in the dense hedgerow we caught slurred glimpses 'of lovely and emerald lit fields'. Trees, drystone walls. Clouds dawdling across the sky. Rape blazing yellow. Birds and flowers everywhere. Fields, in Gurney's words,

> Where the sheep feed
> Quietly and take no heed.
>
> You would not know him now . . .
> But still he died
> Nobly, so cover him over
> With violets of pride
> Purple from Severn side.

1993

Jacques Henri Lartigue

Who better to capture the century in its infancy than an infant prodigy, using an instrument still in its technological infancy? Helped by his father, Jacques Henri Lartigue took his first photographs in 1900, when he was six. Two years later his father gave him a camera and Lartigue began to take and develop photographs 'absolutely by [him]self'. These pictures, of his wealthy family posing or playing, were then arranged in little notebooks and albums by the young boy, who quickly went on to experiment with ways not only of preserving but enhancing images of his abundant happiness. By the age of ten, solely for his own amusement, he was producing the work of a precocious maturity that developed, seamlessly, into the classical poise and grace of his photographs of the 1920s and 30s.

The pictures he made as a boy were not exhibited until the mid-60s when the Director of Photography at the Museum of Modern Art, John Szarkowski, declared Lartigue to be 'the precursor of all that was alive and interesting during the middle of the twentieth century.' By then these images of *la belle époque* had, if anything, become even more alluring. The devastation of two World Wars gave Lartigue's childhood the look of a secular, immensely exciting Eden.

The excitement came, initially, from two sources: speed and

flight. From the outset Lartigue had enjoyed the camera's novel ability to stop time; now, at Grand Prix meetings, he used his developing technical facility both to halt and convey the velocity of emergent modernity. 'I am going to use 300/second,' he noted in 1905, 'because of the cars' speed.' The feeling contained in these pictures is superbly expressed by Colin Westerbeck in *Bystander: A History of Street Photography*: 'It is as if, having got dressed that morning in the nineteenth century, [Lartigue's subjects] are racing now out of control into the twentieth.' The immediacy of one image is such that the car seems to be crashing *through* the film which seeks to arrest it. What the futurists strove to represent, Lartigue captured almost casually.

Like the futurists he was infatuated by the conquest of the air initiated by Wilbur Wright's pioneering lift-off of 1908. France at this time was the winged nation par excellence and at numerous airshows Lartigue photographed the sluggish dawn of flight. He'd used the camera to defy gravity, to freeze jumping people and dogs in mid-air; now he recorded the precarious historical moment when the principles of aeronautics were just managing to keep the available technology aloft (and vice versa). It is as if the century itself is struggling to take wing. Again, the power of these pictures – their temporal concentration – has increased with time: in them the heavy sky of the past becomes scattered with flying machines, symbols of what a contemporary observer called 'the great new future of the world'.

Lartigue retained a life-long fascination with speed but, with the onset of puberty, it was augmented by another, even giddier source of excitement. In July 1907 he suddenly got 'a new idea: that I should go to the park and photograph those women who have the most eccentric or beautiful hats.' Within a year he declared that 'everything about [women] fascinates me – their dresses, their scent, the way they walk, the make-up on their faces, their hands full of rings and, above all, their hats.' Hardly surprising, then, that Lartigue went on to become what the historian of photography, Vicki Goldberg, calls 'the first fashion photographer'. At once restrained and exuberant, Lartigue's pictures of women and their elegance are paradigmatic of the twentieth-century aesthetic of glamour: the stylisation of longing. The Riviera lifestyle celebrated by Scott Fitzgerald provided an inevitable anchorage for themes displayed with a compositional ease – he loved the camera's capacity to isolate the world's weirdly tilted symmetries – that anticipated the signature style of Cartier-Bresson.

By the time of Lartigue's death in 1986, he had been canonised as a sublime recorder of happiness. While this assessment is impossible to refute, it is worth enlarging on. Proust provides the first clue to amending our perception of a man who spent his life happily photographing his friends, relatives and the women he loved. 'I am still too young to know what makes for happiness in life,' he wrote in a letter. 'But I know that it is neither love nor friendship.' The second is furnished by Thomas De Quincey who, in *Confessions of an English Opium Eater*, termed himself 'a Eudaemonist: I hanker too much after a state of happiness . . . I cannot face misery, whether my own or not, with an eye of sufficient firmness.' An obsession with happiness, in other words, resembles a kind of misery.

In 1919 Lartigue met and married Madeleine Messager whom he nicknamed Bibi. They were divorced in 1931 but it is not the facts of the couple's married life that concern us. Rather, it is the strange, mournful quality of the husband's pictures of his wife.

There is only one person missing but, because of that, everywhere is empty: that is the default sentiment of much symbolist longing. In Lartigue's photographs the beloved *is* there, beautiful, pallid, alluring – but *still* the scene is desolate, dark, brooding. The London through which Bibi passes on the open top of an empty bus in 1926 is the unreal city – 'under the brown fog of a winter dawn' – of Eliot's Waste Land. Every shop looks like an undertaker's. The Riviera, in many of his pictures, is not the sun-drenched idyll of the early sections of *Tender Is the Night*; as often as not it is ravaged by weather as violent as the mental storms that engulf Nicole and blight her marriage to Dick Diver. Unlike Fitzgerald's hero, Lartigue kept his eye firmly averted from the carnage of the First World War, but its associated technologies are all the time rumbling through his frames. In a picture of 1920, Bibi, Lartigue and his granny look like they have driven straight from the gas-shrouded wreckage of the Western front.

We have seen how the long lag between their being made and shown deepened the meaning of some of Lartigue's photographs. In at least one extraordinary instance it has, by association, been fundamentally changed. A photograph from 1903 shows Lartigue's brother and cousins – four people in all – in Mardi Gras masks, facing the camera. Between 1969 and 1971 – at the same time that Lartigue's work was becoming internationally venerated – Diane Arbus took some of her most disturbing photos (published posthumously in *Untitled*), of the residents of various mental institutions. Several of the photographs show the inmates in Hallowe'en masks; one in particular shows four masked patients lined up in an uncanny compositional echo of Lartigue's boyish image. The new book of Lartigue's photographs is prefaced with an epigraph from Marguerite Yourcenar: 'All happiness is a kind of innocence'. We are all attracted to the 'extreme innocence' of Lartigue's pictures of his – and the century's – childhood, but the fact that this was the phrase used by Arbus to describe the attraction of her 'retardates' casts a darkly enhancing shadow across the long summer depicted in them.

1998

Henri Cartier-Bresson

Truman Capote remembered Henri Cartier-Bresson at work as 'an agitated dragonfly'; Carlos Fuentes called him an 'invisible butterfly'; John Berger likened him to 'a hare'; Malcom Brinnin recalled his being 'hummingbird-tense', with an eye that was 'polyhedral, like a fly's'. The accuracy of this bestiary of observations lies, precisely, in its suggestive diversity. No single comparison quite catches him. The photo that comes closest to doing so is the one by Beaumont Newhall in which Cartier-Bresson can *just* be glimpsed, disappearing from view. This capacity to disappear is one of the personal traits on which there seems to be absolute agreement.

Cartier-Bresson has compared himself to 'a cat' which 'makes you forget his presence'. Like the one creeping up to painter Saul Steinberg in one version of a famous portrait and which, in another, has slinked off, vanished. In keeping with this feline idea of himself it is, appropriately, one of the dogs – rather than any of the people – aboard the barge at 'The Lock at Bougival in France 1955' who is alert to the photographer's presence.

I met him only once, at a friend's house in the suburbs of Paris about four years ago. I remember he had exquisite manners (an excellent way of avoiding drawing attention to yourself). Quite suddenly he leapt up – that word is too disruptive, too suggestive of commotion: he leapt up *subtly* – and took a picture of our host as he fiddled with the barbecue, totally unaware of being photographed. Up until that point I'd not even noticed that he had a camera. Which is strange, really, since this nimble old man, with his quick and ancient eyes, is probably the greatest photographer of the century.

He was born in 1908 to a wealthy family of textile manufacturers but, by his teens, any hopes his father entertained of Henri becoming involved in the family business were dissolving. He wanted to become a painter and, with that sense of entitlement and ease born of privilege, he was, by the mid-20s, moving freely in the surrealist circles of the Parisian avant-garde. At the age of twenty, though giddy with the liberationist urgings of surrealism, he began studying with the painter André Lhote who encouraged him in the contrary direction, towards a systematic, mathematical analysis of the geometry of art. In 1930 he travelled to the Ivory Coast of Africa where he fell seriously ill with black-water fever. The main effect of this Céline-like journey to the end of the colonial night was to give a vital political edge to a sensibility already aesthetically radicalised. As a person he was evolving that combination of qualities – extreme refinement and an anarchic loathing of 'all forms of authority' – that would distinguish his work as an artist. All he lacked was a medium. Which he found in photography, more exactly, in a 'little device': the hand-held Leica.

The tension between Lhote's rigour and the commitment to chance and spontaneity advocated by the surrealists quickly became a defining quality in his work. According to André Breton the quintessential surrealist image was 'a pure creation of the mind . . . a juxtaposition of two more or less distinct realities'; Cartier-Bresson's style has, accordingly, been likened to a kind of found surrealism: a man reading a paper, his head not obscured but *replaced* by a knotted curtain; a stone statue turning towards the photographer to alert him to a young girl passing by; two pigs leaning on their sties, chatting like suburban neighbours. Taken *à la sauvette* – on the run – these chance encounters are counterpoised and held in place by a perfect and apparently effortless command of pictorial geometry. Again and again the shapes assumed by the human figures rhyme with the arrangement of lines and forms – buildings, hills – behind them: 'the profoundest forms', in Wallace Stevens's words, 'Go with the walker subtly walking there'. The action in the foreground (a man jumping over a puddle, or yawning) coincides with – or is echoed by – some detail (a poster, or a piece of graffiti) in the background. It is as if, for Cartier-Bresson, 250th of a second is all the time in the world.

His influence became so widespread so quickly that the unprecedented character of Cartier-Bresson's work from the 1930s cannot be overemphasised. When the photographer Helen Levitt first came across his pictures, in 1935, the medium suddenly seemed 'limitless'. No sooner had Cartier-Bresson mastered this medium, however, than he attempted to get to grips with another. He studied documentary film-making with Paul Strand in New York and then, back in Europe, assisted Jean Renoir on two features. In the summer of 1940, while working for a film and photo unit of the French army, he was captured by the Germans. He escaped from a POW camp (that famous talent for disappearing!) but in the States it was believed that he had been killed. An exhibition in his memory was planned for 1946, by which time he was on hand to convert this posthumous tribute to a mid-career retrospective.

In 1933 he had met Robert Capa who, in preparation for the publicity generated by this show, advised him to play down the surrealist label and advertise himself instead as a 'photojournalist'. Henri took his advice and, in 1947, together with George Rodger and David Seymour, they co-founded Magnum, the photo agency that has become virtually synonymous with Capa's coinage. For the next thirty years Cartier-Bresson photographed his way round the world.

For some it is that first burst of activity in the early 1930s in which Cartier-Bresson's genius is seen most clearly. His achievement can only really be appreciated, however, if the full range of the work – a surprising amount of which lies outside the style immediately identified as his – is considered. In odd images by him we can glimpse a combination of style and subject matter which would define another photographer's entire contribution to the medium. A picture of agricultural labourers in Mexico is like a visual premonition of Sebastião Salgado's photos of workers in the gold mines of Brazil. The United States, he claimed, was 'too vast' to photograph, but his picture of freights hauling across Arizona shares the visionary emptiness of seminal images from the tradition of American landscape photography; his few pictures of Southern blacks seem as rooted as those by Mississippi-born Eudora Welty. Change the caption – from 'The Seats Opposite, Romania 1975' to 'Ben and Candy, Tripping' – and his picture of a couple sprawled out in a train compartment becomes a monochrome Nan Goldin.

His pictures of writers such as Albert Camus (hunched up like Bogart in his existential overcoat) or Ezra Pound (smouldering like an extinct volcano) or Jean-Paul Sartre (one eye focused on being, the other wandering off towards nothingness) are nothing short of iconic. Simultaneously majestic and familiar, his portraits of Giacometti (striding like an etiolated figure of his own imagining), Matisse and Bonnard (shrivelled by grief after the death of his wife, Marthe) show what it is like to meet genius on equal terms.

Like Bonnard, many of the pioneering modernists who had – directly or indirectly – shaped Cartier-Bresson's early artistic ambitions were photographed by him late in their lives. These photographs – of Georges Braque, for example, or Marcel Duchamp, or André Breton, or Alfred Stieglitz – suggest how modernism itself has aged with the century. At the time they were taken they showed modernism in the process of becoming a mode of memory. Now that the man who made them is himself ninety years old, they evoke nothing else so much as the nostalgia of the avant-garde.

Wherever he went he had the knack – as did D.H. Lawrence, in words – of fixing a place in one or two images. You see his pictures of a country you know well and say, 'Yes, that's it, that's it exactly!' Thinking specifically of his *Mexican Notebooks*, Carlos Fuentes declared, 'the world has found its look'. The photos in that book were culled from two trips, in 1934 and 1964. Since then he has been reluctant to go back, fearing he would find the country changed. This could not happen, according to Fuentes, because he photographed the Mexico that is eternal, changeless. Most obviously in the bleak, elemental image of Popocatepetl; less spectacularly, more characteristically, in the style of semi-detached delight that informed another, more recent visitor, the poet Michael Hofmann. In a well-known photograph Cartier-Bresson balances a wall-painted bottle of Corona on a young boy's head; in *Corona, Corona* (1993) Hofmann finds a similarly tilted symmetry in the Mexico

> Of well-lit drink shops. Of illustrated marriage magazines
> and spot-the-beachball shots in Kodak shops.
> Of *Secrets of a Nunnery*, and two churches
> facing each other on two hills, holding a lofty dialogue.
> (One was a ruin.)

If his geographical range is huge then so, too, is the temporal.

Cartier-Bresson has said that up until 1955–56 France was 'still in the nineteenth century' and some of his subjects – like the taxi drivers he photographed in 1933 – peer at us through the smog of ages. A picture from Thebes in 1950 could have been made in the company of Flaubert on his trip to the 'Orient' a hundred years earlier. Others – give or take a few quirks of fashion – could have been taken yesterday. I have seen his 1959 picture of a young girl skipping through a square puddle of sunlight re-enacted, in exactly the same spot, on an almost daily basis in Trastevere.

Naturally he is praised for his eye. But it is less what *he* has seen than what he enables *us* to see that is so startling. How, then, should *we* look at his photographs? Roland Barthes's idea of the *punctum* – the apparently insignificant detail which makes him *love* a photograph – is not much help. In Cartier-Bresson's work the *punctum* is generalised, dispersed throughout the image. His photographs also suffer from being seen in too close proximity to each other. It is difficult, as a viewer, to sustain the keenness of eye that each individual picture requires. But if we place one of his photos next to a related one by someone else, his distinctive qualities are enhanced. Take, for example, the 1966 photo – not, by his standards, an exceptional picture – of two black men cleaning a *bateau-mouche*, separated from the white tourists by what is, quite literally, a glass ceiling. Over all of this is the Eiffel Tower, like a radio mast transmitting this apparently unpolemical image to the world – just as, two years later, another image of the clenched back fists of American sprinters will be broadcast from the Olympics Games in Mexico. Cartier-Bresson has spoken of his liking for a 'sharp' image but, as this comparison suggests, his is a *discreet* sharpness. Which is why the pleasure afforded by his pictures is both immediate and gradual.

So how does he do it? He has provided a few hints – his dislike of bright sun, for example, which severely limits his angle of approach – but, typically, he is evasive. He insists he is 'an amateur' (thereby allying himself with pioneers like Eugène Atget and Alfred Stieglitz, who made exactly the same claim) and that he knows nothing about photography (thereby declaring himself to be a master of the medium). The key to this paradox is found in a book lent to him by Georges Braque in the early 1950s. Since then Eugen Herrigel's *Zen in the Art of Archery* has served as a meditation on Cartier-Bresson and 'the artless art' – the Zen phrase borrowed by Jean-Pierre Montier as a title for a thoroughly wearisome study of his life and work – of photography. Echoing the ego-dissolving discipline of the Zen archer, Cartier-Bresson has said that he does not take the photograph but allows himself to be taken by it. He becomes part of the scene he is photographing, becomes – to take a famous example – that dusty road in Greece waiting for a boy to walk along it on his hands. Just as the arrow must be released not when the archer decides but when the shot itself is ready, so Cartier-Bresson's much-quoted idea of the 'decisive moment' is less the result of isolating an instant than of being utterly receptive to the moment when the photograph makes itself available. This, needless to say, is an intensely demanding kind of passivity, for by becoming part *of* the scene, Cartier-Bresson also plays a part *in* it, coaxing elements into place (by moving his head 'a fraction of a millimetre') or encouraging – simply by being there – people to play *their* parts. Would the Greek boy have done that handstand had there been no one around to make an 'instant sketch' of his doing so?

His many variants on that phrase emphasise how important drawing has always been to Cartier-Bresson. Since 1974, though, he has more or less abandoned the surrogate activity of photography and devoted himself to drawing. More than anything else it is this long devotion – a quarter of a century! – that defines his greatness as a photographer for the fact of the matter is that his drawings are unexceptional. This becomes obvious if you compare any of his many drawings of nudes with two photographed nudes. The first is from 1933 and, like Bonnard's paintings, shows a woman dappled and patterned – *painted* – by the water in which she floats. The other, from 1989 (fifteen years after he had given up photography), is included as a lovely coda to the main body of work in the book *Europeans*. Captioned 'Break Between Drawing Poses', it shows two women stretched out on a bed, gorgeously, sensuously. The drawings that result from sessions like these are laborious, dutiful, willed. His hand, to adapt Robert Lowell's famous phrase, cannot realise what his eye has seen. Only with the camera can he do that. With the camera a dream of drawing is made flesh.

1998

Robert Capa

D-Day

Robert Capa invented a genre of photography and set the standards by which it is still judged. His fabled daring not only enabled him to take exceptional photographs, it also generated the criteria that deemed them exceptional. 'If your pictures aren't good enough,' he was fond of saying, 'you're not close enough.' Capa was the best because he got closest, close enough, in 1936, to have snapped – or so he claimed – the moment of a Republican soldier's death in action. By the time of the Normandy invasion, the claim made for him by *Picture Post* in 1938 – that he was 'The Greatest War Photographer in the World' – was uncontested.

With his characteristic eagerness to be at the sharp end, Capa arranged to hit the Normandy beaches with the first wave of the 16th regiment of the American 1st Infantry Division – a unit he'd seen action with in North Africa and Sicily. Six-foot waves drenched the landing craft as it dipped and lunged towards the heavily defended Omaha Beach. Mortar and machine-gun fire poured from the German positions. When the ramp went down Capa and the GIs plunged waist-high into freezing water. 'The bullets tore holes in the water around me, and I made for the nearest steel obstacles,' Capa recalled. 'It was still very early and very grey for good pictures.'

The rough weather meant that only a few tanks made it to the beach. Many landing craft had drifted out of position, leaving units stranded and uncertain what to do. Faced with withering German fire and weighed down by equipment, men abandoned the plan to gain the beach and hunkered down among anti-tank obstacles, struggling against the suck and surge of tide.

The panic, confusion and paralysis of the landings are etched into the texture of Capa's photographs. People often recall how, in moments of intense danger – fights, car crashes – things occur in slow motion, the seconds expanding as the senses are swamped by stimuli. The photographic equivalent of this sensation of heightened clarity is a fast shutter speed which breaks the flow of events into the smallest possible increments. In Capa's pictures you get the impression (and I am trying to convey an impression, not to advance a technical explanation) that however fast the shutter speed, it is incapable of freezing time. Too much is happening. The camera's senses are overloaded, they cannot cope. History is moving too fast. For the soaked GIs huddled at the water-line, time is moving too slowly. Seconds are as vast as lifetimes. Capa's pictures capture this disequilibrium in which nothing can be calibrated.

Capa once described a photograph as 'a cut of the whole event which will show more of the real truth of the affair to someone who was not there than the whole scene'. He did not photograph events *per se* but the lived experience of events. No picture offers this 'real truth' in more concentrated form than one of a soldier floundering up to his neck in water. 'There was so much chaos and mass confusion that one was reduced to a state of almost immobilisation,' recalls Edward K. Regan, who was in the second wave of troops. He could have been any one of thousands of GIs at Omaha – he happens to be the soldier who recognised himself in that photograph of Capa's.

After sheltering behind a burned-out tank, with the advancing tide now reaching his shoulders, Capa made a dash for the beach. Lying flat on a strip of wet sand between sea and barbed wire, he finished his second roll of film before wading back out into the sea. He was picked up by a landing craft evacuating casualties to a transport ship where, using another camera, he photographed some of the dead and wounded before crumbling into sleep, exhausted.

In England the two films of the actual landings were handed over to the offices of *Life* for urgent developing. Finished prints had to be rushed to New York by plane on the morning of 8 June to meet the deadline for the next issue. By then Capa was heading back to Bayeux in France where news of his death – a soldier claimed to have seen the photographer's body floating in the water at Omaha – was beginning to circulate.

Capa was a gambler, in his life, in his work. He blew his earnings from photography at cards, at the racetrack. After the war he rescued Magnum from debt by putting what money remained on a horse that came good. According to the novelist William Saroyan he 'was a poker player whose sideline was picture-taking'. The distinction is perhaps not as clear-cut as Saroyan intended for there is always a quality of luck – even if it is carefully manipulated luck – about Capa's kind of photography. 'You never know when things are going to happen,' Capa himself said. 'They may happen just as the light goes.' Various technical adjustments can compensate for inadequate light. Deliberately setting the camera to the wrong ASA, for example, is called 'pushing the film'. For Capa, photography was all about pushing his luck.

Luck: in the rush to process the films most of the seventy-two images of the actual landings were ruined. None survived unscathed – and it was because of this darkroom accident that the photos have that blurred, spray-drenched immediacy that makes them so distinctive. It as if they are still developing, as if they have never quite become *fixed*: as if they are still happening. 'I'd rather have a strong image that is technically bad than vice versa,' Capa said. Now, as a result of an accident that almost wiped out two complete films, he had eleven images whose strength drew in large part from their technical deformity.

Back in France Capa resumed work, photographing the aftermath of D-Day: the consolidation of the beachhead near Colleville-sur-Mer, the massive build-up of supplies ready for the break-out, and the burial of the dead. Like the photos taken before the landings these have been processed faultlessly. They are marked by the stillness that is absent from the blurred frenzy of the landing itself: the stillness of stopped time, the stillness of the dead.

The living, meanwhile, tramp across tyre-churned sand, a column of GIs passing through the dead space of the photograph, beyond the edge of the frame, into future history.

The Battle for Normandy

There was considerable competition for publicity between the various divisions of the US Army pushing towards Cherbourg at the tip of the Cotentin peninsula. Capa ended up with the 9th Infantry – a Division particularly hungry for coverage – and the 82nd Airborne.

The first thing to say about the photographs he took in this period is that they are images of victory. Or at least a succession of hard-fought, often desperate encounters on the road to victory. As a consequence, taken in sequence, they have an unstoppable forward narrative momentum. It is almost as if we follow the same figures from one frame to the next. If we looked at them fast enough they would form a film. But unlike frames of a film each image is entirely self-contained. Some – most obviously the one of three GIs, two of whom are moving through a rubble-strewn street in St.-Sauveur-le-Viconte – even contain this larger narrative within a single image. One is tempted to say they are like film stills but they might better be seen as *still films*.

The second thing about these pictures is that they show war as we like to see it, war as it ideally looks: American uniforms, helmet straps hanging loose (from an early age that single detail suggested a casualness, a freedom from restraint that is, so to speak, *identifiably* American); fighting in trashed sleepy villages. In France. In summer.

The famous photographs – not by Capa – of German troops swarming over the Acropolis give war the appearance of an ultra-yobbish sightseeing binge. Rightly renowned for their unflinching depiction of the bloody reality of war, many of Capa's photos from the summer of 1944 yet have about them an inescapable sense of the idyll (the French even offer wine as you pass by). In contrast to *Granta*'s catchy tag for Raymond Carver and his contemporaries, we might term this quality idyllic realism.

This is seen most clearly in Capa's many photographs of soldiers *not doing anything*. Holiday snaps always show moments of supreme inactivity; glossy magazines present idleness as achievement. One way or another, leisure and repose are two of the mainstays of the image industry. Capa himself is one of the great photographers of *rest* – rest that comes of weariness, fatigue, exhaustion. No one has delineated the hierarchy of rest more precisely: sleeping, lying, sitting, crouching; as a last resort, leaning. 'Better on your arse than on your feet, flat on your back than either . . .' The soldiers in Capa's pictures share Samuel Beckett's fondness for these lines. In the absence of anything else a GI contrives to turn his body into a sofa (the idea is to allow every part of the body to support every other part). Standing is something to be postponed for as long as possible. Happiness is doing nothing, taking the weight off your feet. The minimum unit of rest is the time it takes to smoke a cigarette; smoking, in Capa's photos, becomes a measure of inactivity, of respite.

Capa made a name for himself by photographing the moment of maximum danger, of maximum exposure. In his photographs of resting soldiers, though, the camera which was famous for framing danger, offers a safe haven. After the awful over-exposure of combat a soldier sits reading the paper, doubly insulated from action by window- and picture-frame.

In that crucial photograph from St.-Sauveur-le-Viconte, one soldier props himself on the hood of an abandoned car. Two other GIs walk past with that minimum expenditure of effort you see over and over again in Capa's pictures: trying to make walking as near to sitting as possible. The figure in the lead carries a machine gun over his shoulder. He adjusts himself to the weight of the gun like we adjust ourselves to a pillow, trying to get comfy.

Nothing can beat the real thing, though: sleep. Three soldiers crash out on a sofa of rough ground. One is half-awake, another is dozing, the third is, as the phrase goes, dead to the world.

In his memoirs Siegfried Sassoon commented on the similarity between sleeping soldiers and dead soldiers. And those lines that Beckett liked – 'Better on your arse . . .' – actually conclude, unequivocally, 'Dead than the lot'. Many veterans of the Battle for Normandy have said that at times they envied the dead. Capa's photos of rest are disturbing because the only rest that will not be disturbed is that of the dead. Returning to the liberated town of Gavray in August 1944, two French civilians look at bodies crashed out at the roadside. The dead represent some extreme point of adaptability: whatever the terrain they don't feel uncomfortable. Death, in Capa's pictures, always has some sense of the end of effort, of never having to get up again. For the living there is the burden of further exertion or, for the French woman who has had a baby by a German soldier, humiliation at the hands of her compatriots. Taken in Chartres on 18 August, this sequence of photos serves as a negative affirmation of the almost idyllic quality of many of the others: in the most shocking photographs from this phase of Capa's war, there is not a soldier to be seen. These are photographs not of war but of the ominous rumblings of approaching peace. The war has moved on. This is what is left in its wake.

The Liberation of Paris

Endre Friedmann arrived in Paris from Budapest in September 1933, a few months short of his twentieth birthday. In his first, *centime*-less months in the city, his cunning and charm stood him in better stead than the few photographs of Trotsky that comprised the centrepiece of his portfolio of work. By October 1938 when he left Paris for New York – fearing possible internment, in the wake of the Hitler–Stalin pact, as an émigré and communist sympathiser – he had become Robert Capa, the great photographer. When he returned in August 1944 to cover the liberation of Paris he was also recording his own triumphant homecoming to the city in which he had re-forged himself in the image of his pictures. Paris, specifically the Lancaster Hotel near the Champs Élysées, remained his base for the rest of his life.

It had been agreed between General De Gaulle and the other allied leaders that French troops would be the first into Paris. On the morning of 25 August the French 2nd Armoured Division, led by General Leclerc, began rolling towards the Porte D'Orleans.

Not only was the liberation of Paris to be accomplished by the French but, Leclerc decreed, only French journalists could accompany the column as it made its journey towards the city. Resourceful as ever (a good part of his craft, after all, was not about taking pictures but getting into a position where he could take them), Capa and *Time* correspondent Charles Wertenbaker contrived to enter Paris right behind Leclerc himself.

Capa duly photographed the ecstatic, cheering crowd before following French soldiers and *résistants* engaged in street-fighting against die-hard opposition.

The following day people gathered in the Place de l'Hotel de Ville to witness the victorious appearance of De Gaulle himself. Snipers opened fire on the crowd from the surrounding buildings and people flung themselves to the ground in panic. In the midst of all this Capa shot some of the pictures that reveal, in the most dramatic form possible, the way in which his photographs participate in the events they record.

But his Paris photos do more than convey with unrivalled immediacy the lived experience of 25–26 August. They are also photographs of the Myth of the Resistance. I mean myth in the sense Angus Calder – following Barthes – intends in his book *The Myth of the Blitz*: not fabrication or lie but the construction, manipulation and absorption of an event in and by the nation's memory.

The armed uprisings that began in Paris in mid-August were Communist-led; De Gaulle was impatient to liberate the city lest another Commune be established. Once he had achieved this ambition De Gaulle wasted no time in giving mythic expression to events, in an emotional speech of 25 August: 'Paris. Paris outraged, Paris broken, Paris martyred, but Paris liberated! Liberated by herself, liberated by her people, with the help of the whole of France, that is to say of the France which fights, the true France, eternal France.'

By this formulation, Pétain and the collaborationists are not part of 'the true France'; the deep political divisions within the resistance movement, meanwhile, are subsumed within the unifying ideal of 'the France that fights'.

Capa's pictures show the people of Paris, whether Gaullists, Communists or political indifferentists, combining with French troops to liberate their city. One key image shows a soldier, a woman and a young man, weapons at the ready – or at various stages of readiness anyway – advancing tentatively towards a street corner. Three of them: a black and white tricolour, as it were, reclaiming the heart of the republic whose values they proclaim.

The (implicitly) gorgeous woman in the centre is kitted out in what, to our eyes, is a wonderful outfit of 1940s retro chic. French women don't just get dressed up to go to the *boulangerie*, the picture suggests, they are even immaculately turned out for a spot of street-fighting. What we see here, in other words, is house-to-house fighting of a specifically Parisian kind: café-to-bistro fighting. As Jean Galtier-Boissière remarked in his journal, the nice thing about fighting in your own town was that you could go off for lunch with your rifle. Not only that, but everyone in the *quartier* could watch and applaud. 'The heroes multiplied,' he wrote. 'The number of last-minute *résistants* . . . was considerable.' By 25 August most of the real fighting had been done; what Capa shows in these photographs, then, is a kind of symbolic combat (the enemy, incidentally, is nowhere to be seen).

After the liberation, General Koenig was appointed military governor of the city. It was extraordinary, he said, 'to have liberated Paris without having destroyed its wonders; all the bridges, all the great buildings, all the artistic treasures of the capital are intact.' Some of the credit for this must go to the German General von Cholitz, who ignored Hitler's desperate order to turn the city into 'a pile of ruins'. But perhaps this *was* the great French achievement of the Second World War: the preservation of the architecture of Paris. Much of London was ruined. Dresden was flattened. Hiroshima was devastated. In Paris a few windows were broken. And Capa was there, of course, on 25 August, to capture this triumphant survival of Parisian architecture.

A few days earlier the Communist resistance had appealed to the citizens of Paris in terms that harked back to the revolutionary rallying cry of the nineteenth century: '*Tous Aux Barricades*.' In Capa's photo it is not barricades that are being manned but *balconies*. A vast wide-angled crowd is squeezed into the picture frame. Above them, dominating the whole photo, is a huge V of sky formed by the receding perspective of the street: a V signifying that which it is formed by – the victory of architecture.

With this photo Capa composed the visual anthem of the liberation.

Coda

Works of art urge us to respond *in kind* and so, looking at this photograph, my reaction expresses itself as a vow: I will never love another photograph more.

The caption on the back of the postcard on which I first saw it read: 'Italian soldier after end of fighting, Sicily 1943.' The allies invaded Italy in July of that year; Palermo, the capital, was captured on 22 July, and by 17 August the whole of Sicily was in Allied hands. Victory in Europe was still almost two years distant but Robert Capa's photo is like a premonition of – and coda to – the end of the war in Europe.

When I next saw the picture, in a book of Capa's work, it had a different caption. This time it read: 'Near Nicosia, Sicily July

28, 1943. An Italian soldier straggling behind a column of his captured comrades as they march off to a POW camp'. This is much more specific – but which of the two most accurately expresses the truth of the image (as opposed to the circumstances in which it was made)?

At first it seems that the entire meaning of the picture changes according to the caption but then one realises that whatever the circumstances surrounding the picture-frame, Capa has deliberately isolated this young couple (making both captions misleading since neither mentions the woman). The visual truth of the photo pushes the circumstances in which it was taken beyond the edge of the frame, out of sight. Following Capa's example, I too prefer to 'crop' the narrative, to concentrate on the story contained by the image, to transcribe the caption inscribed *within* it.

Capa's picture recalls and complements another: André Kertész's photograph of 'A Red Hussar Leaving, June 1919,

Budapest'. In the midst of the commotion of departure, a man and a woman look at each other for what may turn out to be the last time. In *Another Way of Telling*, John Berger has written of how the look that passes between them is an attempt to store the memory of this moment against everything that may happen in the future. Capa's photograph shows the moment when all the unvoiced hopes in that photograph – in that look – come true. And not just the hopes of Kertész's couple, but the hopes of all lovers separated by war.

The hot Mediterranean landscape. Dust on the bicycle tyres. The sun on her tanned arms. Their shadows mingling. The flutter of butterflies above the tangled hedgerow. The crumbling wall at the field's edge is the result not of the sudden obliteration of bombs, but of the slow attrition of the seasons. It is possible to grow old in this landscape. All the sounds – the rustle of cicadas, the noise of his boots on the road, the slow whirr of the bicycle (his or hers? it has a cross bar) – offer an irenic contrast to the deafening machinery of tanks and artillery. The photograph would be diminished without the bicycle; it would be ruined without her long hair. Her hair says: this is how she was when he left, she has not changed, she has remained true to him.

Noticing these things fills me with longing. I want to *be* that soldier. Since that is impossible I resolve to go on a cycling holiday in Sicily. I want, also, to know their story. When did they meet? Have they made love? How long have they been walking? Where are they heading? How long is the journey? The photograph itself urges us to ask questions like this, but, if we look – and listen – hard it will provide the answers. Listen . . .

They do not care how long the walk ahead of them is; the greater the distance, the longer they can be together like this. She will ask about the things that have happened to him; he will be hesitant at first, but there is no hurry. She begins to remember his silence, the way it was implied by his handwriting, by the letters he sent. Eventually, he will tell her of the friends he has lost, the terrible things he has seen. He is impatient for news of friends and relatives, back in their village or town.

She will tell about her brother, who was also in the army and who was wounded, about his parents, about the funny thing that happened to the school teacher and the butcher's dog. They will walk along, their shoulders bumping, noticing everything about each other again, each a little apprehensive of disappointing the other in some small way. At some stage, perhaps when they are resting by the roadside or perhaps when they lie down to sleep under the star-clogged sky, she will turn to him and say, 'Am I still as pretty as when you left?' Knowing what his answer will be, feeling the roughness of his hand as he pushes the hair behind her ear, watching his mouth as he says, 'More. Much more.'

And the defeat of Italy, the end of the war? Maybe they will talk of that too, but not now, not now . . .

1994/1991

If I Die in a Combat Zone

*Requiem** is a tribute to 'the 135 photographers of different nations' who died while covering the wars in Indochina, Vietnam, Cambodia and Laos. Designed as a memorial – the endpapers, inscribed with the names of the dead, deliberately echo the Vietnam 'wall' in Washington, DC – it is not just a book of more or less startling photographs held together by an editorial concept. *Requiem* is a great photography *book*: a book, that is, with its own visual grammar and narrative coherence.

The first photos, taken by Everette Dixie Reese in the 1950s, are elegant, classical images of a serene and exotic landscape. Photographs from the war will show combat-haunted GIs with 'the thousand-yard stare'; Reese photographs an old Vietnamese man with a thousand-year gaze. Another irenic image shows a Buddhist monk – the Western ideal of wisdom – but there are hints, too, that this is a part of the world where rivers have run routinely red. A twelfth century stone relief shows a battle between the Khmer and Cham armies in 1177. In a picture by Pierre Jahan, a French sentry's helmet gives him the look of an invading conquistador which, in a sense, he is. An aerial shot of the Red River Delta shows a landscape that seems nothing else

---

*Edited by Horst Faas and Tim Page.

so much as camouflage-patterned. Military aircraft begin to appear in Reese's cloud-strewn skies, followed, in 1954, by French paratroopers. Then, in photographs by Jean Peraud, we get the first of the images of combat that will make up the bulk of the book. A few pages later the death of Robert Capa in the Red River Delta is announced.

Capa's dying in Vietnam provides an essential continuity from images of the Second World War to those in this book. Many of Capa's famous photos, from the Normandy invasion to the liberation of Paris, show soldiers tramping out of the edge of the frame, trudging from one battle to the next. The last photos he took, minutes before treading on a mine on 25 May 1954, show a column of soldiers wading through waist-high grass. They could be the same soldiers he had photographed in 1944. One of them even raises a rifle in familiar salute. Then Capa is blown to pieces. The column of soldiers marches on, invisibly, into the deepening conflict of South-East Asia.

In keeping with this implied continuity, the war in Vietnam looks, at first, pretty much like the Second World War. In the early stages of that conflict, writers tended to see it through a poetic optic derived from the 1914–18 war, specifically through Wilfred Owen. In the same way, photographers tended to view the war in Vietnam through a filter or lens developed to cover the Second World War. The emphasis is on the ordinary, individual soldier, usually in moments of great danger. This is not surprising. After all, details of vegetation, topography and complexion aside, the experience of men at the sharp end of combat remains fairly constant. The uniforms are different but, in every other respect, Dana Stone's picture of South Vietnamese troops on a devastated hilltop outpost in Ha Than in 1968 could have been taken at Passchendaele fifty years earlier (in common with many accounts of the Third Battle of Ypres, a section of *Requiem* is entitled 'The Quagmire'). Robert J. Ellison's shot of an ammunition dump exploding in front of three marines is like a full-colour version of W. Eugene Smith's classic image of four marines cowering from an explosion on Iwo Jima. (The pictures in *Requiem* do not only look *back* in time. Kyoichi Sawada's photo of a dead Viet Cong soldier being dragged behind an armoured vehicle anticipates Paul Watson's even grislier image of a US soldier being hauled through the streets of Mogadishu in 1993.)

As the war progresses so it begins to develop its own visual style. Capa had said that he preferred a powerful picture to one that was technically perfect. In Vietnam – most evidently in Catherine Leroy's images published by *Look* in 'full-bleed' (as the technical term so accurately puts it) – this distinction becomes increasingly blurred. Larry Burrows took carefully composed images, but for many photographers immediacy undiminished and unmediated by anaesthetic formal concerns was everything. This was not simply because of the exigencies of battle; or, rather, developments in *non*-combat photography lent themselves particularly well to the hazards of Vietnam. By the mid-60s Robert Frank's apparent indifference to traditional photographic virtues had become an ordering aesthetic in its own right. In *Bystander*, Colin Westerbeck remarks that Garry Winogrand was trying 'to see what is left of photography, what the essence of it is, after you give up the formal French rationality that Cartier-Bresson always hangs on to.' Where better to explore that question than a war where any vestige of rationality could be annihilated in four hours at My Lai? The Second World War had a shape, a purpose, that became evident both in the larger narrative (from Capa's pictures of D-Day, to George Rodger's images of the liberation of Belsen) and *within* each of the individual, incremental pictures that make up that narrative. As the war in Vietnam progressed so it came to be seen – quite literally – as confused, chaotic, purposeless. Three years before he went missing in action in Cambodia, Dana Stone wrote to his parents that 'the risks were getting way out of proportion to the gains. I seemed to be getting the same pictures that I had made many times before and as I became more accustomed to the war what had initially been interesting and exciting became dull and frightening.'

That was in 1967, by which time, according to Susan Moeller in her book *Shooting War*, three subject areas of combat imagery had begun to define the war visually. The main one of these was 'men slogging through paddies'. She might have added 'in torrential rain'. America's increasingly absurd involvement in South-East Asia is nicely suggested by Henri Huet's picture (below) of GIs wading through a paddy, keeping their weapons dry by holding them above the waist-deep water – even though the sky itself is flooding. (One soldier, incidentally, is holding his rifle one-handed in a way that inevitably recalls the soldier who greeted Capa eleven years previously, further reinforcing the impression that we

are seeing the same column of men, tramping from battle to battle, from war to war to war, eternally.) In another of Huet's pictures a soldier is completely submerged: all that can be seen above the surface of the water are hands and weapon.

The other two subject areas mentioned by Moeller are men calling in artillery and men leaping from choppers. These choppers have become the virtual logo of the Vietnam war. So much so that, through a process of infiltration by media association, songs by Hendrix and the Stones swirl inaudibly around the rotor blades of the choppers in this book. To put it another way, these photos of choppers constitute a kind of visible sound-track. They are immediately identifiable as images from the Vietnam war because they look so like stills from a film. The real is authenticated by the pervasiveness of the fictive – which, in turn, was derived from photos by Tim Page, Burrows and others.

A version of this narrowing gap between the real and the representational, between participants and observers, lies at the heart of the *Requiem* project. The photographers featured in this book talk habitually of using the camera as if it were a gun. On the brink of surrender, while the soldiers destroy their guns and ammunition, photographer Pierre Schoendoerffer destroys his camera and films. Several photographers carry arms as well as cameras; others, like Sam Castan, die as soldiers, gun – rather than camera – in hand.

Operating guerrilla-style on subsistence resources, fighting for the war of national liberation they were documenting, their Vietnamese counterparts were, in William Tuohy's words, 'soldiers first and cameramen second'. Only a few thousand of their negatives and prints survived the devastation of the war and its aftermath. Often next to nothing is known about the photographers themselves: in the biographies at the end of the book are many versions of the following entry: 'No photographs of, or personal information about, Duong Cong Thien survived the war.'

The Americans, on the other hand, operated in a style similar to the government whose policies they came increasingly to oppose. As the military relied on technological might, so the American photographers were possessed of a limitless supply of photographic ordnance. According to Moeller, 'Burrows carried so much [film] that he had rolls stuffed into his socks.' Saturation bombing by the military was matched by saturation photographing by the news media. If it sometimes seems – and I am trying to articulate an impression, not to offer an analysis of military strategy – that the First World War was fought in order that it might be remembered, then the Vietnam war sometimes seems to have been fought by the Americans in order to generate images of combat. In this context the section of the book entitled 'Escalation' refers, implicitly, not only to the war's increasing scale but, also, to its escalating visibility.

While the North Vietnamese died invisibly, 'their photographic deeds unrecorded' (Tuohy again), some of the photographers who covered the conflict from the other side gained considerable renown in their attempts to find images rivalling those of the master, Capa himself. Capa's work is, if you like, the negative from which all the subsequent prints in this book are derived. Following his famous advice that equated proximity – to danger – with quality, many photographers in Vietnam aimed, as one writer put it, 'to edge right up to death'. For these photographers, the thousand-yard stare got apertured down to three or four feet. Soldiers observing Burrows' obsessive urge to get close to the action joked that he must be the most short-sighted photographer ever.

Now, this does not mean that the photographs taken by the men and women in this book are better – because they died – than those by photographers like Tim Page, Catherine Leroy or Don McCullin who survived. But the fact of their having died lends their work – especially their last rolls of film, the shots they were taking hours or minutes before they were killed – a dramatic pathos. These pictures are like a technologically advanced version of the folk idea whereby the last thing a person sees before dying is imprinted on their retina. Sam Castan's last roll of exposed film was taken from him by a North Vietnamese soldier and recovered only when this soldier, in turn, was killed. On occasions like this – especially in Hiromichi Mine's fire-and-water-damaged picture of a chaplain celebrating mass – it is as if the eyes of the dead are flickering open again, blinking through the mud in which they are lying. More importantly, the fact that *Requiem* is devoted entirely to the work of people who died profoundly influences the book's narrative grasp.

When it was published in *Life*, Burrows' picture (not included in this book) showing four Marines carrying the body of a fifth had to be cropped in order to eliminate from view another photographer who had strayed into the frame. In this book, though, the proximity of fellow photographers is immanent in its meaning. A photograph by Dicky Chapelle shows a South Vietnamese soldier preparing to execute a Viet Cong prisoner while, to his left – exactly as prescribed by Auden in 'Musée des Beaux Arts' – one of his comrades stands idly by, hands in pockets, smiling. Then, two pages later, we see a chaplain kneeling over Chapelle's body, her head soaked in gore. In the first picture we saw what she saw; in the second (opposite) – by Henri Huet – it is as if we share the point of view of the soul leaving the body. The photographer has assumed the place of her subject. Roland Barthes summed up the peculiar tense of photographs as 'he is dead and he is going to die'. *Requiem* turns this round and applies it to the photographers: they are dead and they are going to die. Another dramatic picture by Huet shows Larry Burrows, cameras round his neck, helping GIs to battle through the downdraught of the evacuation helicopter to which they are carrying a wounded comrade. That was taken in 1970; in February the following

year Burrows and Huet died together when the helicopter they were travelling in was shot down over the Ho Chi Minh Trail. By the inexorable, terrifying logic of the book's conception and arrangement, in other words, we take our place in the old war song quoted by Francois Sully – another photographer who died – in an article in *Newsweek*: 'To each his turn. Today yours, tomorrow mine.'

1998

W. Eugene Smith

In 1936, after his grain business went belly-up in the Great Depression, W. Eugene Smith's father drove to a hospital car park and blasted himself in the stomach with a shotgun. He died hours later despite a blood transfusion from his seventeen-year-old son. So vividly does this episode prefigure the qualities and concerns of Smith's work that to visualise it except in the brooding, symbolic tones of his photographs is all but impossible. Smith was a method photographer: the only way he could work was by immersing himself totally in his subjects. 'I do not seek to possess my subject,' he wrote, 'but rather to give myself to it.' More than any other photographer – and this is his strength and weakness – Smith sought to *transfuse* himself completely into his material. All too often, the more he gave of himself the more hopeless the situation became.

He was only twenty when, having dropped out of the New York Institute of Photography, he landed a job with the newly launched *Newsweek*. Initiating a pattern repeated several times over, he was dismissed by that magazine and taken up by *Life* – before falling out with them, getting fired, and re-enlisting as a war correspondent in time to cover the landings on Iwo Jima and Okinawa, where he was badly wounded by a shell blast.

It was not until 1947 that he was able to return to work as a photographer. Between then and 1954 he completed some of his – and *Life's* – best-known photo-essays: 'Country Doctor', 'Spanish Village', 'Nurse Midwife'. *Life* provided matchless opportunities for photographers but Smith resented the way they were regarded as purveyors of raw material to be processed, selected and arranged as the editors felt fit. Miffed – to put it mildly – by the way his 'Country Doctor' series had been printed he wrung from the magazine the right to make his own prints but this, as far as Smith was concerned, was a small concession: he wanted total control of the way his work was used.

He had a point. *Life* pioneered a way of arranging the world that achieved such visual hegemony that, in the 1950s, the world seemed intent on arranging itself along similar lines. However important its place in the history of photojournalism, the *Life* aesthetic – its world-view, as it were – has, over time, become so conventional that, in their original context, some of Smith's pictures – and those of fellow regulars like Margaret Bourke-White – seem too, well, *Life*-like.

After an incendiary disagreement over his pictures of Albert Schweitzer in Africa, Smith quit *Life* for good in 1955 and promptly joined Magnum (which he left a few years later). He also accepted a commission to do a small-scale project on the city of Pittsburgh.

When he arrived for this three-week assignment his sponsor was surprised to see the photographer unloading some twenty items of luggage from his station wagon. His refusal to abide by deadlines had strained the patience of all his employers but it was in Pittsburgh that Smith's insistence on taking as long as the job required reached megalomaniacal proportions. For the first month he barely clicked the shutter, preferring – as he always did – to get to know his subject. He eventually spent a year making over ten thousand exposures of every facet of the city. And this was just the beginning. Conceiving the Pittsburgh project as a photographic equivalent of Joyce's *Ulysses*, he spent another two years there trying to print and edit the mass of material into an order that would do justice to 'the tremendous unity of [his] convictions'.

In his biography, *Shadow and Substance*, Jim Hughes paints an unforgettable picture of Smith driving himself to the brink of madness as he grappled with his gargantuan undertaking. Wired on amphetamines, banging out letters full of delirious, teeth-grinding declarations of intent, he would work for three or four days straight and then collapse. Free at last to realise his ambitions of total artistic control he began to suffer from a kind of dementia of seeing. Where Cartier-Bresson saw affinities of shape within a single frame, Smith wanted to preserve visual echoes from different pictures within a vast narrative coherence he could never quite realise.

By 1959, having settled for publishing a mere thirty-eight pages of photographs, Smith lamented 'the final failure, the debacle of Pittsburgh as printed'. As if in recoil from a project in which he had tried to see everything from every point of view, Smith retreated to New York and took pictures from the reas-suringly limited vantage point of his apartment windows. As if intent on becoming an archive of image and sound, he taped all his phone calls and recorded other people's conversations in the building. He also replaced the bulbs in his apartment with photo-floods which were left on day and night to keep at bay the darkness that is an identifying trait of his photographs.

From an early stage he had not been averse to manipulating reality, coaxing people into the shapes and patterns required by his pictures. This 'rearranging for the truth of actuality', as he called it, continued in the darkroom, where Smith pushed the standard techniques of dodging, bleaching and burning to create his characteristic brand of tonal hyperbole. The most famous example is the picture of a mad woman in Haiti whose gleaming white eyes yell out from the all-engulfing blackness around her. In several of the best-known Pittsburgh prints a charcoal smudge drenches the scene so thoroughly that, by an ironic twist, we arrive at a smoggy, heavy industrial equivalent of the blurred, turn-of-the-century pictorialism promoted by Alfred Stieglitz and the Photo-Secession. His pictures of steel workers in their 'devil goggles' – to use one of his own captions – are darkened and de-personalised to the extent that they appear like an 'industrious crew' amid the belching fires and 'rowling smoak' of Milton's – and Humphrey Jennings's – Pandaemonium. Smith's darkroom rhetoric sometimes diminishes by over-enhancing. But in his best pictures, most obviously the Pietà-like image of a mother bathing her young daughter who has been terribly deformed by mercury pollution from a factory, his – and our – sense of outraged humanity is heightened by controlled technical intervention.

That picture was taken in Japan in 1972, the year after a major – and, at his insistence, chaotically hung – retrospective of his photographs opened in New York. In tandem with the many journalistic assignments featured in that show he had also continued working on another huge book to be called – after a cloying photograph of his two children – *The Walk to Paradise Garden*. Intended as a distillation of his entire career, the task of assembling this Key to his Own Mythology – or 'Total Book', as he called it – proved too much for Smith's speed-bleached brain. In 1977 he quite literally shelved the intractable problem of how to arrange his life's work by depositing it at the Center for Creative Photography at Tucson Arizona.

Like the subject of a more sedate photographic vision, he died there the following year, in a grocery store, while buying food for his cats.

1998

Robert Doisneau

About leisure he was never wrong, Robert Doisneau. How well he understood its human place: the way it makes room for – and attracts attention to – itself. In this respect he was the direct heir of the Impressionists; what they sketched in the parks and boulevards of Paris he recorded on its side streets and suburbs. When he photographed workers he tended to show them relaxing, taking a break. A war-time picture of *résistants* shows them sitting on the kerb, rifles in hand, eating, turning the street into a café terrace. The mere fact of being photographed by Doisneau imparts an attractiveness to his subjects. He photographed them as William Claxton photographed jazz musicians. There are potential Chets everywhere in Doisneau's work. This leads to the parochial accusation of romanticising the ordinary.

Doisneau was born in 1912, in Gentilly, a working-class suburb of Paris. An early inspiration was the way that the ugliness of his neighbourhood made 'the people seem beautiful by contrast'; initially, he said, this seemed 'unfair' but then their beauty came to seem 'a type of revolt'. The echo of Camus – Doisneau, incidentally, did an excellent portrait of the author of *L'Homme Revolté* – is felicitous, for Doisneau's spirit, too, was essentially *mediterranean*.

Ideally his approach to photography was leisurely. He did plenty of commercial work but whenever possible he preferred,

Whitman-like, to loaf, drifting through the streets of Paris, waiting – to slip into his own preferred metaphor of fishing – for life to bite (though it turns out he was not averse – as in his iconic 'Le Baiser' – to contriving life into biting, or at least into kissing). People saunter in and out of his pictures, at their leisure.

More than any other photographs, Doisneau's show people *looking*. More exactly he shows people in the *act* of looking. He did not photograph events but the space created by them. ('When we live', he said, 'we occupy a certain space'; visually, he was not concerned with individuals so much as the way 'people seemed to fit into their environment.') In his pictures the space is almost always the same, but the site where it is created is always changing. Its edge is defined by the people watching, but this border is dissolved by the person in the crowd who is paying no attention, who is just walking dully along, who is looking elsewhere, beyond the frame. Often it is Doisneau's discreetly enquiring presence that distracts them from the main event. In a famous photo a man is peering round the shoulder of an artist painting a nude; the onlooker's dog, meanwhile, is staring at Doisneau; a companion photograph shares the point of view of the onlooker, revealing the model who is posing in exactly the same position as the painted nude – but wearing an overcoat. His work as a whole is joined together in this relay of constantly refracted glances. To look at his photographs is, as Doisneau himself put it, to 'walk along [a] visual path'.

Except for the odd detour – in 1960 he was sent by mistake to Palm Springs, California to cover a golf tournament – this path was confined exclusively to Paris. This lends a special interest to the photographs of England which came to light after his death last April, aged eighty-one. They were taken in 1950 and are fascinating because they show Doisneau looking for a space – the space that has become indelibly associated with his name – that rarely exists in England.

He first noticed this lack of expressive space after photographing in railway stations. When people missed trains on the Continent, he said, they would throw up their hands in horror and everyone would look; in England, they would take out a newspaper, sit down and wait for the next one. This, said Doisneau, is why there was no tradition of street photography in England. It's built into the language, this lacuna: with the option of the formal '*vous*' everyone can speak to everyone else in public spaces in France; here, with a single idiom that has to double for intimate and public life, you can't speak to anyone without it seeming like you're trying to pick them up.

This was Doisneau's problem in England: he could not find a way of *addressing* people visually. There was no place for him in a country where loafing is considered loitering with intent. Where events would form themselves around him in Paris, in England nothing happens. He tries out Parisian spots like the lingerie shop where he captures a man whose eye can linger only on condition that he keeps walking. He can't do both, can't dawdle *and* linger on the lingerie. Unusually, the photographer seems to be in hiding, taking his subject by surprise. Typically a Doisneau photo feels like Larkin's railway carriage on that famous Whitsun: 'all sense of being in a hurry gone'. In England he grabs a photo of workers at a building site grabbing a bite to eat.

Because of the man in the beret and the background advertisement for 'Sparkling Wines' and 'Burgundies' one scene *does* look almost Parisian: people are standing around on a street corner, a couple of swells are walking by. Nice. Something else is simmering here, though. Doisneau's Parisians all share the ideal urban space of the picture frame. Everyone is at home in it. Here it is a *contested* space. The walkers are having to make an effort – 'ignore them, darling' – to appear relaxed. It's not just a question of looking and walking: some kind of rights are being asserted. There is a *spatial* tension.

There may be no public space in England but there are public houses. It is when Doisneau retreats indoors that he stumbles on a scene more akin to his Parisian streets. A picture of a boxer working out seems authentically Doisneau-esque because of the peculiar combination of absorption and inattentiveness of the people looking on (and off). As in his characteristic work the subjects are at home in the picture frame. For once there is plenty for him to look at.

The most telling of these uncaptioned English photos, however, shows two young women on a sofa. Where normally his subjects' gaze takes us beyond the frame, to another event, another photo, here they are totally unseeing. The woman on the left stares at the photographer as though he is not there. As in some of Edward Hopper's late paintings emptiness encroaches on the human subjects like the damp stain on the blank wall.

1995

Leaf Reed Land-er

Asked what he reads, a character in Italo Calvino's *If on a Winter's Night a Traveller* replies:

> Nothing. I've become so accustomed to not reading that I don't even read what appears before my eyes. It's not easy: they teach us to read as children, and for the rest of our lives we remain slaves of all the written stuff they fling in front of us. I may have had to make some effort myself, at first, to learn not to read, but now it comes quite naturally to me. The secret is not refusing to look at the written words. On the contrary, you must look at them, intensely, until they disappear.

The narrator pauses to consider the significance of this strange declaration of verbal independence: 'You try to picture how the world might appear, this world dense with writing that surrounds us on all sides, to someone who has learned not to read . . . and you can't stifle a feeling of jealousy.'

In the first half of *Letters from the People*, Lee Friedlander has photographed the world as it appears to this non-reader. Cropping a letter at a time from signs (the K of Car Park, the B of Bar), window displays, notices and advertisements, the alphabet

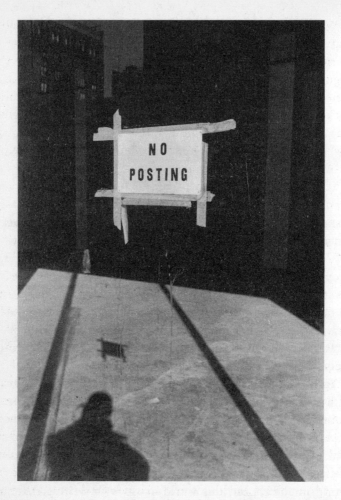

is broken down into its constituent segments. Once the alphabet is complete he moves on to numbers.

The lexical reservoir at his disposal is immense. In no time at all the vast anagram of the city provides all the components necessary to replicate the entire written culture of the English-speaking world.

What emerges is culture in the bacteriological rather than literary sense of the word. Signs breed a fungus of graffiti, what Norman Mailer calls a 'plant growth' of scrawl. Even when it begins to form words – CASH, GOD, EYE, SIN, STEAM (in wet concrete) – this found language evokes Calvino's vision of a world packed with unread meaning. Messages appear but the sense leaks from even the simplest announcements. 'WHILE U' is excluded from the frame; now a shop window commands: 'WAIT'.

Not that there is anyone around to take notice. Except in one instance there are no photos of people reading or writing (and even in that one picture, of the Vietnam Memorial in Washington, they might more accurately be said to be pointing out and looking at names rather than reading them). In all but half a dozen of the 200-plus images in the book there are no people to be seen. The only human presence is Friedlander's spectral shadow – his signature, one might say – stalking the empty city, recording rather than reading. The language seems to have spawned – to have written – itself. Often the quantity of scrawled additions renders language not simply unreadable but illegible.

Yet this photographic lexicon becomes more intensely human with every page. Names begin to appear. Then dripping expressionist shrieks: TERRIBLE, PAIN, ACID. A few pages later, almost imperceptibly, the word ART makes its first discreet appearance. Dialogue emerges. Below a lavishly aerosoled HURT'N an abandoned municipal sign advises CARE. Soon there are brief, frenzied essays on politics and philosophy – COMMUNISM IS NOT EXISTENTIAL – and pieces of frazzled, enigmatic advice: RING IT 100 TIMES IF NECESSARY (needless to say, there is not a bell in sight, just an abstract expanse of white wall).

Friedlander is not, of course, the first to photograph the graffiti of the city. In 1933 Brassaï commented that the 'succinct signs' preserved in his own photographs of Paris walls 'represent none other than the origins of writing'. Between 1938–48 Helen Levitt photographed chalk drawings and messages on the buildings and streets of New York. What is special about Friedlander's book is an implicit narrative trajectory – from clumps of letters to pieces of writing – that obliges us, quite literally, to *read* the photographs. Perhaps it is too narrowly literary to suggest that *Letters from the People* stands or falls, ultimately, by the quality of the writing it depicts, but the act of reading quickly and inevitably arouses the instinct for critical evaluation. And so, in the midst of all the cock-suck exhortation, we seize on a daubed declaration of love and jealousy as a species of almost-poetry, at once intimate and public:

> She's my friend
> And I'll tell you
> She Ain't no good
> She don't love you
> Like I do.

Once embarked on this process of critical discernment we begin to wonder what principle other than chance has governed Friedlander's method of selection for this photographic anthology. On the salt flats near Wendover on the Utah–Nevada border, for example, lovers scratch their sweethearts' names on the frost-white crust of salt. Each winter the flats are flooded. Through the blue water you can still read the names, floating, eerie, almost not there. And that traffic sign in North Carolina where the command to STOP had been sandwiched between 'Can't' and 'Hiphop' . . . Or that warning on the London Underground, anarchically defaced so that law-abiding commuters were urged to 'OBSTRUCT[ing] THE DOORS CAUSE[s] DELAY [and can] BE DANGEROUS.' Or – my favourite – the exquisitely subversive suggestion in Brighton: 'Go on – call in sick.'

Why weren't they in the book? I found myself thinking – unreasonably (obviously) and inevitably, for the chief effect of these self-captioned photos is to make you aware of the sheer quantity of language out there. Probably only the unlettered can appreciate how much. The joy of *Letters from the People* is that we are rendered illiterate and then taught to read again. We return to the written world with fresh eyes, better able to appreciate the scrawled beauty and tender lyricism of the message on a sea wall that closes the book:

> Everyday I calls a phone to her
> Every night I dreams for her.

1993

William Gedney

A few days short of his thirty-ninth birthday, William Gedney spent the evening in his book-crowded Brooklyn apartment, poring over a copy of E.J. Bellocq's *Storyville Portraits*. Bellocq had made these photos in about 1912 and for almost half a century they were forgotten. Then, in 1958, Gedney's friend Lee Friedlander came across the glass-plate negatives. In 1970 he exhibited a selection of the prints he had made from them, in the hope that Bellocq's name could be inserted retrospectively into the photographic pantheon. When Gedney saw them, he found himself entranced by these images made by a man who had come to exist exclusively in terms of what he saw, a man who had disappeared from history, whose work had been so fortuitously rescued from oblivion by Friedlander.

Storyville Portraits contains just over a third of Bellocq's eighty-nine surviving pictures, which Gedney had first seen at Friedlander's house. As he looked at them again on that 'depressing day' in the fall of 1971 he was struck by 'how, in just thirty-four pictures, so complete a world is rendered, an all-encompassing wholeness. Each one of his photographs seems to contain the germ of all his work. If only one of his pictures existed . . . you would still sense he was a great photographer.'

Although Bellocq abided by the photographic conventions of

his time, Gedney thought there was a 'subtle but telling difference that [made] him a great artist'. The same girl, it seemed to
Gedney, could be posed in the same way, in the same setting in
front of the same camera and photographed by a hundred different photographers,

> and each would come up with a slightly different picture.
> But I wonder, would any come up with a picture better
> than the rest? If Bellocq was one of those photographers, I
> believe he would. It is a continuously amazing thing that
> this impersonal machine, the camera, should render not
> only the surface of the visible world, but is capable of ren-
> dering so sensitively the personality of the photographer.

Gedney attempted to develop these ideas over several more
pages of his notebook until, amid much crossing-out, his
thoughts gave way to unconnected jottings. After copying out a
passage from W.H. Auden that took his fancy he conceded, 'Have
not been able to finish writing on Bellocq.'

The notebook in which he sketched these ideas on Bellocq was
made by Gedney himself: part of his programme of intensely
private, creative self-sufficiency. Several of these home-made
notebooks are filled with notes on how to make notebooks, a
task he liked because of its exactness: the precision, the sharp
angles. It pleased him also to learn that certain cities in ancient
Egypt had been arranged along the lines of a grid, a street plan
of rectangles. In 1985 he copied out a passage from a book by
Nan Fairbrother that elevated this personal preference to the
level of a universal template:

> the shapes we make for ourselves are geometrical, and the
> background of civilised life is more or less rectangular. Our

rooms and houses are arrangements of cubes, our doors and windows, furniture and rugs, books and boxes – all their angles are right angles and all their sides are straight.

Square things, then: like photographs or books; ideally, books of photographs.

He filled little notebooks with lists of books that he needed to read or buy. Then he filled larger notebooks with passages that he liked from the books he had acquired and read. Like an ascetic cleric in the Dark Ages, he transcribed other people's words, making them his own, customising them, on occasions, to render them more appropriate to his own situation. 'I go to encounter for the millionth time the reality of experience,' wrote Joyce. Gedney marked that with an asterisk and inverted the terms – 'the experience of reality' – to distinguish the photographer's quest from the novelist's.

He also transcribed his *own* notes, transferring the scrawled entries – the negatives, let's say – from little store-bought notebooks and, by analogy, printing them up in his definitive, home-made ones.

A cliché: he read avidly. Everything he could. Spotting someone reading a book on unfamiliar, offbeat subjects people sometimes ask, 'Why are you interested in that?' To which, for an autodidact like Gedney, there was only one reply: because it is interesting. He amassed and hoarded knowledge and then, if something caught his eye – a potential photograph – he would bring to bear on that instant or incident everything he had learned and read. It didn't stop there, though, because his ideal of self-sufficiency was underwritten, naturally, by self-generating curiosity. The more he saw, the more he wanted to learn. The more he learned the more he saw. It wasn't enough to train himself to see, he had also to understand what he saw, to become more articulate in the language of sight.

Coleridge, it is often claimed, was the last person to have read everything. This voracious appetite for reading was matched, in his writing, by a chronic inability to finish anything. Walter Benjamin, an obsessive collector of books, thought that the most satisfying way to acquire volumes was to write them yourself, but he, too, was able to bring only a few of his most cherished projects to anything like completion. It is a trait they share with Gedney.

Although he reproached himself, on occasions, for not making the best use of his time this inability to bring any of his varied projects to completion was not the result of laziness but, paradoxically, of immersing himself so thoroughly in his work. Early on he acquired Marguerite Yourcenar's wisdom, that everything undertaken for its own sake is worthwhile – irrespective of the outcome. He lived out the ideal of the artist who produces – who works – for his or her own sake; more exactly, for the sake of the task itself. And his ability to do this was unaffected, perhaps even facilitated, by his apparent lack of success. A selection of photographs from Kentucky and San Francisco was exhibited at the Museum of Modern Art in New York in 1969 but Gedney appears to have felt little or no impulse to capitalise on this early recognition of his work. After the critic John Canady had commented favourably on these photographs in the *New York Times*, in March 1969, Gedney wrote that 'compliments even from someone you admire (most are from fools and not meant) warm you for about one minute and then mean nothing. The work in progress is the only thing that matters.' Ideally, his self-sufficiency would extend even to doing without the praise of others.

It is difficult not to make a connection between on the one hand, Gedney's obsessive urge to collect and accumulate – books, materials – and his reluctance to share his life with anyone else and, on the other, his inability, finally to let go, to share his work with the world. He kept trying to refine his work down – selecting and rejecting, rejecting what he had selected – but could never edit it down quite enough. No finished form could do justice to what he had in mind. To complete was to compromise. Always the archivist's urge to curate and catalogue overcame the editor's obligation to dispense with and discard. And so he went on accumulating. Effectively, he became the sole collector of his own work, thereby completing the circle of artistic self-sufficiency.

Probably the irony of his dying of AIDS was not lost on him. He amassed and amassed and amassed – and then fell prey to a disease that, little by little, pilfered away his immune system, a volume at a time, until there was nothing left: a new mutation of the classic, the perpetual destiny of the miser.

Except that is not the whole story, of course. He gave himself utterly, freely, to the nocturnal world of gay clubs and casual encounters. He even penned an unfinished account of one such experience, titling it – somewhat optimistically: it was only two pages long! – 'A novel of degeneracy'. What they shared, the autodidact who lived reserved, austere, and the 'degenerate' sexual adventurer, was a love of – and need for – anonymity, darkness, obscurity. This was a major theme in his work: people living out their lives in obscurity.

One day, after making a characteristically scrupulous study of Lewis Hine's prints in a library, Gedney came across some pictures by a Brooklyn photographer whose name meant nothing to him. The photos were 'of no aesthetic interest, taken only for documentary reasons' but they made Gedney reflect that 'it is not easy to be unpretentious, simple, direct, honest and yet intelligent'.

There were precedents, however. Most obviously, Eugène Atget, who, after hearing Man Ray praise his photos of Paris streets, responded that he only provided what the sign above his *atelier* modestly claimed: 'Documents for artists'. Devoting himself to the task of preserving a Paris that was in danger of disappearing, living as *un anonyme*, insisting that he was 'an amateur', Atget only consented to his pictures being published on condition that his name was not used.

Closer to home, there was the artist Francis Guy. Gedney was so taken by Walt Whitman's speculative account of Guy's method of working on *Snow Scene in Brooklyn* that he copied it out in his notebooks:

> a position and direction were fixed upon, looking out of a window if possible, and when the place to be pictured was well conned and determined Guy would construct a large rough frame and fix it in the window, or in such a position that it enclosed in its view whatever he wished to portray – and outside of the frame all was shut off and darkened . . . This picture of Guy's, we believe, was thus a literal portrait of the scene as it appeared from his window.

Virtually a photograph, in fact: a photograph not unlike Gedney's own picture of the Myrtle Avenue El in the midst of a swirling snow storm. He made many pictures of that view at different times of the year, always of the same scene, with the same lens, from exactly the same window – his own – at 467 Myrtle Avenue.

Gedney was fascinated by the history of his street and spent long hours in the local library, excavating its past, transcribing quotations and pasting newspaper accounts of significant events of the street's history into what he designated his 'Myrtle Avenue Notebooks'. Whitman – whose grave Gedney photographed – had also lived on the Avenue for a while, and the paper he had edited for several years, the *Eagle*, boasted that this first paved and graded street in the area was 'the pride of the old-time Brooklynite'. That was in 1882; by 1939 Henry Miller considered it 'a street not of sorrow, for sorrow would be human and recognisable, but of sheer emptiness'. In the 'Myrtle Avenue Notebooks' Gedney uses these two quotations as terminuses between which he shuttles back and forth, preserving the history (through newspaper cuttings) of the street whose contemporary life he was recording in his photographs. To that extent the 'Myrtle Avenue Notebooks' are the record of a homely, straightforward enterprise.

But they are also like sketches of a grandiose project of retrieval and meditation. Passages culled from books Gedney had read transform Myrtle Avenue into a discursive thoroughfare: a place where the *idea* of the street is contested. There is also an implicit traffic between the photographs he made of Myrtle Avenue and the verbal ambitions set down in the notebooks. The pictures are redefined by and feed back into the larger theoretical or conceptual idea of the street that is being developed through the quotations copied or pasted into the notebooks. 'There must be eyes upon the street,' wrote Jane Jacobs in *The Death and Life of Great American Cities*:

> eyes belonging to those we might call the natural proprietors of the street. The buildings on a street equipped to handle strangers and to insure the safety of both residents and strangers, must be oriented to the street. They cannot turn their backs or blank sides on it and leave it blind.

What the street needed above all, according to Jacobs, was 'effective eyes'.

It would be difficult to exaggerate the novelty of what is going on here: a photographer in the classical American tradition, steeped in the swirling legacy of modernity, conceives a postmodern text, and executes it, in his best school-boy handwriting, in little notebooks of his own making, in 1969.

Gedney often found that other people's words served him better than his own, but he continued, throughout his life, to try to coax and twist his own view of the world into his own words. His spelling was inventive, to say the least, his grammar frequently wayward, but his fascination with language and its capacity for generating – and hindering – insight is everywhere apparent. After Diane Arbus's suicide, for example, he remembered her as a 'rare species of bird loaded down with that bulky green canvas bag hung over one shoulder, pulling her body to one side and a camera with attached flash strung around her neck, constantly persistent in pursuit. A small being physically, always weighted down by her equipment, the necessary burden.' The fleeting impressions he was able to sketch verbally, with difficulty, he could fix, unerringly, in a photograph. Almost always, though, his photographs are informed by an active and ambitious literary sensibility. 'I am attempting a literary form in visual terms', was how he summed up one of his extended photographic projects.

If not exactly Whitman's 'laughing party of mechanics', the men Gedney photographed in east Kentucky were certainly amicable with him. These photographs are among Gedney's best but the seeds of this project lie in his own autobiography, and can already be glimpsed in the early pictures of his grandparents collected under the detached title 'The Farm'.

A farm boy himself, Gedney was always fixing things: repairing, mending, adjusting, tinkering (he loved the *mechanics* of the camera and darkroom). This was one of the affinities he shared with the two families of unemployed coal miners – the Couches and the Cornetts – he lived with and photographed for a month in 1964. He became especially close to the Cornetts, to Willie, Vivian and their twelve children, staying in touch with them for years and returning, in 1972, to make further photographs.

Gedney liked the grace and lightness of the Cornett girls. When he returned in 1972, they had grown up, succumbed to the heavy chore of breeding, and his eye was drawn overwhelmingly to the malnourished strength of the male Cornetts (he saw that strength itself is a *skill*), to their elegance and economy of movement.

Thinking specifically of Gedney, whom he knew, the artist Peter Bellamy observed that 'gesture is the ballet of photography', a remark that reminds us how Gedney's men often have the grace of dancers. Again and again in his Kentucky ballet the traditional *poses* of gender are reversed: two women, one pregnant, one in curlers, both smoking, stand looking at a young man arranging himself seductively on the hood of a car; Vivian sits on a bench while Willy stretches out, draping a long leg over her . . .

'I do not consider myself a "social problem" photographer', Gedney wrote in a draft letter intended to interest publishers in his Kentucky project. 'I am concerned with making a good photograph – an uncropped blending of form, value and content. I prefer the ordinary action, the intimate gesture, an image whose form is an instinctive reaction to the material.'

There was another aspect of the Cornetts' life – getting loaded, and the violence that inevitably resulted from it – which does not come under the rubric of 'the intimate gesture', but this absence in Gedney's photos does not compromise his Kentucky work (he was not, after all, aiming to be comprehensive). A similar lack does become a problem, though, in the project that intervened between his two sessions in Kentucky: photographing the disaffected youth – hippies in the process of formation – in the Haight-Ashbury area of San Francisco in 1966–7. He could photograph them going about their business – more accurately, he could photograph them *not* going about their business – but the core of the Haight, the thing that defined it not only as a place but as a historical moment, was the psychedelic experience. And that was unphotographable.

If initially it seemed difficult for onlookers to understand the special energy of the Haight in 1966, writes Jay Stevens in

Storming Heaven, his seminal account of 'LSD and the American Dream', it soon dawned on them that 'on any given day roughly half the people in the Haight were either tripping, or had been tripping, or were about to trip.' The elaborate multi-media lengths to which the likes of Timothy Leary and Ken Kesey went to simulate acid trips – for those unwilling to sample the drug – served mainly to prove the unrecordable nature of the experience. Armed only with a camera and black and white film, Gedney faced an almost impossible task – albeit one of his own choosing. Gedney never worked on assignment; he went and photographed wherever and whoever he was drawn to. He was drawn to this place and these people by something they shared with the Cornetts: they were a distinctive group, disenfranchised, on the fringes of society. The difference, of course, was that the disenfranchisement of the hippies was voluntary, self-elected. The Cornetts lacked material things (and therefore treasured them); the hippies were discarding them. And while the Cornetts seemed to have been marooned by history, in the Haight a radically new, potentially revolutionary, structure of feeling was making itself apparent. Gedney was unconvinced by the larger, narco-ideological imperatives, preferring to travel at 'the bottom of pyramids. By that I mean I don't often meet the higher ups in a movement or scene, the ones who will tell you what it's all about, which is something quite different from what is happening. I am a walker of streets, talking to people, taking pictures.'

On the basis of these pictures Gedney seems to have felt ambivalently about what he was witnessing: drawn to the almost tribal feeling of kinship and community, but not entirely comfortable with people who, so to speak, did not share his affection for squares. This is what gives his pictures their unique historical importance. After intense media attention the Haight became a popular destination for tourists eager for a glimpse of what was going on beyond 'the beaded curtain'. Whether outraged, fascinated or simply aghast at what they were witnessing, these observers from the straight world effectively shared the hippies' own idea of themselves: namely that they had reinvented themselves totally, moved on to another, virtually unrecognisable way of living. Taken from *within* the world by someone who remained sceptical of many of its grander claims, Gedney's photographs show 'hippies' for what they *were*: teenage boys from Illinois, girls from the nice suburbs of middle America. The extraordinary thing about the people in these photographs, in other words, is that they are so ordinary. Haircut aside, the guy stretched out on the hood of a car might as well be in east Kentucky as northern California. For Gedney the essential gestures remained the same. 'The power of youth, the proclamation of a new way,' he noted, 'but it is only the old way made to look new.' In keeping with this guarded view his own pictures make the new look old, as if the photos somehow *pre-dated their subject*. Or, to make the same point the opposite way, they make the 1960s seem like they happened a long time ago: in the 1950s, in fact!

Unable to find *himself* in the people he saw, he documented an emergent lifestyle that could not be articulated by the photographic aesthetic at his disposal. Tellingly, a dummy of his planned book, *A Time of Youth*, starts with a shot of a closed door on which is scrawled an exhaustive list of all those who are not welcome to enter. Gedney could record the people who passed through but, photographically, the doors of perception remained closed.

Whereas the world of the Cornetts – to which he was welcomed back, in 1972 – was far more accessible. Photographs here were easy to come by (on one occasion, three potentially distinct photographs share a single frame) and their focus, the hub of the Cornetts' world, was the car.

'Junior and his girlfriend wanted to get married,' Gedney noted archly,

but the only justice of the peace they could find was work-ing all day at a gas station so he performed the service there. It seems appropriate since so much of the thoughts and actions of the male Cornetts involve automobiles that one of their clan should be married in a gas station.

Cars, for the Cornetts, are to be repaired, plundered for spares, patched up. To be gathered round, examined, discussed. The car is a mechanical *agora* or forum: a meeting place to exchange bare-chested opinions about carburettors or brake lin-ings. Familiarity with such parts is expressed by kicking them; knowledge of engines by letting cigarette ash drop into the com-bustible tangle of tubes and sparks.

The best caption for these pictures of the Cornetts and their cars is provided by another photographer. When Diane Arbus learned to drive she 'loved the feel of the steering wheel and the gearshift'. It was, she said, 'like getting to know universal gestures [she had] always been aware of'. That is exactly the function of the automobile in Gedney's photos: the site and generator of universal gestures. For the Cornett children an automobile engine is a mystery to be initiated into. A man holds his baby up for a first peer into the engine, a baptism of oil at the altar of mechanics. A teenage boy genuflects beneath a jacked-up wheel, worshipping. As a car sinks into utter uselessness it becomes a part of the landscape, a relic. A truck looks as site-specific as the stoop of a house. Its tyres are like wooden poles sunk into the ground. A boy lies under the hood of a car, reaching up an arm as if pulling a shiny car-patterned eiderdown over himself. Someone else leans on the hood like he's ordering drinks at a bar. An adolescent girl with famine legs stands in front of a huge truck that looks nothing if not immovable. The one thing the Cornetts never seem to do with their vehicles is *drive* them. They're stuck.

Long after he had abandoned plans of publishing a book of his Kentucky photos – or any others, for that matter – Gedney singled out a phrase from Auden's 'In Praise of Limestone' – 'short distances and definite places' – as a 'possible title for a book of photos'. There are no establishing shots (to help orient the outsider) or panoramic vistas in Gedney's Kentucky photos. The Cornetts' world is circumscribed absolutely by the known, the familiar. Careworn she might be, but Vivian on the porch is sheltered from the fathomless despair of Dorothea Lange's iconic 'High Plains Woman' in which the surrounding sky suggests an infinity of distress. Of course this situation breeds its own claustrophobic pressure as well as consolations but, for Gedney, an overall truth is always predicated on precision of circumstance and closely observed detail. If these are outstanding pictures of hardship and resilience that is because they are also outstanding photographs of *belts* – more precisely, of belt loops – pockets, zippers and shoes. His people are individualised so sharply that they are recognisable by their shoes and trousers. So much so that, in a photograph of half-a-dozen pairs of trousers hung out to dry, their owners are all implicitly *there*.

Those who lack things are defined most conspicuously by what they own, and in Gedney's photographs every *thing* – a can of brake fluid, a bag of Henderson's sugar – is valued, used. It has been said that if Balzac describes a hat that is because someone is about to put it on his head. If there is a wrench in Gedney's photographs that is because it is going to be picked up and used to mend something, to fix something, to repair something. The only useful noun is a verb. Hand, for example. The mechanical world is a problem to be solved and hands are the medium of thought, of *figuring*. The knowledge – and ignorance – of generations is in the hands of the Cornetts.

Hands alert us also to the fact that Gedney was one of the great photographers of *touch*. Stieglitz's claim – that 'the quality of touch in its deepest living sense' was inherent in his photographs – applies just as accurately to Gedney's. He remembered, as a child at his grandparents' farm, 'the delight of being able to touch so many things of different textures'. As a mature photographer he saw – literally – that the idea of tactile value held good for photographs as well as painting and sculpture. Many of the best photographs do not work only on the eye but engage at least one of the other senses: touch, in Gedney's case.

Like so many tendencies in Gedney's work, this responsiveness to the tactile is felt most powerfully in the photographs he made in the course of two extended trips to India, in 1969–71 and 1979–80. 'Everything in India is handled personally . . . India is a place of direct contact,' he noted. The way Indians sit 'involves much more physical contact with their own bodies . . . The clothes Indians wear, of simple light fabrics draped with many folds, make one aware of the movement of cloth against the body'. Even the walls and roads have a direct, 'man handled feeling. Tea is drunk from clay cups made to be thrown away. Delicately fluted on the potter's wheel it gives the tea an edge, a subtle taste of the hand that made it, of the earth that gave it birth.' He was delighted by a sign in a museum which stressed not that it was *forbidden* to touch the exhibits but only, more mildly, that 'Touch Is Discouraged'.

India's culture of 'direct contact' enabled Gedney to visually *handle* the spiritual life of the people he was photographing. In the gnarled hands of an old woman we do not just see someone praying, we see *prayer itself*. The physical everywhere bore the imprint of the spiritual. Wherever he looked he saw 'men of the crudest, lowest uneducated classes standing in positions of the utmost refinement, rivalling Greek sculptures without the stillness of idealised form.' He also found himself seduced, visually, by Indian women who embodied precisely the grace and lightness that he had observed, fleetingly, in the Cornett girls and, more enduringly, in their brothers. He had long been alert to those moments when life briefly patterned itself on the classic images of Western art. In Benares (where Gedney stayed for most of his first Indian trip) the way people's limbs echoed the forms of the deities they were constructing was a tangible illustration of something that was far more difficult to capture: a momentary gesture's capacity to contain the timelessness of myth. To enable himself to recognise such moments Gedney immersed himself in the study of every aspect of Hindu history, culture, ritual, thought and myth.

Like any traveller cut adrift from his own stock of books, he also read whatever came to hand. And the highly contingent nature of his reading proved serendipitous. A crucial insight into the ancient city of Benares, for example, came from *Tom Jones*.

Mankind has always taken great delight in knowing and descanting on the actions of others. Hence there have been, in all ages and nations, certain places set apart for public rendezvous where the curious might meet and satisfy their

mutual curiosity. Among these, the barbers shops have
justly borne the pre-eminence.

Having transcribed this passage Gedney added a note of his
own: 'All of Benares is a large barber shop.'

By the terms of Fielding's analysis, the barber shop that featured
prominently in each of Gedney's earlier pictures of the El was the
hub, the focus of Myrtle Avenue. Which meant, by extension,
that Benares was like that focal point of Myrtle Avenue *infinitely
dispersed and refracted*. 'How do Indian streets differ from
American streets?' Gedney asked himself in Benares. Partly by
the way that, in America, at some point, life inevitably retreats
indoors, becomes hidden. But in the barber-shop streets of
Benares everything was on display constantly. 'Indian streets serve
as much a part of an Indian's life as his home . . . one of the great
freedoms of Indian life is its streets. The right of people to squat
anywhere . . . people sleep, work, play, eat, fight, relax, relieve
themselves, die in streets. All human activity takes place there.'

Everything was revealed all the time and the effect was overwhelming, exhausting. 'You see too much, your eyes want rest,' he
grumbled from the relative tranquillity of Delhi. It was the constant hassle that got to him. On occasions the man who had seen
the smallest increment of the quotidian touched by the sacred
could feel only loathing for a people who 'devour each other in the
pig-sty of their soul-less existence'. The next day he explains and
retracts this outburst: 'The above was of course written after a very
tiring day. My work puts me into constant close contact with
mass public. I work in the midst of the daily existence.'

Which is what he had always wanted, of course. The difference was that in Brooklyn he could retreat indoors to his
apartment, his books. In Benares there was no possibility of
retreat, no window from which he could observe, unseen,
detached. Life was clambering all over him. The struggle,

photographically was to find his own space, to find quietness in the midst of perpetual bustle. Tourists photographing people washing on the ghats of Benares saw only the event, the spectacle. Gedney had to train himself to find a pictorial equivalent of the space that each of those bathing individuals found for themselves. He had to enter that space, find room for himself. Which was difficult for a westerner (nothing irritated him more than being mistaken for 'a tourist or hippie'), especially a westerner with a camera. Either people would yell out that he could not photograph here or, as soon as they saw him, would pose, smiling. If he said 'Don't smile, act natural' – one of the first entries in the customised Hindi phrase book he compiled – they would become even more self-conscious. The solution? To learn to dissolve into his surroundings. To become invisible. Which was far, far easier to do at night.

The dummy of his book on youths in the Haight began with a closed door. His night series from Benares, by contrast, opens with a road, a way into 'the wealth of shadows' where the 'bodies of citizens sprawled on narrow ledges', where limbs were 'bent in unconscious grace', where he could observe 'movements unobserved by the mover'.

In an undated manuscript fragment he had written of the – by no means uncommon – pleasure of looking 'at the one you love while he is asleep'. In the night streets of Benares he photographed all sleepers as if they were the beloved. These pictures of people dreaming are like a dream come true for Gedney. He became a guardian, a custodian of dreams, passing among the sleepers like Whitman:

> I wander all night in my vision,
> Stepping with light feet, swiftly and noiselessly stepping
>   and stopping,
> Bending with open eyes over the shut eyes of sleepers,

> Wandering and confused, lost to myself, ill-assorted,
>   contradictory,
> Pausing, gazing, bending, and stopping . . .

And photographing, unnoticed, invisible. That is why he had felt so
at ease among the Cornetts: they took no notice of him (they might
have paid more attention to him if he'd been a car part) while he
noticed everything about them. Look at his photograph of Indian
boys playing (football?) in the street: how close he is, how indifferent they are to him, as if he were not there. It is this absence that
enables us to identify the picture as quintessentially Gedneyan.

In 1969 he had taken a series of self-portraits in which nothing
of his head could be seen. In the picture of those kids playing
there is, in the background, a figure whose head has been similarly
amputated by the picture frame, not participating, watching. By
association, then, this figure is a self-projection of Gedney, an
explicit reminder of how the bulk of his self-portraits were of *other*
people. Alerted to that figure, we become conscious of others who
go almost unnoticed in the background, in the margins of Gedney's

pictures: the *fourth* girl, for example, who is almost completely hidden by one of the three girls in the Cornetts' kitchen above.

This, then, is how Gedney was most emphatically himself: going about his business, unnoticed, unobserved. If the corollary of this was that he should not be recognised, that his achievement go unrecognised, that was a price he was prepared to pay. Which was why, as Gedney's friend Christine Osinski suggested, it was the worst 'of all curses to get something where he would get noticed'.

He suffered from increasingly poor health throughout the mid-80s. In March 1987, he learned that he had AIDS. He had always loved fixing things but the rest of his life would be spent trying to fix, to repair himself. In 1985 he had moved to a new house in Staten Island where he did not set up his darkroom, where his books remained in crates. His plans for a book on Benares came to nothing. Nothing came to anything. He had glimpsed this tendency in himself in India: 'Withdrawn, detached too far, become not objective or subjective but beyond. Beyond photographs or thought, capable of action no longer. It happens sometimes, the futility of all being.' Now it began to seem like a destiny.

He seems already to have lost interest in taking new photographs before becoming seriously ill. He took some pictures of gay marches in New York, a few more in Paris in 1982, but, after returning from his second Indian trip in 1980 he made relatively few new photographs. Who knows? Perhaps he had seen enough in India to last him the rest of his days. Mainly he devoted himself to developing and printing hundreds of rolls of films, sifting and sorting, choosing and discarding, arranging and rearranging his life's work. He began to live posthumously.

He spent more and more time reading and transcribing what he read. George Steiner has written that learning a poem by heart means that we make it part of our blood stream, and Gedney, by dint of tireless transcription, was attempting something like a total blood transfusion. In India he had sought to dissolve almost entirely into his surroundings. Now he began to dissolve into what he read. In his final book of 'Transcriptions and Notes' his own life becomes reduced to a few entries in red ink: 'Nov. 9, 1985 finally completely moved in to 24 Van Tuyl St, Staten Island after one year in the Pratt faculty house.' Everything else was given over to other people's words, other people's lives. And yet, at the same time, everything he read began adding up to a surrogate biography, a vicarious commentary on his own work. He saw his life refracted through the prism of other people's words. It was another way of not being noticed, of revealing himself in terms of what he saw and read.

The last half-dozen pictures of what seems to be Gedney's last roll of exposed film were shot in March 1987 (the month he learned he had AIDS) and developed eight years after his death, in 1997. Possibly he clicked off a few photos of things close to hand, just to use up the film. Still, they are the last photos we have and, as such, have an inevitable place in the narrative of his life and work. They show the clutter of his desk, the things he used on a daily basis (paper clips, brushes, stamps, pencils), the things he used for seeing: magnifying glass, spectacles. On an index card is written 'EYE EXAM'. The last properly exposed frame is a close-up of his art books and exhibition catalogues, packed tightly on the shelf.

The last picture we have *of* him is on his Gay Men's Health Crisis card. The card is valid 'through Dec. 31, 1989' – six months longer than he would need it for. It shows a bespectacled middle-aged man in a scruffy brown sweater: unexceptional, a bit sad-looking, his neck and chin marked by dark blotches. If we had to sum up in a word the impression conveyed by this photograph of a man who had devoted his life to teaching himself to see, our first choice might well be 'myopic'. His gaze is neither penetrating nor alert but, on reflection, we would amend that verdict to 'accepting'.

It is a picture taken by a machine that didn't see, know or care what it was photographing.

His death, on 23 June, 1989, merited only the briefest obituaries – three cursory paragraphs – in the *New York Times*. He left his work to his friend Lee Friedlander.

1997

Nan Goldin

There is something rather irritating about some of the essays sandwiched between the photographs of *I'll Be Your Mirror**, especially Luc Sante's 'All Yesterday's Parties' and Darryl Pinckney's 'Nan's Manhattan'. 'Life was bleak on the Lower East Side in the late 1970s, but it was a purposeful bleakness,' declares Sante. 'We liked it that way.' After this cringe-making overture he gives an account of the parties, the drugs, the sex, the being-part-of-Nan's-world delirium of those heady nights. From the start it was the people in Goldin's photographs that comprised the main audience for her incrementally evolving slide show, *The Ballad of Sexual Dependency*. These images of Alphabet City transgressives had achieved hip notoriety well before they found fixed form as a book in 1986. Ten years later there is a major retrospective at the Whitney but, in keeping with the project's hermetic genesis, the catalogue essays celebrating Nan's entry into the American canon are written, so to speak, *from the inside*. This was a mistake – a loyal one, it has to be said – for little is added to our appreciation of the photographs by speaking of them *fondly*. Goldin has said, absolutely accurately, that she has never used her camera 'in a cruel way'

---

*Edited by Nan Goldin, David Armstrong, and Hans Werner Holzwarth.

erhaps the case for the importance and value of her extraordinary body of work is best made sceptically, caustically.

'The world will not see such a one as Cookie Mueller again soon,' reckons Sante. Why? What was so special about her? She did a lot of drugs, went to parties, wrote some mind-numbingly crappy prose, and died of AIDS. Sure, she was special to her friends but that's pretty much what a friend is. Put it another way: the one thing we all have in common is that we all think we're unique. Cookie's main achievement turns out to have been precisely the same as Brian's, Bobby's, Siobhan's and the rest: namely that she was photographed by her friend Nan.

Given that everybody in this circle was some kind of aspirant, it's striking how spectacularly unsuccessful most of them have been. There is no equivalent here, for example, of the then unknown Robert Mapplethorpe's shots of the then unknown Patti Smith. The truth is that Nan's are picture of losers. As such they alert us to a very recent phenomenon: the glamour of failure. What gives them their peculiar mood, however, is a very old one, dating back, at least, to the libertines of the eighteenth century: the boredom of hedonism. John Cheever claimed you could taste the loneliness in Hemingway's writing, and in Goldin's photographs the boredom is palpable, terminal. Look at the picture of 'The Monopoly Game'. Take away the board and you'd think they were in a doctor's waiting room. In this respect Nan's people are like the Goncourt brothers who, in 1861, declared that they were reassured by only 'one thing': the boredom that afflicted them. Tormented by their lack of success, they believed that their capacity for boredom was what made them special.

A hundred and twenty years later this affliction-election is not simply complemented but *measured* by one's capacity to be photographed. Goldin's camera was totally unobtrusive in even the most intimate circumstances because the world itself was a tacit camera. Even better, by a neat Warholian conceit, to be photographed sitting on the toilet, in the shower, or shooting up, was tantamount to proof of one's vocational identity *as an artist*.

With prophetic impatience D.H. Lawrence had claimed in 1925 that

> as vision developed towards the Kodak, man's idea of himself developed towards the snapshot. Primitive man simply didn't know *what* he was . . . But we have learned to see, and each of us has a complete Kodak-idea of himself . . . The picture of me, the me that is *seen*, is me.

Goldin – who regards 'the snapshot as one of the highest forms of photography' – records the apotheosis of this tendency. A spooky self-portrait from 1984 shows the photographer with two black eyes, pointing her Nikon straight at the mirror; on the right hand margin of the frame looms a second reflection, a *doppelgänger*. Even alone, the picture suggests, a photographer is lurking. In 1981 she photographs her boyfriend, the repulsively handsome Brian, smoking, next to a TV showing the *Flintstones*. A few years later she photographs him again, the Flintstones photo taped to the wall behind their bed, exactly like a thought balloon in a comic.

That picture also illustrates how the photographs in *I'll Be Your Mirror* tend to render the accompanying essays superfluous. Taken as a whole Goldin's *oeuvre* forms a narrative that mixes the simultaneous and the successive; but this is also a *critical* narrative, constantly reflecting on itself, generating its own commentary. The picture of Brian on the bed 'quotes' the Flintstones picture; very often, pinned or stuck to the walls behind Goldin's friends we see other, earlier photographs which modify – and are modified by – the later context. Sometimes the light in one photograph is so similar to another, apparently unrelated one as to bring them into sudden, touching, shocking or poignant proximity. To make the same point the opposite way: we do not properly appreciate just how extreme is the artificial light that drenches the photos from Goldin's years of heavy drug use until, following a period in rehab, we get the first glimpse of the subtleties of natural light. (In fairness to Sante, he is right to point out that Goldin was always able to 'take the most squalid corner of the worst dump and find colors and textures in it no one else saw. The blues were oceanic, the oranges crepuscular, the reds seductively hellish.' The orangey-yellow glow of many of her interiors is so distinctive that it might be called 'goldin'.) The photographs also insist, unashamedly, on assuming their place in the tradition of fine art: the famous picture of 'Bobby Masturbating' recalls Schiele; 'David on my Red Couch' evokes memories of Modigliani and Matisse; suggestions of Bonnard crop up again and again in photographs of women bathing.

The nakedness of these art historical appeals did not prevent a certain amount of indignation about the allegedly decadent content of Goldin's work (druggies, gays, transvestites) but it takes a quirkier, non-moralistic point of view to see the traces of depravity in her world. My girlfriend Valeria – when writing about Nan it seems inappropriate not to name names – looked through *The Ballad of Sexual Dependency* and, naturally, didn't bat an eyelid at the pictures of 'Bobby Masturbating' or somebody else 'Getting High'. Then she came to a photo of a couple fucking, 'Roommates in Bed', and that was too much for her. 'Ooh!' she said. 'Look at their dirty feet.' Now nothing I have read about Goldin *caught* her work – in the same way that photographers catch their subjects – as precisely as that exclamation. This, if you like, was the decisive detail. Here is Brian, hairy and smoking, sitting naked on the toilet. No big deal. Then you look at the *floor* of the place and suddenly it *is* shocking – not that he's naked, but that he is barefoot.

That observation about the dirty feet also alerts us to how, while Goldin's work is utterly of its time, it has also achieved true timelessness. So much so that the best sustained commentary on her photographs is to be found in a poem written over a half a century before any of them were taken: the third of T.S. Eliot's 'Preludes'.*

1996

---

*The Eliot Estate granted permission to quote only four of the thirteen lines I hoped to reproduce here; no matter, the complete poem is easily consulted in numerous anthologies as well as the standard editions of Eliot's work.

Andres Serrano

Hanging on the walls of the Portfolio Gallery in Edinburgh are large, very beautiful, colour photographs of corpses in a morgue. Men, women and children identified only by cause of death: 'Rat Poison Suicide', 'Knifed to Death', 'Burned to Death', 'Knifed to Death', 'AIDS-Related Death'. The victim of violent death (Christ) has been a mainstay of Western art for centuries; photos of the dead and dying (in Rwanda, in the Tour de France) appear every day on TV and in newspapers, but Andres Serrano's photos – his *still deaths*, as it were – affect us differently, more profoundly. We look at them and feel . . . nothing. No sadness, no horror, no pity. Photographs, especially of the dead and dying, tend to contain a narrative, a story. Here there is no narrative except the title, nothing to take you beyond the frame, beyond the duration of the shutter speed. There is no time in the photos (whether they achieve the timeless condition of art to which they ardently aspire is another question). We look and look at what many of us have never seen in real life and try to articulate what we feel. Nothing. Numb. Looking at them is probably as close as one can ever come to seeing what it is like to *be* dead.

And Serrano himself, how did *he* feel when he was making these pictures?

In the morgue I was all right, there was nothing that affected me adversely but I'd get home and get all bent out of shape about other things which in retrospect seem insignificant. I think it was my way of dealing with whatever uncomfortable feeling I had in the morgue. When I was there I did not allow myself to feel anything that might distract me from technical things. Lighting, focusing, these were my only concerns. If I was repelled or horrified in any way I would not allow those feelings to enter into the picture. Instead I'd get annoyed about other things. A kind of displacement.

Initially my interest was in photographing John and Jane Does, I don't know what you call them in England, you know, the unknown corpses, people who died without any known identity. They have just one or two things in common. They're dead and they have numbers tagged to them. I wanted to explore the uniqueness of such people. But they actually come in very infrequently so I decided to photograph everyone I came in contact with.

The most dramatic picture in the series is of a Jane Doe. It shows the head of a woman, already decomposing (the eyes are gone). I ask Serrano about this, referring to it, slightly inaccurately as 'Jane Doe Murdered by Police'.

Killed not murdered. Murder is more of an indictment and I'm very non-judgmental in the way I present things. She was in a stolen car. The driver got away. She was hit by five shots. She'd been in the morgue two months and if you look closely there's white skin peeling through the black skin. I asked the doctor about that and he said that's how it is: there's white skin beneath the black. And this doctor, he'd had a teacher who once took a thin slice of skin off a cadaver and said that was the thickness of racism.

So there *is* a narrative, but, as is often the case with Serrano's work, it lies outside the picture frame. Most obviously in the case of the infamous 'Piss Christ'. Look at the picture and you see a crucifix suspended in a reddish-golden amniotic light. An image bathed in its own holiness. Except, as the title hints, the crucifix turns out to be suspended in a tank of the artist's urine.

The piss artist was born in 1950 and brought up in Brooklyn by his African-Cuban mother, who spoke no English. He dropped out of High School at fifteen but subsequently spent two years at the Brooklyn Museum School. Keen to become an artist but unsatisfied with his ability to paint he turned to photography. At twenty-eight, after a street period (drug addiction and dealing) he underwent a familiar New York reversal: breaking his habit and getting serious about his work. His big break came when The American Family Association mounted a vociferous campaign against him after 'Piss Christ' was exhibited as part of a group show in Virginia. In a dramatic if somewhat predictable piece of performance art, a copy of the exhibition catalogue was ritually torn up in the Senate. Serrano was made. More precisely he had made the transition from being an artist (i.e. someone who nobody gives a toss about) to a *cause*. In the course of a transition like this scandal not only obfuscates but actually takes the place of a reasoned critical evaluation of the work. In Serrano's case, however, the controversy surrounding his work – as well as immersing icons in urine he had also made blurry photographs of his own semen in a series quaintly entitled 'Ejaculate in Trajectory' – went, so to speak, hand in hand with the unavoidable recognition that a skewed obsession with Catholicism and a perverse seriousness ran throughout his work: he had used urine, he explains, so that his colour range could be expanded to include yellow as well as red (blood) and white (milk). Love it.

His photographs since the 'Piss Christ' episode reveal a broadening of scope beyond those hoary old chestnuts, the sacred and profane (who'd have thought they still had so much life in them?). In 1990 he exhibited a series of portraits of New York's homeless intended to parallel Edward Curtis's pioneering images of American Indians. He also photographed members of the Ku Klux Klan decked out in full absurd and sinister regalia: a potentially dangerous undertaking for a Hispanic. How had they reacted to him?

Quite well actually. When I first arrived in Georgia I called Bobbie, this woman I had been put in contact with who had been the ex-Imperial Wizard's secretary for about forty years. I said I wanted to photograph Klan members and she said that if I came down in three weeks they'd all be here for a rally. She could introduce me. I said, 'That's fine but I got to tell you one thing, I'm not white, I'm Hispanic.' She said, 'Don't worry about it baby, that won't be a problem at all.' It was a slight problem though because when I turned up to meet the ex-Imperial Wizard, Bobbie was not around! I showed up with two white women. It was a hot day and everyone's sitting round in lawn chairs talking about niggers, Jews and queers. The old man was very hospitable. He asked us to sit down but there was actually a lot of tension. I stayed in Georgia about a month and slowly but surely the Klan came round to me.

It is easy to see why. Like many people who have succeeded in creating enormous offence, Serrano turns out to be courtesy and charm itself. You meet him and you share immediately in the aura of extreme relaxation that surrounds him. His eyes put you at ease because (strange for a photographer) they do not seem to be looking for anything. But they *are*, of course. To make his art – to gain access to places, to persuade people to enact the fantasy tableaux he then records on camera, to reveal things normally hidden from sight – Serrano has to have not just a photographer's but a hustler's eye for what can work for him.

Having produced a 'portrait of Budapest as [he] found it', he is currently doing a project in Rome. 'Not about Rome really, something about a state of mind. Rome is just my background. I have ideas, I look for models, I look for locations, and sometimes ideas present themselves.' Mutual friends in Rome are more precise. Andres would call and say 'I need a dog, a big dog, a big Great Dane.' He also needed ageing prostitutes to enact a couple of scenes he had in mind but they – or their pimps – wanted too much money so he asked a friend if she could get her grandmother to do it: pose nude, that is, and kiss the dick of a man who was lying down, supposed to be the dead Christ.

'No way!' the friend replied. 'You get *your* grandmother to do it.'

'My grandmother's dead,' said the artist.

So much the better, I'd have thought.

1995

Richard Misrach

Richard Misrach photographed the aftermath of the Gulf War – a cratered desert littered with bombed-out troop carriers and fire-mangled tanks – five years before it started, thousands of miles from Kuwait.

Misrach took these photographs in Nevada, at a site known as Bravo 20, which the US Navy has been using as a bombing range since 1944. We think of desert as nature stripped to its bare minimum: the absence of everything that could define a landscape as something other than desert. The desert is what is left when nothing else is. Misrach's photos show a landscape that, having been reduced to nothing by the actions of millions of years of wind and sun, has been pulverised into a state of less than nothing. There was nothing here to ruin except emptiness: what resulted was a zone of ruined emptiness. The desert had been reduced to something less than desert.

Large tracts of the American West are given over to the military but Bravo 20 was exceptional: the Navy's permit to use the land had expired in 1952. Since then the area had been bombed illegally. In 1985 local residents began camping out on Bravo 20 to protest the devastation of the area. They won a partial victory when new laws governing military use of the land were introduced – but a further lease of fifteen years was granted to the

Navy. When that expires, in 2001, Misrach plans to set up Bravo 20 as a national park, the world's first environmental memorial. In the meantime – a couple of seconds from the desert's point of view – Bravo 20 takes its licks.

It is approached by twenty miles of unsurfaced road. A sign – 'Road ahead washed out' – has been swept aside, either by a later instalment of the floods it warns against or by a vehicle determined to refute that claim. Twenty miles is a negligible distance here in Nevada, barely meriting the word 'distance'. Unless you're running on empty, or inching over gashes and trenches like us, it hardly even qualifies as a unit of measurement. The further we go the worse the road becomes. Eventually it becomes indistinguishable from that which is not road. To our left are low hills; off to the right is a glare of pale emptiness which gradually surrounds us.

We stop at a locked gate. Silence pours into our ears. Beyond the gate is Bravo 20, cordoned off by forty miles of wire fencing. The only vertical thing in sight, the fence, is a pure expression of the horizontal. Stretching out taut and level it looks like a trio of contour lines extending themselves in indefinite pursuit of some slight deviation in altitude.

Just beyond that fence, arranged and labelled in low heaps, is the detritus of bombing: shell casings, tyres, wrecked vehicles, ravaged metal. A scrapyard on the edge of nowhere.

The sky throbs. Military aircraft are specks of glinting silver, flying so high that you lose them even as you track them across the sky. The throbbing grows louder. The specks become planes, ripping the sky apart. By Lone Rock, the epicentre of the range, there is a noiseless flash and puff of earth, a drift of smoke before the noise of the explosion lumbers towards us.

The Bravo 20 pictures comprise one of Misrach's *Desert Cantos*, the name he gives to the ongoing project of photographing the American desert begun in the late 1970s.

On TV the American desert is often depicted as an incentive to thirst: a parched tongue of land whose long shadows point always to a glacier-cold beer. Polarised sky, red-filtered sand: the ad agency desert: one pint of lager to two pairs of 501s.

Misrach's desert is less hospitable, often not immediately identifiable as desert. His work explores the multiplicity of meanings in the idea of 'desertness'. Misrach's desert is a place – as the titles of some cantos suggest – of events and fires, floods and seas. Steering clear of theme-park deserts like Death Valley or Monument Valley he records the residue of human activity inscribed in these apparently uninhabited lands. These traces are never more powerful than when they are invisible, when the desert basks in the aftermath of the early, carefree days of atomic testing.

The traces are not always so ominous. At Pyramid Lake, where Misrach is working on his Desert Seas Canto, they have been left by one of the founding fathers of wilderness photography. In 1868 Timothy O'Sullivan took a famous picture of the lake and the pyramid-shaped rocks that give the place its name. Like his contemporary Carleton Watkins (who made some of the first photos of Yosemite), O'Sullivan was born in the East but did much of his work under the auspices of government surveys as America pursued its Manifest Destiny, forging its way west, mapping the wilderness.

Stooped down at his bellows camera, legs protruding from the shrouding photographer's cloth, Misrach seems a figure more akin to his nineteenth-century antecedents (with their unwieldy equipment and long exposure times) than to his contemporaries (with their bags of versatile Nikons). His work also has explicit compositional resemblances with O'Sullivan's. An 1868 photograph of a covered wagon becalmed in the sand hills of Nevada offers a vivid pre-echo of many of the Bravo 20 photographs. In O'Sullivan's picture the sense is of the dwarfing scale and implacable power of the land. In Misrach it is of its vulnerability.

Unlike these early photographers, Misrach was born in the West (in Los Angeles, in 1949) and is gradually working his way east, making manifest what has been left in the wake of America's military-technological destiny. The framing of the wilderness by O'Sullivan and others was a necessary prelude to preserving it for posterity in the national parks – but a corollary of enshrining the beauty of the Grand Canyon or Yosemite in this way was that what happened outside these magnificent natural preserves was implicitly unimportant. The desert was just desert.

At Pyramid Lake Misrach is covering O'Sullivan's tracks; more often he strays far from them, photographing places previously cropped from America's inherited frame of visual reference. In doing so he also registers a shift in our conception of and need for the wilderness. American landscape photography grew out of the European tradition of landscape painting, specifically Romantic rapture in the face of the transcendental power of mountains. In America this fed directly into the cult of Yosemite which culminates, photographically, in the work of Ansel Adams. Increasingly, however, it is the sun-scorched emptiness of the desert, a place that is at once pre- and post-historic, that exerts a hold on us. Don DeLillo has described the desert as 'a container for emptiness' and, in a world stripped of transcendent values, we are drawn increasingly into that vacuum.

An hour's drive from Pyramid Lake, near the desert town of Gerlach, is a narrow track called Guru Avenue. The track's edge is lined with messages written on stones: DO YOU BELIEVE WHAT IS BELIEVED; THE DEVIL IS AN ANGEL NEXT TO SADAM HUSSEIN. There are dozens of these pronouncements and questions, always in the same careful handwriting, the hand of the desert sage who signs himself simply 'Dooby'. ON THIS DATE IN 1991 NOTHING HAPPENED. The strange thing about this comment is that it is *un*dated. Here and there a particular individual is singled out for praise on inscriptions that seem like epitaphs to the living: THE WORLD NEEDS MORE PEOPLE LIKE YOU ANNETTE MARSHALL. As we continue along the avenue we move deeper into this world of deranged wisdom, of profound banality. BREATHE THE POWER; IF YOU WANT DIRECTIONS ASK BILL STAPLETON; THE ENTIRE WORLD IS CRAZY I CAN PROVE IT.

These messages are interspersed with more elaborate pieces: a skeletal wigwam made of sagebrush; near the doorway is a sheep's skull with an arrow through its eye socket; from the apex of the roof a can of faded Bud dangles over the words ARE YOU READY FOR ETERNITY.

Near the end of the Avenue we come to 'The Imagination Station in Dooby Vision', a straw and wood hut with all the dusty comforts of home: armchair, TV set, sideboard, magazines. The windows are made of the glassless frames of TV screens, about six of them, each facing a different direction. It is dark and cool inside the hut. Stretched out in the armchair, I sip beer and watch the most perfect TV images ever seen: on one channel there is a square of aching sky; on another, a shadow-sloped hills; on a third, the dust expanse of desert.

All stations of Dooby Vision are broadcast in absolute silence, a silence so extreme that the slightest sound receives maximum amplification: a fly buzzing, a lizard scuttling drily, grit crossing the road . . .

We actually run into Dooby at the gas station in Gerlach. I'd expected an acid-ravaged Manson but Dooby is in his fifties, splinters of old-timer stubble sprouting from his chin. He's a regular guy – workshirt, baseball cap – but it's impossible to read his eyes; they have taken in so much sun and distance it is impossible to get close to them.

*

Fifteen miles out of Gerlach we turn off the highway again, on to the dry lake bed – or *playa* – of the Black Rock Desert. An endless elongation of flatness. Heavy winter rains have left some parts of the *playa* spongy, treacherous, and at first we drive cautiously through the darker patches of whiteness. Soon a dry plume of talc is billowing in our wake and we accelerate to a state of pure momentum. Speed is meaningless because nothing changes. To say that there are low hills in the distance makes no sense for everything here is in the distance. The *playa* is pure distance.

I walk from the van until eventually it shimmers, floats and disappears. Further on I cross two narrow channels of thick brown water, flowing rapidly in spite of the total lack of gradient. The mud is silky and emits a soothing odour of calamine. The sun is directly overhead. My shadow is buried beneath my feet. I put my tennis shoes on the ground and in moments they look like they will be there for ever (which is another way of saying they look as if they have always been there). This applies to oneself also. It is easy to imagine sitting down, achieving some state of heatstroke meditation and remaining here indefinitely. Becoming petrified, turning into a sun-dried Dooby sculpture that is neither living nor dead, part of the natural process of wind and light.

The silence in Guru Avenue was nothing compared to this. Sound here is the red surf of blood in your ears. The trick is to subdue the clamour of thought, to let your head become as empty as what surrounds it.

In the hands of some photographers, film becomes as sensitive to sound as it is to light. The best photographs are to be listened to as well as looked at. Misrach is the great photographer of silence.

We drive across the *playa* in the direction of Black Rock. Herds of clouds roam the sky. A fluke of shadow turns Black Rock – a light shade of grey most of the time – into a jade slag-heap surrounded by a blaze of light. Part of Misrach's craft has nothing to do with the camera. It involves roaming the desert in his van for weeks at a time, putting himself at the mercy of the landscape, waiting for moments like this, for the light to happen. He uses no filters. The colours we see in his photographs are the colours that were there at the time. He uses the same film, the same lens, the same 8″ × 10″ Dierdorff camera. In the same way that our own field of vision remains constant, all Misrach's pictures are, in a sense, the same. Like the landscape depicted, they are all-engulfing. And just as the overwhelming scale of the landscape is implicit in each part of it, so each photo within each Canto contains the vaster project of which it is a part.

Many times in the course of our trip I am struck by the inherent photographability of the desert. Misrach's pictures have internalised both the space of the desert and the space of the gallery wall in which they will hang. The horizontal space of the desert and the vertical space of the photograph are interchangeable. It is possible, therefore, to lose yourself in Misrach's pictures.

We drive along Highway 50 – the loneliest road in America, apparently – before heading north to Wendover where, in the spring and early summer of 1945, last-minute preparation and training for the dropping of the atom bomb took place. The town itself is on the border of Utah and Nevada. Like the 'high place of darkness and light' in Dylan's 'Isis', the dividing line runs through the centre of town, splitting it into two states, two time zones. At the airbase itself time stands still and the buildings are still standing – but fading. This is Misrach's theme: *fading*. Colours fade, the graffiti on the walls of the offices and hangars fades, the memory of what happened here is fading. History fades. But history for Misrach is, precisely, this fading. His photos preserve and arrest the history of fading.

I wander through the disused, wooden buildings. Beyond the perimeter fence, lines of blue hills are backdropped against each other, becoming bluer until eventually they are backdropped by the sky. Apart from shadows inching their way around the site, nothing moves. The scene is still and silent as a photograph. It is like tripping, like walking through a Misrach photograph in 3-D, experiencing with all your senses the virtual reality of the photograph.

Presumably the Wendover airbase looked like this before Misrach photographed it. Or perhaps, more radically, the place has taken on and absorbed the qualities of his pictures, adjusted itself to them (in an almost literal sense there was nothing to see before Misrach photographed here).

On the edge of Wendover the salt flats are so extensive that you can see clearly the curvature of the earth. Every year the Bonneville world land speed championships are held out here on the flats. Misrach will return later in the year to photograph the event itself – which is to say he will not photograph the event itself but the peripheral activity surrounding it (in his Canto 'The Event', the ostensible focus of attention, the space shuttle gliding into land, is visible only as a speck in just one of the pictures). An underlying irony draws Misrach to this particular event. In 1846 a group of emigrants en route to California became lost near here; half of the so-called Donner party perished in the ensuing winter. Later this year, on the same flats, vehicles will reach speeds of 500 mph.

Now, in early summer, parts of the flats are still under a couple of inches of water. Some way off, like a contemporary monument to the Donner party, a family car has sunk up to its axles in an area of sudden mud.

Whether there is water here or not, the frost-whiteness of the salt always gives way to a glisten of blue. You approach and the blue recedes. In the distance a rock floats above the horizon, perfectly reflected in a sea that doesn't exist. Misrach photographs the illusion but the whole landscape, in any case, is like a mirage: an Arctic frost of salt, a crystal mirror throwing the white-hot sun back into your eyes.

Towards evening the flats change colour by the second: violet, lavender, turquoise, purple. Even my shadow is blue against the white salt. Car tracks are silver, yellow, gold. The flats blaze like the brightest colours there have ever been – but infinitely faded. No sooner have the colours been noticed than they have changed, resolved themselves into something even more beautiful and wondrous and still.

Beyond the salt flats a road shimmers with cars and trucks; beyond the road a Union Pacific freight hauls itself beneath a horizon of snow-crowned mountains. In the sky is a pale smudge of moon. Landscape and light arrange themselves into a photograph.

1993

Atkinson Grimshaw

It was in the early 1870s, in his mid-thirties, that Atkinson Grimshaw began producing the dockside and street scenes for which he is best known: the moon climbing over the bay, rising clear of a forest of masts and rigging; a few strollers bathed in the warm glow of shop fronts. After mastering the moonlight thing in the 1880s he began, in the few years before his death in 1893, to extend his meteorological range somewhat. *Lights on the Mersey* and *At Anchor* of 1892 and 1893 respectively are small, intensely calm, Whistleresque nocturnes. *Sand, Sea and Sky*, a daylight beach scene from 1892, shows distant but colourful figures on pale sands; in *The Turn of the Tide* these figures have vanished, leaving the scene to fidgeting gulls and sand, sea, clouds. At the same time, he seems also to have returned to the Pre-Raphaelite style that marked his early, unexceptional beginnings. *An Extensive Meadow with Geese by a Stream* is like a Pre-Raphaelite landscape seen through eyes that no longer have the sharpness of vision that characterised the Brotherhood in its heyday.

A hardened modernist could accuse Grimshaw of using a limited repertoire of effects to serve up endless permutations of the same scene, usually overlain with a patina of Tennysonian genre sentiment: 'So sad, so strange, the days that are no more.' *The*

Old Gates, Yew Court, Scalby (1874) seems like a crepuscular premonition of scenes routinely yearned for by David Inshaw and the Brotherhood of Ruralists. The moonlit scenes of the late 1870s and 80s, however, repay sustained attention.

Typically, as in *Under the Leafless Trees* or (pictured here) *Silver Moonlight*, they show a solitary figure on a deserted lane, moonlight smouldering through clouds, the gas lights of a mansion visible through the black branches of leafless trees. I'm lazily tempted to describe them as haunting since this adds a sense of unease to their enduring fascination (Bram Stoker was an admirer), but this is a consequence, probably, of my first coming across his work on the cover of a Penguin edition of *The Turn of the Screw*.

Similarly, despite the fact that his paintings appear so frequently on the covers of Victorian novels, it is a mistake to see Grimshaw either as their painterly equivalent or, as is claimed in the catalogue to the exhibition at the Richard Green Gallery, as the painter of the 'spirit of the Victorian city'. Even in his dockside scenes there is none of the crowd and bustle of Dickens (though there is Dickensian fog: so thick and brown that the mud on the streets seems to have simply fallen from the air). Instead, we have promenaders or lone figures beside the homes of northern industrialists. These figures are not only excluded from the rooms glimpsed through the windows but separated from the grounds of the house by high walls, by wealth. There is always a gate, however, so that the house, while safe, is not inaccessible. The Englishman's home might be a castle but, as depicted by Grimshaw, it is not a castle besieged by the poor. He shows the Victorian era untouched by class conflict: the security brought by wealth with no reminders of the squalor on which it is built. The figures (a lone serving-girl or two lovers) pose no threat; they exist only to enhance the atmosphere of the painting.

Grimshaw did many of these paintings for the owners of the homes depicted. Once the picture was installed inside they could enjoy a view of their house from the outside without leaving the comfort of their own home. Grimshaw's work depends on exactly this paradox of domesticity: to truly appreciate cosiness you have to imagine what it might seem like from the outside (that's why people leave their curtains open). But the lonely figures in Grimshaw do more than enhance the domesticity that can only be glimpsed through the toast-coloured windows. They are to the Victorian ideal of domesticity what Caspar David Friedrich's lone figures by the sea are to the vast, unspecified longings of German Romanticism. Grimshaw's enduring achievement is to make this Victorian ideal as mysterious and resonant as the Germanic.

How? Unlike Knostrop Hall, the Jacobean mansion that, from 1870 onwards, was Grimshaw's own home, many of the houses he painted had only recently been built. A miscellany of turrets and decorations from earlier architectural styles gave them an air of instant agedness and Grimshaw painted them in such a way as to make them look older still.

The importance of this becomes apparent when we consider another distinctive quality of his paintings: their stillness, their damp silence. In *Autumn Morning* no leaves are falling: most have already fallen, a few are still to fall. Only that which is still remains. However hard you listen to the moonlit scenes there is only the sound of old rain in puddles. No wind, not even the sound of the woman's shoes splashing through the puddles. The reason for this, I think, is that the painting's *effective* duration extends sufficiently to include the time when she has disappeared round the curve of the lane. Old photographs often make city streets seem deserted because the long exposure time 'vaporises' moving people or falling leaves. People and houses cannot exist in the same time- or picture-frame. In the same way, Grimshaw's figures seem constantly about to dissolve into the time contained within the painting. An old photo elides a few seconds; Grimshaw's paintings, decades. His dusks are also strangely like memories of all other dusks like this – *even those that are still to come* (when the woman has disappeared down the lane, when the recently built house is as old as he makes it – and the owner wants it to – seem). In other words, the painting looks forward to a time when what it depicts will be a memory of what was to be.

This process is inscribed in the paintings themselves. The mud on the wet lane is criss-crossed by the wheels of coaches and the feet of pedestrians, which, over time, will reveal a reflection at present glimpsed only fragmentarily in puddles. Eventually, however, the wet lane will show a perfect image of the scene – without the people and the coaches who lent it its meaning. Perhaps, then, these pictures *are* haunted after all – by future ghosts.

1990

The Life of Paul Gauguin

It was in Moscow, a city I hated, that I came to love Gauguin. By my last day there I had conceived such a loathing of the place I could hardly be bothered to do the one thing that I wanted to do: visit the Pushkin Museum. In the end it was only the brown awfulness of my room that persuaded me to venture out into the grey awfulness of Moscow and head for the Museum.

And there they were: four great Gauguins, negating not only the ugliness outside, but also my own petty irritation. Squares of canvas where beauty had kept faith with itself. They were there every day, *waiting to be seen*.

Like everyone else I knew a little about Gauguin – dim memories of *Lust for Life*, memories that were probably as far removed from the film as the film was from reality – but from then on I was on the look-out for a comprehensive biography. Now there is one. David Sweetman has performed a great service, arranging years of travel and research into a painstaking, absorbing account of every facet of Gauguin's life.*

He opens with one of those chest-beating prologues in which the biographer announces the specialness of his endeavours. In this overture the discarded *Moon and Sixpence* myth of the

---

Paul Gauguin: A Complete Life.

stockbroker gone native is invoked in order that it might be re-debunked to reveal Gauguin as a 'renegade, syphilitic paedophile'. Six hundred pages later, the notoriously twisted record having been set as straight as it is ever likely to be, one's sense of awe at Gauguin's life and work is enhanced rather than diminished by his biographer's sores-and-all ministrations. What better tribute could there be to Sweetman? One should feel indebted to him – one *does* feel indebted to him – but there is something about the book that turns one against it, something that brings to a head all one's generic reservations about biographers.

'Without biography there is only speculation,' Sweetman declares, implying that *with* biography there can be an end to speculation, with biography there are *answers*. No, what a biography provides is a convenient assembly of materials to be drawn on as Gauguin drew on the unwieldy scholarly under-takings of Jacques-Antoine Moerenhout and Gerald Massey, or as he drew on the Maori art exhibited in Auckland, New Zealand. Gauguin's cavalier behaviour in Auckland gnaws at Sweetman: 'Had he glanced at the *New Zealand Herald* of Tuesday 20 August,' he chides. 'Had he taken the trouble to find out . . .' Biographers are always puffing themselves up in these terms: *until me no one had bothered to consult this archive, to chase up that correspondent* . . . Good luck to them too – but to reproach the subject, even tacitly, for not being as diligent as his biographer! Beware the great temptation of biography: to bury the genius you seek to elucidate beneath a wealth of detail.

Especially since the commitment to thoroughness means, paradoxically, that things get overlooked. Biographers need to be as alert as novelists to the small movements, gestures or details that enact the larger psychological profile they are trying to build. Sweetman dutifully describes what Gauguin was wearing when he first arrived in Tahiti but he also misses the opportunity to convey one of his main themes – the artist's complex relation to imperial adventurism – in the most concise fashion imaginable. Here is art historian Kirk Varnedoe on Gauguin's arrival:

> Though he recognised that his inner nature was divided between an 'Indian' side and a 'sensitive' side, he was apparently less aware of the confusion in his mind between Indian and cowboy as models of uncorrupted courage. Thus, while he practised with bow and arrow on Brittany's beaches after seeing the Indians in Buffalo Bill's Paris show of 1889, he arrived in Tahiti wearing a cowboy hat over shoulder-length hair, in the image of the scout himself.

In a nutshell! Varnedoe's masterly essay also casts light on another of Sweetman's deficiencies. While he provides a great deal of socio-economic background, Sweetman's Gauguin is always, as it were, *pasted on to* this background rather than moving within it. It is another aspect of the biographer's craft that requires something of the novelist's – remember how John Berger made Spanish history course through Picasso's bloodstream? – whereas Sweetman is essentially a text and context man. Much of this context is extremely useful and even if some of it – like the pages defining the exact nature of Gauguin's dealings on the stockmarket – is superfluous to the needs of a general reader like myself, it is good to know it is there, to be consulted should the need arise. What is lacking is, in Raymond Williams's terms, 'the dramatisation of a process'.

Perhaps one should not be surprised at this. If Gauguin was in some ways a representative of the French imperial expansionism to which his art offers an apparent counterpoint, Sweetman is an exemplary type of the modern, industrial biographer. Years of research and then a gruelling schedule of so many thousand words a day, banging it out, banging it out. Copy editors are often the unsung heroes of this mode of literary production but in this case it has been impossible to quality-check all the verbal components. Stylistically it is not so unpleasant to have Gauguin's life aboard ship described within two pages as 'hardly pleasant' and 'far from pleasant'; and it may not be a particular sign of literary impoverishment to refer to Theo Van Gogh as 'the poor man' twice in two paragraphs; to write of *The Four Breton Women*, however, that it 'was clearly a satisfying achievement, but there is clearly more to the picture than just its "abstract" qualities' is clearly less than satisfactory. Here as elsewhere Sweetman tries to render the not-quite-right word right by putting it in inverted commas. Evoking the character of *Japonisme* he attempts to pass the linguistic buck by writing of '"the look", as a fashion writer might put it', when what he really means by this is 'as a biographer in a hurry might put it'.

One is almost resigned to this kind of thing in whopping great biographies and it can seem like nit-picking to point out little infelicities, but Sweetman's 'rather relaxed' (in the previous line Gauguin was 'rather aimlessly pondering his future') attitude to the finer points of writing leads to some rather relaxed, aimless thought: 'Fortunately for his sanity, Gauguin was basically an optimist . . .'

With so weak a psychological grasp of his subject, some of Gauguin's actions perplex Sweetman more than they need. A little speculation – a useful quality when dealing with a one-time stockbroker – can take us nearer the truth precisely because it goes beyond the facts. Take the instance noted earlier when Gauguin, overcome with lethargy, neglected the opportunity to investigate Auckland and the Maori art exhibited there. He had just made the momentous, massive decision to leave France for good. Once he had done that nothing else mattered. He could abandon himself, for he knew now that the momentum of this decision was enough to carry him through to the end of his destiny.

No other artist's life or work compels us to confront this notion of destiny as nakedly as Gauguin's. Compare him with Van Gogh, who would have turned out more or less as he did no matter what happened to him. His life is like a wire tightened to breaking point. The tension of the entire life is there at every moment of it. Gauguin, by contrast, could have washed up anywhere; his life is full of abandoned lives: sailor, stockbroker, tarpaulin salesman, artist-carouser . . . Interludes of slack despondency and periods of feverish activity come together in a tangle of strong impulses and uncertain direction. At the same time there is a massive driving egotism, a streak of cunning – Pissarro, his one-time mentor, thought Gauguin a 'schemer' – that saw the potentiality for harnessing this recklessness, compacting it into a determining core.

It is completely in keeping with the essential trajectory of Gauguin's life that the decision to leave France for good was forced on him, as was so often the case, by converging circumstances. Again and again in Gauguin's life, a series of apparently unrelated actions, often accidents, bears the imprint of his will. 'It has been like this all my life,' he wrote. 'I get to the edge of the abyss but never fall in.'

Gauguin knew that his work would always be at the mercy of his existence. The technical struggle with paint (and that, Sweetman's account makes plain, was protracted enough) was secondary to this struggle to live on the brink of the possible – even though that existence would be forged in the name of painting. We are always moved by those artists who come perilously close to failure and defeat; Gauguin's story persists as a myth because the journey to Tahiti, to the ends of the earth, gives such literal expression to the idea of someone going to the edge, pushing himself as far as possible. Either he would be a *great* painter or he would be nothing. This was a massive gamble – he had earned, he said, 'the right to dare all' – and we know now that it paid off in a way that Gauguin himself could never have been certain of. This is one of the virtues of Sweetman's method: bogged down as he is in the immediacy of circumstances, Gauguin's struggle is not lost in the redemptive glare of the great works. Significantly, the one painting Gauguin kept with him was *Self-portrait near Golgotha*, a totem of the suffering to which he was 'hardened'. Once completed, the rest of the paintings were rolled up and shipped to France so Gauguin was able to draw scant comfort from the imaginative world he had realised on canvas. There is therefore something very moving about the happy interlude he spends contemplating the achieved mystery of *Where Do We Come From? What Are We? Where Are We Going?*

Sweetman offers a dutiful reading of this vast canvas but he is far more competent as a researcher into the life than as a commentator on the work. When it comes to the paintings he taps away at his desk like Teha'amana on her bed, the spirits of Berger (in early-70s *Ways of Seeing* mode, prodding him about representations of the female nude) and Edward Said (the artist as imperialist poacher) looking over his shoulder. Like a timid magistrate he is all the time weighing up the 'charges' against Gauguin but, as Norman Mailer pointed out in *The Prisoner of Sex*, 'literary lawyers cannot do criticism, they can only write briefs'. The transcripts of Sweetman's less than magisterial deliberations contain some critical equivalents of classic courtroom dodges: he makes a point in the full knowledge that an objection to it will inevitably be sustained – because even when subsequently cancelled out the point will have lodged in the mind. *The Four Breton Women*, for example, could be seen as 'a rather harsh comment on a group of indolent peasant women – which could in turn be seen as a reflection on [Gauguin's] attitude to women in general', even though, as Sweetman concedes in the following paragraph, 'this is probably going too far', forcing him to conclude inconclusively that

'Gauguin had no fixed ideas about what he was doing as yet, and was still trying things out in a random way'.

Sweetman's whole critical procedure shuttles back and forth at this dull level of 'readings' and 'interpretations' which can be 'pushed further' even though it invariably turns out to be a mistake to take things too far. The idea, presumably, is that a kind of critical average will eventually emerge. But the paintings cannot be averaged out like this, that is not what they are waiting for.

The tendency to average out is especially apparent in Sweetman's treatment of Gauguin and women, Gauguin and sexuality. Much of this stuff, one feels, comes not so much from heartfelt indignation as from a sweet man's need to show that he can hold his own at some dismal ICA conference on 'revelation and concealment and . . . issues of male sexuality, the eroticism of dress, the nature of sexual identity and masking' and God knows what else. His characteristic procedure is to outline a parody of the feminist case against Gauguin as a 'sexual tourist' searching out a place where there is plenty of 'cheap-and-easy sex for wealthy white males' and then qualifying and amending his way back to a suitably neutered version of the artist's greatness. Since it refuses to be averaged out, a painting like *The Spirit of the Dead Keeping Watch* is deemed 'prurient' – but what could be more prurient than the critic's daubing it with smutty little clichés about the young girl's 'pert buttocks'? It's still fun to read Kate Millett giving D.H. Lawrence a caning in *Sexual Politics*, but Sweetman's art historical feminism is, as Lawrence said of Gauguin, 'a bit snivelling'.

Besides, how weary and parochial all this fretting about the representation of women sounds. It so happens that I am writing this in an ancient urban paradise where the light blazes as it did on the first day of creation. To have eyes is to be a god here. And there are women, beautiful women everywhere, women with long black hair, tanned skins, wearing only the simplest dresses.

Everywhere there are women's limbs and men's eyes on them. The sun itself stares down and touches these women's limbs: that is why they are so tanned. And here and there, in the markets, with the fruit ripening all around, you see the girls who are becoming women, beginning to be looked at – becoming aware that they are being looked at – in a different way. You don't need to have a thing about young girls, or to want to play Our-Little-Secret with a thirteen-year-old to feel the eye beginning to linger, to sense how watching merges into a kind of waiting. What cloudy, northern arrogance to claim that women are diminished by the male gaze when here, in the south, away from the drizzle of political morality, a woman feels men's eyes on her as easily as the sea feels the sun, warming to it.

One watches Sweetman grapple with the spectre of art historical feminism like Jacob Wrestling the Angel, but this vision proves so unilluminating that the wrestler himself is forced to submit, rather wanly, that it is not those who 'study his paintings and his writings' – people like himself, in other words – but the 'average gallery-goer, the ordinary member of the public' who may well have the best 'appreciation of Gauguin's legacy'. Quite a climb-down from the earlier, vaulting claims on behalf of biography! It comes close to swinging Sweetman round to Gauguin's own tacitly *anti*-biographical suggestion that 'the work of a man is the explanation of that man'.

In his explanations of that work Gauguin comes back again and again to the 'mysterious' – i.e. *in*explicable – nature of one or the other of the symbols he is explicating. This abiding sense of mystery is at the heart of Gauguin's art. It is especially haunting in the gaze of his women because this look seems, precisely, to contain, to *hold* the resolution of the mystery they suggest. Earlier visitors to Tahiti had commented on the peculiar grace and stillness of its inhabitants, often interpreting this as torpor or boredom, but Gauguin saw something more: 'Animal figures rigid as statues – something indescribably ancient, august, religious in the rhythm of their gestures, in their extraordinary immobility. In the dreaming eyes, the blurred surface of some unfathomable enigma.'

This description of what he saw conveys perfectly what *we* see in Gauguin's images of women. Looking at them I am reminded of Picasso's remark that the African masks hanging around his studio were 'more witnesses than models'. It is the same with Gauguin's women. They are witnessing themselves being painted – being seen – by Gauguin. They gaze out of the paintings as if they are staring into them, like ideal all-comprehending spectators who see them exactly as Gauguin intended. 'The title has two meanings,' he said of *Manao Tupapau*, 'either she thinks of the spirit, or the spirit thinks of her.' A similar self-circling movement joins Gauguin and the women in his pictures.

In *The Vision after the Sermon: Jacob Wrestling the Angel* Gauguin used the diagonal of the tree to divide the naturalist scene of the Breton women from the 'vision' that appeared to them. In late paintings like *Te Rerioa* there is no telling where the dream begins and ends, each level of signification – the oneiric and the real, the dream and the woman dreaming – is contained in the space of the picture. There is no time – or sound – in this or any of the other Tahitian paintings. The horseman in the background is so still that he might as well be a figure in a canvas hanging on the walls as a scene glimpsed beyond them. The raised axe in *Matamoe* or *Man with an Axe* will never fall. Despite the plethora of symbols all narrative in his paintings is suspended. Seen in this light Gauguin's rejection of impressionism was important not just as a move from representation to invention but as an attempt to free himself from the primacy of the momentary and the fleeting in favour of the non-temporal, the eternal. In Tahiti, goaded by the timelessness of the great images of Western art, against which he never ceased to measure his own endeavours, this ambition coincided with what he imagined to be his subject's experience of time. Typically the paintings fuse the timeless poses of high art (Western, Egyptian, Javanese: never Polynesian) with the immemorial stillness of the Polynesian women. To look at the pictures is thus to enter a little loop of eternity. The experience is best evoked not by a description of the paintings but by D.H. Lawrence in a letter describing his reactions to the Pacific coast of Mexico which he saw, as it were, through the eyes of Gauguin's art:

> It's very like the South Sea Isles in quality . . . a queer bay with tropical huts and natives very like islanders, soft, dark, some almost black, and handsome. That Pacific blue-black in the eyes and hair, fathomless, timeless. They don't know the meaning of time. And they *can't* care. All the walls and nooks of our time-enclosure are down for them. Their eternity is vast, they can't care at all. Their blue-black eyes . . . I have learnt something from them. The vastness of Pacific time, unhistoried, undivided.

1995

Pierre Bonnard

With the woman he loves about to try her luck on the Genetic Lottery – a gamble that will change her, physically, beyond all recognition – the narrator of Peter Carey's story, 'The Chance', finds himself moved by images of constancy. By an elderly couple helping each other down the street, or by the paintings Pierre Bonnard made of his wife Marthe:

> Bonnard painted his wife for more than twenty years. Whilst her arse and tits sagged he painted her better and better. It made my eyes water with sentimental tears to think of the old Mme Bonnard posing for the ageing M Bonnard, standing in the bathroom or sitting on the toilet seat of their tiny flat.

Actually it was more like forty years. They met in 1893 when she was twenty-four, Bonnard a few years older. And Marthe, as they grew older together, did not exactly pose for Bonnard. As she went about her business, he made rapid sketches of moments he found compelling and then worked from memory in the studio.

The resulting paintings, the ones Carey's narrator has in mind, show a domestic paradise where the sexual power of the beloved is enhanced by utter familiarity. Bonnard evokes that stage in a sexual relationship when you cannot take your eyes off the beloved, when the most ordinary gesture fills you with longing. In Bonnard's paintings this phase lasts forever.

As we learn more about the couple's life together, however, a different impression emerges from the paintings. If we follow Bonnard's own advice and 'bring back certain elements which lie outside the rectangle' then what we see in the rectangle of his art changes. One of the reasons Bonnard so often painted Marthe in the bath, for example, was that she spent so much of her time in it. (When, in 1926, they bought the Villa du Bosquet, near Cannes, one of the first improvements they made was the installation of a luxurious bathroom.) Marthe was difficult, reclusive; as she got older she became neurasthenic, incapable of being left alone, obsessed with keeping herself clean. According to Robert Hughes, she was 'a nagging, neurotic shrew who made life miserable for Bonnard and his friends, knew nothing about painting, and could not even cook'. (What, no *tucker* for poor Pete?)

Actually Marthe *did* know something about painting – she had a joint exhibition in Paris, Monet admired her work – but in this harsh light Bonnard comes increasingly to resemble the figure of the pet dog who waits adoringly on his mistress in many of the paintings. In the context of this relationship of obsessive, claustrophobic mutual dependence, Bonnard's work becomes not exactly anguished, not troubled even but considerably more poignant. In the current show at the Hayward, a painting of 1927 shows Marthe on the steps of the Villa du Bosquet, dressed to go out. What, by normal standards, is an unremarkable activity in daily life (but an extremely rare one in the life recorded by Bonnard's paintings) results in a painting, made with infinite tenderness and care, of extreme vulnerability. Imagine this picture, as it were, five minutes after the moment it depicts. She will still be there, an image of *paralysed volition*. Continue to imagine Marthe's life at le Bosquet – it remained their principal home for the rest of their lives – for a few moments more. The house and studio – which she is increasingly reluctant to leave – are constantly filling up with pictures of herself, naked, stunning, blazing with light. Everywhere she went – which was practically nowhere – she saw herself in the wonderful glow of Bonnard's art. Carey's narrator says he painted 'her better and better' but in practice this meant *less and less like she had become*. For the last twenty years of Marthe's life Bonnard painted her as she had been in the first years of their relationship: unchanged, held in the agelessness of his paintings.

All the testimony we have about the couple's life together is hearsay. Bonnard's art provides such an abundance of circumstantial evidence – rooms, furniture, plates – about life at le Bosquet that, as Sargy Mann remarks in the catalogue to the Hayward exhibition, we come to feel *at home* in his paintings. But these paintings, which reveal the Bonnards' lives in such intense detail, veil the privacy they display. The beauty of Bonnard's colours, moreover, dissuades us from seeing just how strange – how troubling – many of his paintings are. In a bath painting of 1936, Marthe's face has been, so to speak, painted to a pulp; in a painting of 1930 she seems like a corpse, floating Ophelia-like in her bath.

When Marthe died, in 1942, Bonnard told only a few close friends. To Matisse he wrote: 'You can imagine my grief and my solitude, filled with bitterness and my anxiety about the life I might have to lead from now on.' He had painted Marthe everywhere in their house except in her bedroom. Now he kept that door locked. And he went on painting her. In *Nu dans le Bain au Petit Chien*, which he worked on from 1941–46, the bath has lost all hardness, has become an amniotic sac, adapting itself to her shape. Marthe floats like an elongated embryo. The painting is pregnant with her memory.

1994

Edvard Munch

Neurosis seems too mild a term for the protracted bouts of dementia, angst, dread and hysteria that regularly convulsed Edvard Munch. 'Sickness and insanity', reads a characteristically jaunty reminiscence, 'were the black angels that guarded my cradle.' Death came soon after: his mother died in 1868 when he was five, his sister nine years later; his father in 1889.

Munch was in Paris at the time, where, having worked through the influences of naturalism and impressionism, he was avidly absorbing the lessons of Gauguin and symbolism. Back in Norway his work was greeted with widespread derision, but powerful figures within the avant garde of Christiania – now Oslo – encouraged and championed his obsessive pursuit of his own style.

Almost as soon as this style emerged, in the early 1890s, he began to think in terms of arranging his paintings in a series. In the works grouped around the theme of 'Love' in 1892, he assembled the visual components, archetypes and forms that would serve as imaginative templates for the rest of his life.

A rippling shoreline, a desolate figure in the foreground. A woman on the edge of a lake-side forest, the reflection of the moon like a yellow test tube on the water. What light remains in these late summer evenings emanates from the figures it has shone on during the day. Women glow like candles, with flaming wicks of hair. Ghostly, weightless, they hover in space, as if figments of the imagination of the jealous man (a self-portrait of the artist, invariably) wounded and brooding in the shadows.

To this initial group of paintings Munch added works on the themes of anxiety and death which make up *The Frieze of Life*, a constantly evolving, almost sentient project. Paintings mutated into each other as a limited set of motifs was endlessly re-worked, often in different media (woodcuts, lithographs). The pale corpse-like figures making their way down Karl Johan Street in 1892 are, by 1894, flowing over the bridge where Munch, in his best-known painting, 'felt a great, infinite scream pass through nature'.

When Munch first arranged his paintings for *The Frieze* he noted how, in a phrase uncannily reminiscent of the remark quoted above, 'suddenly a single musical note passed through them all'. That single note is sounded by *The Scream* which becomes visibly audible, so to speak, even in the still silence of the other paintings. In a harmless sketch of a figure leaning over a Paris balcony you can hear the first compositional pre-echo of *The Scream*. By *Despair* of 1892 the sunset is beginning the delirious ripple which will soon curdle around the foetal, skull-like creature of *The Scream*.

Most paintings in *The Frieze* date from the last decade of the century. Although Munch continued adding works, the looser, scrappier handling of paint that characterises his style after 1902 dilutes the imaginative density of his vision. After a complete breakdown in 1908 he went on to create huge sun-engulfed allegories but the grandness of their ambition seems almost to compensate for a control and intensity he could no longer achieve.

'I need my own paintings,' Munch insisted. 'I must have them near me if I am to continue working.' Rather than adding significantly to *The Frieze* the last thirty years of his life were spent re-jigging, re-producing and rearranging a world he had already created. On his 75th birthday he was photographed in front of his *Frieze* on an ornately uncomfortable sofa. Dressed up – trussed would be a more appropriate word – formally, like a man in a coffin, he might as well be dead.

A problem for commentators is that Munch himself provided a perpetual gloss on his works and the incidents that gave rise to them. Few artists have provided handier epigraphs – 'I was born dying' – for subsequent monographers. Even adverse comment has tended to adopt the artist's favoured vocabulary of sickness and instability. In 1895 a critic dubbed Munch's work 'a sick mind's similarly unhealthy and repulsive nightmares'. Munch's reputation has been radically upgraded since then, but admiration is still expressed in more or less equivalent terms. Reinhold Heller, a leading authority and author of a standard work on Munch, is quick to notice the 'streaks of red symbolising [his] tortured striving.' Put like that, the striving doesn't sound remotely tortured. Heard through this kind of critical filter *The Scream* sounds like art historical easy listening.

The first step in removing this filter is to remember, without in any way playing down the traumas of the artist's life, that in the bohemian circles of *fin de siècle* Christiania and Berlin, anyone with a vague inclination to the arts had to aspire to be, as Munch put it, 'an aristocrat of the nerves'. Everybody was perpetually on the verge of breakdown. What distinguishes Munch is not simply his talent or propensity for delirium but his *tenacity*. Munch worked up a highly individual pictorial language and established a set of visual conventions to express what, as much as private anxiety, we might term a larger *de*structure of feeling. In a passage hauntingly evocative of Munch's canvases, Marshall Berman has described how an 'atmosphere – of agitation and turbulence, psychic dizziness and drunkenness . . . self-enlargement and

self-derangement, phantoms in the street and in the s[
atmosphere in which modern sensibility is born'.

A century later, on the far side of modernity, this t
world of Munch's now seems relatively alluring. While the catalogue claims that the 1906 *Self-portrait with Bottle of Wine*
reveals 'the depth of his despair' it would come as no surprise, a
few years from now, to find it used as an advert for Scandinavian
rosé. Similarly, with the whole of the art historical past being
ransacked for commercials it is difficult, when looking at his
Death and the Maiden – a voluptuous woman embracing her
skeletal lover – not to wonder if this will end up being used in a
safe-sex advertisement. (On balance, probably not: in Munch,
the erotic urge is at its most powerful when it is entwined with
the thanotic.)

As for torment, let's not underestimate the trauma of visiting
a major art show these days. Coping with crowds, queuing at the
cloakroom, fighting off the knee-aching weariness that overwhelms you the instant you're inside a gallery . . . And that's just
for starters. It's afterwards that the real contemporary force of
Munch's vision becomes most apparent. It would be a relief to
step out of the National Gallery and find yourself not in the
pigeon-congested, bomb-threatened grimness of Trafalgar
Square but in the hallucinatory brightness of Karl Johan, the
street of 'pale corpses'. Munch's world seems attractively psychedelic by comparison. These days, you can be sure, despair
doesn't come in swirls of blood-red and flaming yellow – it just
drizzles down greyly. Typically, it will not be a scream you hear
but a *mutter* passing through London as the traffic clogs up over
Waterloo bridge. In an era of imaginative recession, in other
words, Munch's vision strikes us as imaginatively abundant, luxurious even. A psychotic twilight in Christiania seems
increasingly akin to the paint-drenched idyll of Gauguin's Tahiti.

1992

Egon Schiele

'At the end of the puritanical nineteenth century,' writes Milan Kundera, 'erotic taboos were still powerful, but the loosening of morals awoke an equally powerful longing to overstep those taboos. Shame and shamelessness transected each other at the point when both had equal force. That was a moment of extraordinary erotic tension. Vienna encountered it at the turn of the century.'

Egon Schiele, who was born in Tulln in 1890, came to Vienna at precisely this moment, in 1906, to study at the Academy of Visual Arts. He left the Academy in 1909, by which time, encouraged by Gustav Klimt, he had begun accepting commissions and submitting his work to exhibitions. Schiele had a number of influential patrons and although imprisoned for his sexually explicit drawings he was not the hounded martyr of many self-portraits. By the time of his death, aged twenty-eight, in the influenza epidemic of 1918, he had already produced a massive body of work that established him as the foremost Viennese painter of his time. It was not until the 1960s, however, that his reputation grew internationally, and it is only since the late 1970s that he has become known to postcard buyers and monograph readers the West over.

This is no accident for the angular contortions of Schiele's figures correspond exactly with the gestures and haircuts that had their origin in punk. Otto Benesch, son of one of Schiele's first patrons, recalls the artist's 'dark brown hair which stood out in all directions'; Arthur Roessler, tireless champion of Schiele's work, remembers his 'narrow shoulders, long arms and long-fingered, bony hands'. These are exactly the qualities Schiele emphasised in the self-portraits whose distinctive style of compulsive skinniness anticipates the dominant aesthetic of the last dozen years.

One of Schiele's first commissions was as a designer for Wiener Werkstatte whose clothes were modelled by the artist's sister, Gerti. Not only have today's fashion illustrators totally absorbed Schiele's style but, to us, Schiele's *Self-portrait with Winter Cherry* makes him look like a leather-jacketed Lou Reed; likewise the operatic portrait of himself and Klimt dressed as *Hermits* puts us in mind of the nightclub excesses of the New Romantics. What is important is not the poses but the *idea* of posing that the twenty-two-year-old Schiele shared with style-conscious art students seventy years later. This was the time, you may remember, when it was considered hip to be constantly looking in the mirror – and Schiele's mirror was the most important part of his studio.

For other artists the mirror was a tool, for Schiele it was his subject, a site of frenzied experimentation, the cage and theatre in which he staged his balletic autopsies of the self. In *Self-portrait, Kneeling* of 1910 we see him imprisoned, Houdini-like, by picture frame and mirror, right hand pressed hard against the restraining glass, as if desperate to escape from what he is into that which he appears to be – and (for this is the nature of mirrors) vice versa.

One of the received opinions of expressionist portraiture is that the artist probed into the psyche of his subject. If this is the case

then it is remarkable how Schiele seemed to find again and again
in his subjects exactly the same angst that characterised his own
self-portraits. In fact even Schiele's subjects were mirrors and his
pictures of them are vicarious self-portraits. Schiele notoriously
(and ambidexterously) painted himself masturbating, and many
of his female nudes are, by the same token, vicarious portraits of
himself masturbating. This elision of gender is intensified by
the way that, on occasions, Schiele depicted his own genitals as
an androgynous blob and gash; whether painting himself or his
models there is always the same rash of colour,

> always the one face, regardless of sex,
> the mouth a pursed carnation-red, the eyes
> asking a need they can't realise
> the pose convulsively provocative . . .*

Schiele's critics have often gone to considerable lengths to claim
that the nudes are, in Frank Whitford's words, 'in no way sexually stimulating'. Even when the pictures' overwhelming erotic
content is conceded, a sub-*Ways of Seeing* investigation of the
similarities and differences between his images and those in
Playboy is not far behind. To see Schiele's pictures as the crux in
a debate about pornography and erotica is to think in clichés.
The paintings have nothing to say on this point. That is not the
question they are asking, it is not the issue they are addressing.
You see, art puts us in the dock too, it tests us as surely as we
examine it. Simultaneously it questions and answers our gaze.
This is especially so with Schiele whose nudes – like initiating
mirrors, mirrors that simultaneously anticipate and adjust themselves to my every glance – seem to be articulating what I feel as
I look at them. What, then, do they say, these figures

---

*Verse quotations from 'Egon Schiele' by Jeremy Reed, *Nineties*, 1990.

> In their solitary abandonment,
> mauve stockings, black necklaces, still half dressed,
> skinny, underdeveloped, tauntingly
> consumed by a blood-heat that won't relent [?]

They say and hear me say: even if there had never been such a thing as pornography, even if there had never been paintings like this, men would want to look at women in this way. They say and hear me say: look at these hips, these biceps and the curve of the spine. They say and hear me say: what a pleasure it is to draw as easily as this, to feel the pencil moving swiftly over the paper, to feel it glide along a thigh in one long line.

No single work expresses this as clearly as a sketch showing a model in front of a mirror which reflects both herself and Schiele glancing up from his sketchpad, scrutinising his own image.

Although it has none of the languor of Klimt (Schiele's art historical importance is as the link between the *Jugendstil* of Klimt and the full glare of Expressionism) this sketch is calmer than much of his work, especially the larger paintings. In these raw portraits and the numerous variations on the theme of Death and the Maiden, a recent critic sees 'a panic and a fear that closely borders on hysteria'. Collector Rudolf Leopold talks of 'the torment of solitude, the terror of being haunted by one's own visions'. What is striking about these descriptions is how *un*tormented they make Schiele's representations of *homo extremis* seem. If these comments are accurate – if the experience of the paintings can be formulated so comfortably – then they have exactly the opposite effect to that intended, diminishing Schiele's stature in the act of affirming it.

The torment in much of Schiele's work is nothing if not contrived. Paintings of 1911 like *Self-Seer* (which shows the artist in a state of psychic meltdown) or *The Poet* (in which Schiele's glimpsed chest and stomach resemble a huge decapitated and chancred phallus stroked by skeletal fingers) are *too* self-dramatisingly saturated in the effect they seek to elicit to be genuinely confessional. The angst is only pigment deep, a product of a way of painting rather than the expression of a crisis of being.

Schiele died at twenty-eight; past that age it is difficult to respond to many of his paintings with the same intensity of feelings they provoke while your own age is in tandem with his. Joyce has grown old with the century; Schiele remains the century's perpetual prodigy, full of the swarming hormones of modernism, wired on his own abundant talent. This is not to denigrate Schiele's achievement or youth; it is a way of seeing his achievement more clearly, of acknowledging how what is seen in the mirror of his paintings changes over time.

1990

The Airfix Generation

We were the war children. Born a decade and a half after the Second World War ended, we devoted all our energy to re-creating it. If the 1930s saw a period of escalating military expenditure then the 1960s saw us imaginatively rearming. All our games and toys were designed to enable us to relive the heyday of Overlord and El Alamein; even now my first choice in a video shop is always a couple of episodes of *The World at War*. I would gladly trade any holiday in Italy for the chance to have been a GI in Sicily in 1943 . . . OK, maybe not: let's say being on holiday in Kent in the summer of 1940, watching the Battle of Britain rage overhead. Looking at Constable's cloud studies in the Tate I find myself thinking how much better they would look with a Spitfire swooping down through the cumulus. Show me a picture of any Allied or German plane and I will identify it without the aid of conscious thought: Junkers 88, Gloster Meteor (first British jet fighter, my father worked in the factory that built them), Hawker Typhoon, Heinkel 111, Dornier 215, Focke-Wulf 190 . . .

We can call this condition, common to all boys of my gener-ation, *Airfixation*. There were many strands to our war experience – comics, films, toys – but the core experience is represented by Airfix. Designed to reproduce the machinery of war in miniature, Airfix represents this whole condition in miniature. Airfix provides us with all the necessary parts; if we assemble them piece by piece and glue them together we will have a model of the larger experience and process by which the War was recycled.

The first kit I bought was a Curtiss P40 Kittyhawk (famous for the snarling teeth insignia); the second was a Spitfire and from there I moved on to other fighters: Me 109, Hurricane, Focke-Wulfe 190, Mitsubishi Zero, Me 262 (Germany's first operational jet fighter). There was a clear route from these fighters, whose sole feature was a moving propeller (DO NOT CEMENT), to two- or three-seaters like the Avro Anson, the Stuka dive-bomber (Junkers 87), the Boulton-Paul Defiant (the poetry of aircraft names!), and fragile, ungainly spotters like the Fieseler Storch and the Westland Lysander. From these I moved on to light bombers like the De Havilland Mosquito and the Bristol Blenheim (a useless plane but a good kit) before graduating to the big night bombers: Lancasters and Halifaxes, moulded in black plastic with half a dozen crew members, moving gun turrets, opening bomb doors and yellow chevron transfers on the tailfins.

Fighters came in polythene bags stapled to an illustrated card – 'instructions on reverse' – which hung from a display stand; bombers came in hangar-sized boxes. I remember my parents buying me both a Wellington and a Halifax for Christmas one year and I still only really appreciate presents that are box-shaped (books and CDs as opposed to sweaters) because, during those seminal Christmases, anything that wasn't in a box wasn't an Airfix model (I loved the tell-tale rattle) and was therefore a disappointment. The Boeing B-29 Super-Fortress came in the biggest box but, by common consent, the most challenging kit was the earlier, slightly smaller B-17 Flying Fortress. The B-29 was a more advanced plane than the B-17 but there is no correlation between the performance of an aircraft and its MP or Modelling Potential. It was the B-29's near invulnerability to attack that made it a boring model: a long silver tube with wings; by contrast the B-17's abundance of vulnerable perspex gun turrets (along with an awesome wingspan and the insignia of a scantily clad woman) greatly enhanced its MP.

I was ten or eleven by the time I made my first Flying Fortress and I made it very badly. I made all my models badly. I didn't bother filing the parts to make them fit snugly, I got glue on bits that were meant to be left unstuck: propellers didn't spin, undercarriages didn't so much retract as collapse, cockpits were blurred with smears of glue.

The only thing I was consistently scrupulous about was painting the propeller tips yellow. Often these were the only parts I did paint (though I carefully added the purple V on the wing of my B-17); instead I just stuck the insignia on to the naked grey plastic (what a rare pleasure it was to watch the decals slip free in a saucer of lukewarm water before sliding them into place, unripped, drops of water falling from your fingers). Later, I sometimes painted round the transfers but, ignorant of the difference between gloss and matt, the planes often ended up with a high-visibility glisten of green and brown camouflage.

When you had finished building the planes there was the problem of what to do with them (whirling them around your head and making spluttering Rolls-Royce Merlin noises through pursed lips, blowing at the propellers to make them rotate – these were transient pleasures). The best bet was to mount them on the perspex stand, but I always forgot to clear the plastic niche away in advance and so had to prise open the two halves of the fuselage in order to ram the stand in. The only alternative was to hang them from the ceiling by string, leaving you with a view of their wings (sky blue against squares of polystyrene cloud) while the top halves gathered dust invisibly.

Statistically the war-time odds were against a bomber crew lasting out their tour of duty and the chances were that, in time, most models would be blasted apart by flak from an air rifle or set ablaze and thrown out of a bedroom window.

These days, under the challenge of computer games, Airfix no longer enjoys the position of uncontested dominance that it did back then, in the 1960s and early 1970s. After the war many planes were scrapped as new defensive needs and technological change (the development of the jet engine, most notably) rendered them obsolete. In the same way many stalwarts of the Airfix Second World War range are currently unavailable and the catalogue is increasingly dominated – especially in the wake of Desert Storm – by hi-tech jets. The Stealth bomber, the Tornado, the F-15 Eagle and the YF-22 Lightning are now pushing back the edge of an envelope represented, for us, by the Phantom, the Buccaneer, the BAC Lightning and the vast, delta-winged Vulcan.

The 1:72 ground forces that complemented the planes have been hit even harder by cuts in Airfix defence spending. Only a fraction of the battalions of soldiers that filled toy-shop shelves twenty years ago are around now. These came in boxes with an oblong Cellophane window through which you could glimpse a few of the soldiers inside, arranged randomly on little plastic stems (like 'decal', the word 'sprig', after lying idle in the attic of my vocabulary for more than twenty years, leaps suddenly to mind). The soldiers were attached to these sprigs by their bases and if, contrary to instructions, you twisted and pulled them free (instead off slicing them off cleanly with a razor) the remaining twist of plastic meant that instead of standing flat they ended up balanced awkwardly on a kind of wobble-board.

There were forty-eight men per set. As well as the expected action poses – firing from kneeling, lying and standing positions, running, marching, crawling, throwing grenades – there were always a few men wounded, dying or surrendering. This was standard issue but each set also had a few special features.

U.S. Marines had a dinghy (in two parts) with men to row it (difficult to sit them on the side without their falling overboard); men with anchors or grappling hooks; flame throwers. Japs were sand-coloured, one or two waved flags, at least one wore a cap and brandished a sword. Significantly, none was surrendering. British Paratroops had someone rolling in a 'chute, a bazooka, long supply cylinders and a couple of strangely baseless men doing nothing (freefalling? writhing in agony?). Commandos had canoes (the canoeists were amputated at the waist, a long plastic stump enabled you to plug them into the canoe), ladders, several men brandishing knives and another crouching at a det-onator (he actually looked like someone kneeling down to take a bottle of wine out of a picnic hamper).

First World War British Infantry featured two men running with a ball of barbed wire, officers with swords and pistols, stretcher bearers. Their German foes had a man crawling with a bangalore (a long broom-like thing), officers looking through binoculars, machine guns. Oddly, these Germans of the Great War were fractionally bigger than some of the other sets so that if you scaled them up to an average real-life size of five foot ten the German Infantry of a generation later was, by comparison, a pygmy army in which the average height was five foot two inches. Conversely, if we use the later army to establish the norm, their ancestors were a race of six foot six *Übermenschen*.

In addition to these armies there were various other sets like Cowboys (shiny brown gunslingers and bucking broncos) and Wagon Train (covered wagon, boxes of supplies, women in Victorian dresses). Bright green and slightly ridiculous, the Robin Hood set included one Robin, one Maid Marian, a Friar Tuck and dozens of unnamed extras with bows and staves. In the entire Tarzan set there was basically only one good piece – plus a monkey, a little boy, a few white hunters and hordes of natives.

Although this inclusion of named individuals contravened some ethic or convention of the series, my mania for collecting meant that I had to have them. In fact, in the interests of completeness, I not only had the massed ranks of the Grenadier guards (the only interesting piece was a man with a sword, stamping his foot) but Civilians and Farm Animals.

These aside, the other sets were issued in such a way that they formed conflicting pairs:

Ancient Britons	Romans
Robin Hood	Sheriff of Nottingham
Confederate Infantry	Union Infantry
Cowboys	Indians
French Foreign Legion	Arabs
WWI Brits	WWI Germans
WWII Brits	WWII Germans
Eighth Army	Afrika Korps
US Marines	Japs

Unlike the model planes the 1:72 series of figures has not kept pace with recent events: you look in vain for SAS versus Iranian terrorists, picketing miners versus riot police, Chelsea fans versus Leeds supporters (an excellent Subbuteo accessory). Instead, the depleted 1:72 series remains rooted firmly in the past – a past which, as the above Pools Check of armed conflict reveals, adds up to a fascinatingly static dialectic of history. History is a series of battles between two roughly equal sides. Only the costumes vary. No side is ever out-numbered in the Airfix version of military history (there are as many Commando raiders as German Infantry) and, regardless of the conflict, the casualty rate remains the same: typically four per cent (two per box). Similarly, although by the age of nine, words like bulk head, fuselage, aileron and undercarriage were staples of my vocabulary, and though I had absorbed an extraordinary quantity of aeronautical technical data (turning circles, speeds, ceiling altitudes) there was never any sense of the real purpose of bombers like the Lancaster: to rain indiscriminate death and destruction on the civilian population of Germany (over 42,000 died in the raid on Hamburg, for example).

This becomes more significant when we remember that Airfix represents in miniature a much larger process of reproduction and re-presentation of war that dominated our childhood. The full experience includes the 'Gott in Himmel' heroics of Battle Picture Library comics, American equivalents like *Our Fighting Forces*, bubble gum cards (there was a series devoted to winners of the Victoria Cross) and films (the 1969 production of *The Battle of Britain* was practically an advert for Airfix). Documentaries, meanwhile, offered the chance to authenticate the accuracy of the various details in these models and toys. Even now, on the few occasions when I see a real Spitfire, I am struck by how like a *model* Spitfire it is. This is crucial: untouched by the actual conflict, the deepest layer of our memory of war is derived from a network of simulation. Our first memories are not of the reality but of a highly contrived and simplified – and yet painstakingly realistic – representation of it. The reproductions came first and their accuracy was subsequently authenticated – because the correctness of the details was confirmed – while simultaneously being revised, supplemented and enlarged but never *discredited* by documentaries.

The Rat Patrol was a 1960s TV series about the activities of American and British soldiers of the Long-Range Desert Group. Far more popular with my friends than *The Man from U.N.C.L.E.* even, it was taken off the air after a few episodes because British veterans complained that there were in fact no Americans in the North African campaign. It makes no difference, incidentally, if I have got this wrong; what matters is that this is how I remember the controversy. Accurate or not, my interest in the North African campaign has its origin in *The Rat Patrol*. In a sense every documentary or book about Montgomery and Rommel, the Eighth Army or the Afrika Korps takes as its starting-point, and elaborates on, that first fictive documentary, *The Rat Patrol*, which, in memory, still looks entirely accurate. The case of the feature film *Memphis Belle* is especially illuminating: I went to see it because of a model of the plane featured in the documentary (which I had never seen) on which the fictional film was based. And yet, throughout, I was anxious that some scenes were not quite *realistic* enough.

My abiding interest in the whole war is similarly motivated. If it fascinates more than any other period of history it is partly because of this entwining of successive layers of simulation and fact. But it is also a nostalgic harking back – a harking back not only to some high point in our island story (in Churchillian phrase) but also to a high point in my childhood – in *our* childhood. For boys of my generation, the Airfix era, like the Battle of Britain and the Blitz, retains its power because it was something that we all went through *together*: a unifying experience that has become part of our collective consciousness. That is why, even if I live for a hundred years, I will still look back and say: *this* was our finest hour.

1992

Action Man

I knew about Action Man ahead of many of my contemporaries. The American superhero comics I collected were full of ads for GI Joe, a foot-high 'doll' with moveable limbs and changeable weapons and uniforms. These ads featured squads of model GIs inching their way up a beach in simulated combat. Action Man, when he hit our own beaches in 1966, was obviously just Joe under an assumed name. Like Joe, Action came with brown, black or blond (banana yellow) hair and a disproportionately large dog tag round his neck. On his right cheek, a scar imparted, to the blond one at least, a hint of the duelling Prussian aristocracy. Although there were three shades of hair, Action came in only one skin colour, white, i.e. off-pink. (Did Palitoy undertake market research to establish the commercial feasibility of producing a number of black Actions? In America is there now a quota system specifying a minimum ratio of black to white models?) Although there were no black Action Men there was, or so we liked to joke, an Italian one: he came out of the box with his hands raised, ready to surrender.

These boxes (with stencilled bullet holes in the M of Man) depicted men from each of the three services in appropriate action (camouflaged soldier bursting through exploding foliage) but the models inside were in a state of extreme combat unreadiness. Green, blue or grey fatigues – together with boots and matching plastic caps – identified him as soldier, sailor or pilot. To get Inaction ready for any kind of battle you had to start shelling out for accessories. In terms of expenditure 29s 11d for the Man himself was not the end, nor even the beginning of the end – it was, simply, the end of the beginning.

My Man first saw action beneath the waves, in his frogman kit: wet suit, black plastic flippers, oxygen tanks, orange airhose and matching mask. I loved frogmen from *GI Combat* comics, especially when they flippered out from a sub, caught a Jap diver attaching a limpet mine to the side of the conning tower and ripped out his airhose. I remember thinking how nice it must have been to swim back into the sub after an underwater fight like that: getting dry and having a hot drink.

Like all accessory packs the Frogman's outfit came with a number of red stars. The more expensive the item the more stars you received (Action himself came with five). When you had saved twenty-one stars you sent them off and got another Action Man free. These were a disappointment. Flesh-coloured, naked, they arrived by post with knee joints so weak they could barely stand, and were too limp-wristed to hold a rifle. If the models in the shops were A1, these were D4, the dregs of production line conscription. Following any war's tendency to recruit the fittest first before being forced, subsequently, to lower standards, our Palitoy armies came increasingly to be made up of men who were initially rejected as unfit for duty.

But this growing army of seconds needed equipment. And so, just as war generates its own momentum, so we had to keep forking out for munitions and uniforms. The more equipment you bought, the more stars you accumulated; the more stars you collected the more men you ended up with and the more accessories you needed . . . The French Revolution initiated the idea of the citizen-soldier; Palitoy pioneered the idea of the soldier-boy-consumer who, in the kind of inversion so loved by The Frankfurt School, became the *plaything* of the product in his hands. At the peak of his popularity there were estimated to be four Action Men for every three boys in the country. Bear in mind that this was also the great era of Airfix models and you see that the whole toy economy had been put, so to speak, on a war-time footing: Buy for Victory!

And buy we did! For my birthday in June I got the Snow Patrol outfit. My mother took a photo of my father and me in the garden with our shirts off while Action sweated away in white snow suit, green goggles and skis, black and white rifle slung over his book. (I can't remember the actual event, only the photograph – which I haven't seen in ten years. A *Blade Runner*-style implant?) The following Christmas, Action joined the Military Police and was issued with a brown tunic with a row of medal ribbons above the breast pocket, red cravat and arm band, white helmet and buff-coloured truncheon. By Easter he was a jet pilot with grey flying suit, green-visored helmet and oxygen mask, fluorescent plastic life-vest and clipper board – similar to those used by market researchers – with a pencil tucked into one side.

Pocket money went on half-crown, single-star accessories like map cases (grey tubes with a map inside and MAPS stencilled on the side), ammo boxes (green attaché cases with AMMO BOX stencilled on the side), camouflage netting or mess tins with knives, forks and spoons inside . . .

Palitoy prided itself on attention to detail and these details have been flawlessly imprinted on our collective memory: the plastic lace patterns on Action's boots; the khaki elastic strap of his carbine; the little buckle on the helmet strap and the plastic niche into which it was anchored; the serrated edge of one part of the diver's knife; the genetic logo embossed on his back: 'Made in England by Palitoy under Licence from Hasbro © 1964'.

Palitoy aimed to equip Action with all the paraphernalia of combat in reduced scale. Rival firms aimed to reproduce all the paraphernalia of Palitoy at reduced price. Asia entered the price-war with a whole range of bootleg militaria from Hong Kong at a fraction of the Palitoy price: shoddy rifles, bright green helmets, camouflage trousers that were too big round the waist and sagged around Action's buttocks like builders' jeans.

On the home front, my dad built a house fit for heroes, a hardboard barracks-pillbox where my four Action Men were stationed in celibate readiness. In an effort to cut costs and keep up with the insatiable demand for materials, my mother contributed a lime green combat jacket, a fluffy sleeping bag, a turtle neck sweater (from an old sock), a corduroy jacket and beige slacks (Action Man Undercover Agent).

Things escalated to a state of total consumption when, in an exact reversal of the chronology of the actual war, the British joined in with Tommy Gunn, a home-grown, slightly smaller and vaguely inferior version of Action Man. This may have been an accurate reflection of the way better diet and higher living standards made the Americans more robust specimens than the under-nourished, Blitz-weary Brits, but Tommy was doomed, like Britain itself, to economic defeat. With his slightly red face, elastic boot laces and gaiters, there was something strangely First World War-ish about him and he failed to make a significant contribution to the retail effort.

Besides, Action's range had by then spread to the uniforms of other armies: British, Russian and Australian Infantrymen and French Resistance fighter in black beret and polo neck (only the revolver and shoulder holster prevented his being mistaken for a beat poet). Best of all was the German Stormtrooper, which meant that the massive build up of American arms was no longer ornamental. Action finally had someone to fight against.

Except his fighting effectiveness was severely hampered by a chronic ability to hold anything (I wrapped a rubber band around the handle of the knife to enable him to at least make a stab at holding it). This was remedied in 1973 – 'which was', as Philip Larkin said of the same year in the previous decade, 'rather late for me' – when Action developed gripping hands. By then he had already sprouted realistic hair. His voice broke soon after, rasping out a few random commands when you tugged a cord in his back. In the case of the sailor he even grew a beard. Action man, in other words, hit *technological* puberty at exactly the same time that we did.

Having achieved maturity and won the war for toy-shop supremacy Action had to find peacetime employment. By the time I bought my last kit he was slogging away as a Deep Sea Diver: brass helmet and breast-plate, dry suit elasticated at wrists and ankles (almost impossible to get off and on), sledgehammer, weighted shoes that looked like the customised DMs that women wore in the mid-80s, asserting their right to look as unattractive as they pleased.

The tendency to take his cue from contemporary rather than wartime events had been heralded by the silver foil astronaut suit and space capsule of 1969. The 1970s became increasingly future-oriented. As the past began to lag behind the inspirational tug of the future so, in terms of all-round performance, real humans began to lag behind pseudo-humans. Palitoy had struggled to render Action more and more lifelike. In the 1970s the tables began to turn. Model humans – cyborgs, androids and replicants – set the standard that plain humans aspired to. Action Man as traditionally conceived was human, all too human. From now on toys had to become less lifelike not more. Dragged frantically into a bionic, laser-intensive future, he did not so much disappear from shops in 1984 as dissolve into a growing army of Robo-toys.

Disappearance and death, though, are only necessary preliminary stages on the road to rebirth as a cyborg. And now, after
eight years in suspended animation, Action is back in action.
The four new models on the market look like they were modelled on cartoons rather than people. They are mere *toys* in fact,
floating free of any anchoring in real history. This is a shame, for
Action, in his original incarnations, was much more than a
simple plaything.

In recent years much has been made of ideas of the simu-
lacrum and virtual reality. By the late 1960s though, you could
experience all the thrills and spills of virtually anything in the
privacy of your own home: football (Subbuteo), Grand Prix
racing (Scalextric), driving (Corgi and Dinky), building a house
(Lego). The world, in short, was reproducing itself in miniature
on a scale never before seen and Action Man represented the climactic development of the most comprehensive part of this
process: the recycling and miniaturisation of the Second World
War. Until then miniature soldiers had been either toys or
models; Action Man was both. The *largest* miniaturisation so far
undertaken (not one sixth of life-size but, from the child's point
of view, one third) he was also the most lifelike. This narrowing
gap between recycled and real war was almost closed during the
Vietnam War when 'GI Joe Must Go' demos were held outside
toy-shops in America. Action had become stitched into the history he was designed to mimic.

We British children were untroubled by thoughts of Vietnam.
As we arranged our Action Men in various attitudes of combat
we had only one concern: did they look realistic? We looked at
them, in other words, as if through a camera. What we effectively constructed in these mock combat scenarios were 3-D
photographs. Our sense of how these sculptural photos should
look may have been inspired by – and fact-checked against –
films and comics but, in their obsessive interest with details,

these early assays at combat-*verité* reveal the first throb of a concern with the real history of the war. In its mildest form this might amount to no more than a fondness for *The World at War*; at its most intense it can mean that, by your mid-thirties, you are well on the way to reading nothing but military history.

These early strata of Action-derived memory have not accumulated passively, moreover, but have actively shaped our sense of how the war should be remembered.

A friend and I recently visited the American military cemetery just outside Cambridge. Lines of white crosses curved into the distance. The names of men whose bodies were never recovered were carved on a white wall so long that the inscription stretched out along the top was impossible to take in. Every ten yards or so the columns of names were framed by carved figures of airmen, sailors and marines. By the standards of Action Man and Airfix these figures were very poorly sculpted. By contrast, the meticulously rendered figures in the Great War memorials of Albert Toft, for example, represent the scaled-up fulfilment of an aesthetic first embodied in miniature by Action Man and Airfix figures. These were, if you like, the moulds from which my taste in memorial art had been formed. For boys of my generation it is scarcely an exaggeration to say that, in their way, Action Man and Airfix figures are to the Second World War what statues of the Unknown Soldier were to the First.

1993

Unpacking My Library

'I'm unpacking my library. Yes I am.'

It's something I've been looking forward to ever since my books went into storage in 1989. During that time, when I was on the move constantly, living in different countries, books, which are the only things I have ever cared to own (and which are, in a sense, my bread and butter) became a hindrance. Although I continued to write not just fiction but what might generously be called semi-learned articles, I had to do without them. Sometimes I called my parents and asked them to check a reference or quotation from the stack but it was easier, in the end, to cut down on references. Living abroad meant a move out of quotation marks.

There was also, I discovered, an impressive tradition of people doing without the books on which they depend. The most famous example is probably Erich Auerbach, whose magisterial study of 'the representation of reality in Western literature', *Mimesis*, was written in exile in Istanbul where, he notes (what joy to go over to my shelves and check this reference!), 'the libraries were not equipped for European studies'. Dispensing 'with almost all periodicals, with almost all the more recent investigations, and in some cases, with reliable critical editions of my texts', Auerbach yet wondered if this deprivation were not a blessing in disguise: access to everything he needed might have prevented his ever reaching 'the point of writing'. Auerbach was at least in *one* place; nomadic to the point of frenzy, D.H. Lawrence relied on whatever books friends posted to him. 'Do you still have that book *Early Greek Philosophers* which I bought when I was last in London? If so, would you send it me, I want to do some work on the Apocalypse, and consult it,' runs a characteristic request to a much-put-upon friend in 1929. The next sentence is even more characteristic of Lawrence's method of radically contingent research: 'If you haven't got it, no matter.' In authentically Lawrentian vein, John Berger once remarked that although he admired a certain writer's intellect, there was always an off-putting sense that all this writer had to do to find something out was lift a book from the shelves.

Now I'm a shelf-lifter too! I've been assembling and arranging my books for days, compulsively, relentlessly, staying up till three in the morning. 'Nothing highlights the fascination of unpacking more clearly than the difficulty of stopping this activity.' Now that I have most of my books together again I want them not simply in one place but in one room, with all the friendly adjacency – Bachelard, Barthes – and ironic intimacy – Amis's *The Information* and Machado de Assis's *Epitaph of a Small Winner* – decreed by unwavering alphabetical arrangement. This proves to be impossible: there are too many rogue volumes which are too tall for the vertical shelf-space available, and which have to be consigned to a special over-sized section. Since novels tend to be smaller than non-fiction books this can be resolved by arranging by subject, but this generates its own problems: what do I do with Williams, Raymond? Lump everything together under W or sub-divide between fiction, criticism and politics? And what about *Quasi Una Fantasia*? Do I put it under music or, with the rest of Adorno's output, under the vague classification philosophy/cultural theory (i.e. difficult books translated from the German)?

These problems are a source of unresolvable pleasure but I am determined to keep to the principle of one room only. This means throwing out some books. Which ones? Non-fiction is always useful, but novels, the bulk of them are worthless! That's why you end up keeping them, because they're not even worth selling: *no one* wants them. Once one rejects the principle of completeness, in fact, the main feeling is of how few books you need. Over the last five years I rarely had more than twenty books with me wherever I lived, and although it generated a little inconvenience it didn't cause any major problems. Now I've suddenly got thousands. Throw away three and, according to the same criteria by which they were excluded, you can get rid of another 30 or 300 or 3,000. Peter Carey used to be one of my favourite authors; he is the author of what remains one of my favourite books of stories, *The Fat Man in History*, which I have in Faber's original English edition. I didn't rate *Bliss*, his first novel, and since I have it only in paperback I put that in my 'to be sold' box. As a piece of writing, the sprawling *Illywhacker* no longer means anything to me but since it's a signed first edition I want to hang on to it. And if I keep that then I'm somehow obliged to keep my hardback of the Booker-winning *Oscar and Lucinda*, even though that was the book that made me give up on Carey – and since I'm keeping *that* then I might as well hang on to the Picador *Bliss* for the sake of completeness. And so it goes on. I take them out of boxes, put them on to the shelves, take them down and into a box to be sold and then haul them out and up again. *Vox* by Nicholson Baker: a paperback of a crummy book but you never know: it might, as they say, come in handy one day . . .

These are the marginal cases but there are many books which I see again with unalloyed delight, like *Illuminations* by Walter Benjamin, whose essay, 'Unpacking my Library' (source of all unattributed quotations throughout this piece), I am at last able to consult. The nicest way to acquire books, suggests Benjamin, is to write them. I think not. The books I care least about in my collection are my own. In a sense they're not in my collection (they are the only ones in which I haven't written my name). They're replaceable in a way that the others are not, because although I could get another identical *But Beautiful* I could never again get that copy of Russell Banks's *Affliction* which I bought from Barnes and Noble on Fifth Avenue the day Fi had terrible cystitis. Or that copy of *Something Happened* I was carrying the night Nigel Raynsford and I got 'our heads duffed in' (as we used to say) outside the Suffolk Arms during the summer holiday after A levels. Or that copy of Herbert Lottman's (out-of-print) biography of Camus, which is slightly buckled because it got drenched with spray one afternoon in Tipasa . . .

I keep hauling them out of boxes, and 'what memories crowd upon' me as I do so. 'Memories of the cities in which I found so many things'. Not least because, for the last fifteen years I have dutifully written on the fly-leaf, in pencil, the date and place of either acquisition or reading, whichever is the more glamorous (hence Alistair Horne's *A Savage War of Peace* is inscribed 'Algiers, Oct' 91' even though it was actually bought in Foyle's, Charing Cross Road). These inscriptions mean that my books add up to a massively unwieldy diary. If my library were the only source to go on you could get a fairly accurate idea not only of where I lived at any one time but, to a degree, of my employment history. The gradual transition from paperback to hardback in the mid-80s, for example, marks my progress from reader to critic (i.e. from buying books to getting them free). You would see from the period of greatest accumulation, 1987–89, that I almost certainly worked for a particular London publisher where books were there for the taking. Less concretely, it would also be possible to follow the contours of my intellectual development, or, more accurately, of my intellectual decline. The evidence of my library suggests, unequivocally, that the period of greatest advance (when I devoured Raymond Williams, Foucault, Nietzsche and Barthes) took place in the three years after I left university – well over a decade ago.

Not that I care. I don't even need an intellect, now that I've got all my books around me. Finding myself, at last, in the perfect situation for work I don't want to do any work. I can't go for more than a few moments without sliding back my chair and gazing with massive self-love at my library. Needless to say, I have no impulse to *read*. Books are to be arranged and classified, shuffled around. At the very most I want to take a volume from the shelves, consult it, perhaps smell it, and replace it, carefully. Sometime in the future I may want to add a few incremental volumes but, for the moment, I just want to sit here, gazing at my life. For that's what it is, this library; it's not just the story of my life, it *is* my life. More exactly it is, in a sense, my life *over with*. Assembling my books in one room is the fulfilment of a life's ambition. There's nothing else I want. Except to sit here, purring. 'O bliss of the collector, bliss of the man of leisure!' exclaims Benjamin at the end of his essay.

> Of no one has less been expected, and no one has had a greater sense of well-being . . . For a collector – and I mean a real collector, a collector as he ought to be – ownership is the most intimate relationship that one can have to objects. Not that they come alive in him; it is he who lives in them.

Whatever may happen to me, even if I end up, as I almost certainly will, decrepit, impoverished, lonely and celibate (you see, it *was* a good idea to hang on to that copy of *Vox*!) this library – that is, the part of my being of which it is the external manifestation – will grant me a kind of immunity. I think of people living on my street, couples with children, families, and

I feel a kind of pity for them because they are not here, they are not me, in this lovely lamp-lit solitude, surrounded, at last, by the books acquired over twenty years and from which I have been separated for the last six. At this moment, as far as I am concerned, the world could blow itself to bits and I wouldn't mind. I probably wouldn't even notice.

1995

Comics in a Man's Life

In 1928 D.H. Lawrence wrote a beautiful essay, 'Hymns in a Man's Life', in which he reflected on the way that the hymns he heard as a boy 'mean to me almost more than the finest poetry, and they have for me a more permanent value, somehow or other'. It didn't matter that the words of these hymns were often banal or incomprehensible to him; what mattered was the 'sheer delight' they inspired in 'the golden haze of a child's half-formed imagination'. Even at this late stage of Lawrence's life – he had less than two years to live – the sense of 'wonder' engendered by these hymns was 'undimmed'. I feel the same about the superhero comics in my life.

I remember with absolute clarity the first Marvel comic I bought. *Spider-man* #46, 'The Sinister Shocker'. This was the issue of March 1967 and it cost 10d. I was eight, a working-class boy in a small town in the mid-west. The *English* mid-west, that is: specifically, Cheltenham, in Gloucestershire – the heart of the Cotswolds.

I was entranced, obviously, by the costumed acrobatics and spectacular fights but I also liked the ongoing soap opera of the life of Spidey's alter ego, Peter Parker. This was the phase in Parker's life when, having been spurned as puny and stuck-up, he was at last becoming integrated into the fashionable, semi-alternative life of college. At the end of issue 46 he moves out of his Aunt May's place and into an apartment with Harry Osborne (whose father, unbeknownst to him, is Spidey's recurrent enemy, The Green Goblin). At one point in #46 Peter turns up at a coffee bar with Mary-Jane, one of two gorgeously hip women he's become friendly with.

'What's shakin', Tiger?' says Mary-Jane.

'Nothing much! We were just getting set to spin a few platters!' replies Harry (who, as if having the Green Goblin for a father were not trouble enough, will later, in issues 96–98 – notoriously unapproved by the Comics Code Authority – develop serious drug problems). In Spider-man guise, Peter has injured his arm mixing it with The Shocker; when he asks M-J if she wants to go for an ice-cream she replies, 'Not while the juke is jumpin' dad! Since you can't shake up a storm with your wing in a sling I'll take a rain check till the coins run out.' Also on the scene is Flash Thompson, one of Peter's long-time tormentors – and, in one of the ironies milked to death by Stan Lee, Spidey's biggest fan – who is about to be drafted into the army and will go to Vietnam ('Mmm! There's something about a male in uniform! It's wow city!' sighs Mary-Jane).

Lots of this, it goes without saying, went way over my English head. In future issues I would come across all sorts of references – to Woody Allen, to Dear Abbey – that meant absolutely nothing to me but, from issue 46 on, I was caught in Spidey's web. By the age of twelve, I was fairly fluent (albeit with a Gloucestershire accent) in the kind of Marvelese quoted above, that sanitised version of hip American youth-speak. Although Spider-man remained my favourite I also got into Thor, Daredevil and The Fantastic Four.

Now, one of the reasons Marvel had an edge over its main rival, DC, was the way that its brand of superheroics did not take place in a fantasy vacuum but in the turbulent here and now of

American life. In issue 68 (January 1969) Spidey becomes caught up in the 'Crisis on Campus'. In issue 78 (November 1969) Hobbie Brown, a young black window-cleaner burdened by domestic problems, is fired by his racist boss and decides to try his luck as a supervillain, The Prowler. Spidey beats him but, instead of turning him over to the cops, tells him to go back home to his girlfriend ('that's where it's really at'). In this racially diverse respect *Spider-man* lagged behind *The Fantastic Four*: The Black Panther (who was subsequently granted independence in the form of his own magazine) made his first appearance in issue 52 of July 1966. DC would later follow suit with the famous – and now extremely valuable – 1971 'drugs' issues of *Green Lantern/Green Arrow* (with outstanding art by Neal Adams) but, back in the late 1960s, Marvel's knack for siphoning the *zeitgeist* into the action meant that a version – albeit a heavily distorted one – of contemporary American history was finding its way across the Atlantic to me in England. After family memories of the Battle of the Somme and the Airfix-generated re-creation of the Second World War, this fantastic version of American life was, without question, my most important exposure to extra-curricular history. Like the two world wars this comic book America was something I learned about – began to find my way around, to make sense of – independently.

Even more importantly, especially when Spidey battled The Vulture (in issues 48 and 49) in a vertiginous city of spectacular skyscrapers I began to get a sense of – to feel imaginatively at home in – the architecture of Manhattan. The cityscape in these comics – fifty-storey buildings, billboards, water towers, fire escapes, elevated trains – was, of course, unlike anything I had ever seen in real life. When – as children do – I tried to imagine myself in Spidey's place, web-swinging through Cheltenham, it was impossible: the buildings were too spread out, too low, too *homey*. (Spidey never made it to Gloucestershire but he did come to London, in April 1971 – issue 95 – after Peter Parker accidentally got caught up in a terrorist sky-jacking!) From my earliest exposure to it, by contrast, the Marvel New York was a place where the quotidian was suffused with the mythic (most obviously – and ludicrously – in the case of Thor).

The *Dandy* and the *Beano* were simply comics; Marvel was a *universe*. The more deeply you got into them the more encompassing Marvel comics became: characters from one title would guest in another (The Human Torch and Spider-man were always crashing into each other's pages) so that each magazine offered a different glimpse of – and take on – a world that was imaginatively complete. Events in one corner of this universe (in issue 38 of *Daredevil*, for example) have a knock-on effect in another (in issue 73 of *The Fantastic Four*, for example).* Events in the various titles are 'cohesive and interconnected'. 'There is no such thing as the isolated Marvel event'; Marvel 'gives all of itself in each of its fragments'. These quotations are from Roberto Calasso's book about the Greek myths, *The Marriage of Cadmus and Harmony*: I have simply substituted the word 'Marvel' for 'myth' or 'mythic'.

Ken Kesey said that the superheroes sagas were the real myths of the United States; the United Kingdom did not have any contemporary version of the mythic (for that you had to go back to

---

*A few days after seeing Ang Lee's film, *The Ice Storm* (which nudged me into writing this essay) I saw John Woo's *Face/Off* in which John Travolta and Nicholas Cage end up inhabiting each other's bodies, thereby reprising the storyline of *Daredevil* #38, 'The Living Prison', in which we see (to quote 'The Mighty Marvel Checklist') 'Daredevil in the body of Dr Doom, battling against Dr Doom – in the body of Daredevil.' By the time of *FF* #73, Daredevil and Dr Doom are back in their respective bodies but the FF are unaware of this: cue a 'Guest Star Bonanza' in which Reed takes on Daredevil, Thor hammers it out with The Thing, and Spidey and The Human Torch run rings around each other.

Second World War, to 'our finest hour', the Battle of Britain). This was the first glimmer of what in later years would become a critical position associated – often by virtue of parodic refutation – with a number of young English critics, namely that American novelists (Don DeLillo's *Underworld* is simply the latest case in point) had the advantage over their British counterparts of automatic, unlimited access to the mythic, the vast. And this, in turn, was why it was American – rather than British – writers who shaped the literary sensibilities of the generation of British readers who are now cresting forty.

I have always tended to assume that my life began to stray from the template laid down by class and family when I fell under the influence of my English teacher at grammar school, when I was encouraged to read books like *Sons and Lovers*; that is when I took my first steps on the well-worn path of the scholarship boy. Now, I realise, it started much earlier, when I bought that copy of *Spider-man* #46.

Superhero comics not only had what Lawrence called 'a profound influence on my childish consciousness', they also formed my tastes as a reader and, to a degree, my style as a writer. The very pervasiveness of their influence in this regard makes it difficult to pin down precisely.

In a well-known essay on the composition of *The French Lieutenant's Woman*, John Fowles recounts how he saw his first film when he was six and has, since then, seen at least one a week. 'How can so frequently repeated an experience not have indelibly stamped itself on the *mode* of imagination?' Fowles concludes that this 'mode of imagining is far too deep in me to eradicate'. For me, that mode of narrative imagining was, initially, *comic*-derived. A question asked by an American interviewer gives a more concrete – literally – indication of what I have in mind. Was it difficult, as an English writer, to do the scenes involving American jazz musicians in New York in *But*

Beautiful? No, I replied, because I was living in America when I wrote it. But it was also – I realise now – because of the super-hero comics I read as a kid. Here are a few lines from a scene in which pianist Bud Powell is wandering through Manhattan, on the brink of one of his periodic intervals of insanity:

> Out in the street again burnt-out buildings reared up like a tidal wave of masonry. Shadows coiled around him. He caught a glimpse of himself in the red and silver lights of a store. Wondering if he were made of glass, he kicked at the window, saw his reflection shiver and frost until there was a slow drizzle of glass and his face lay in pieces in the floor.

Those lines are like a condensed memory of any one of the numerous scenes in which the buildings of New York are routinely trashed by fighting superheroes.

Marvel comics – which, for a three-month spell, from September to November 1965, billed themselves as 'Marvel Pop Art' – also provided me with the first sense of discrimination in the visual arts. It wasn't just that I liked some artists more than others; some artists were *better* than others. Accordingly, after a hiatus of six or seven years, from O levels to university, instead of unswerving loyalty to Spider-man or The Fantastic Four, I collected whichever issues of any comic happened to be drawn by particular artists: Neal Adams, Berni Wrightson, Barry Smith and, especially, Jim Steranko. Artists like these had begun to carve out more and more freedom for their own highly personal visual styles. Typically, they would peak in a few masterly issues and then, unable to keep to the gruelling deadlines of monthly production, there would be a marked deterioration or they would move on to another title. Steranko's best work, for example, is scattered among a dozen panel-bursting, genre-advancing issues of *Nick Fury: Agent of S.H.I.E.L.D.*, three sensational issues – 110, 111 and 113 – of *Captain America* and an iconic cover of *The Incredible Hulk* King-Size Special #1. The work of Neal Adams was even more widely scattered: after several extraordinary issues of *The Avengers* and *The X-Men*, he moved to DC where he revivified *Batman* and *Green Lantern/Green Arrow*.

The years passed. Through comics I became interested in other artists: first, Roger Dean, then the really big hitters like Dali. Even when I got a broader sense of art history my preferences and special interests were profoundly influenced by that early exposure to Marvel comics. To put it simply, I liked Michelangelo because the obsessive and extreme torsion of his figures was so obviously derived from that of Jack Kirby (virtuoso creator of the FF and mentor of Jim Steranko).

Then, in the autumn of last year, I experienced what I can only think of calling a moment of intensely *heightened* autobiography. The church of Saint Ignatius in Rome is famous for the *trompe l'oeil* cupola by Andrea Pozzo. Before you get that far into the church, however, you look up at the vault of the central nave, at the epic fresco, also by Pozzo. Completed in 1694, *Entrance of Saint Ignatius into Paradise* shows the dead saints of antiquity slugging it out in a zone of sheer spectacle. Amid dizzy perspectival foreshortening, the continents of the world are represented by four corbels. On one of these – on one panel, as it were, of the huge graphic myth of the ceiling – a woman with a spear sends two beefcake figures tumbling from her precarious perch (identified by the single word 'AMERICA') into the emptiness of illusionistic space.

According to Freud there is no time in the unconscious; at certain intensely charged moments there is no time in consciousness itself. Looking up at the image-crammed ceiling I experienced a sensation that mirrored what was depicted above, a kind of temporal vertigo. The thirty years that separated the

man staring at this baroque fresco in Rome from the boy who had bought his first Marvel comic in Cheltenham *fell away*, became compressed into a single instant of undimmable wonder.

1998

Albert Camus

Algeria

I'm here too late: in the day, in the year, in the century . . .

In the day because all the hotels are full and I end up tramping round in the dark, lugging my pack and money (all of it in cash, a great wad of hard currency), nervous of the hordes of youths who watch me meandering round, concentrating so intently on making it look as though I have lived here all my life and know exactly where I am heading that I soon have no idea where I am on the mapless streets of Algiers.

By the time I find a room it is too late to do anything except drag a chair out on to the balcony and gaze down at the still-warm street, the signs. Arabic: it looks like handwritten water, it flows. The characters have no beginning and no end. Even the sign for the Banque Nationale D'Algier looks like a line of sacred poetry: elongated, stretched out like a horizon of words. It is strangely comforting, looking at an alphabet that is totally incomprehensible, a liberation from the strain of comprehension. Plus there is nothing else to look at, no neon or bars, and nothing to hear. The only sound is of metal shutters coming down – even though, as far as I can see, all the shutters are already down.

I came here because of Camus. Algiers was his city, the place that formed him and sustained him. During one of his first trips abroad, to Prague, he ended up in a hotel like this and 'thought desperately of my own town on the shores of the Mediterranean, of the summer evenings that I love so much, so gentle in the green light and full of young and beautiful women'.

In bed, drifting on the edge of sleep, I think of November evenings in my own town that I hate so much, London, with its sky of sagging cloud, where all the beautiful women already have boyfriends.

Too late in the year because the seasons Camus celebrates are spring and summer, when even the poorest men walk like Gods beneath the heat-soaked sky.

It was only a few months ago, when I read the three slim volumes of so-called 'Lyrical Essays' – *Betwixt and Between*, *Nuptials* and *Summer* – that I realised how essential these Algerian summers were to an understanding of Camus. Before that I'd been happy to think of him vaguely in terms of Sartre, De Beauvoir, Paris cafés, existentialism, absurdity . . .

Everything that is most important about Camus, though, lies less in what identifies him with these names, these ideas, than in what distinguishes him and separates him from them – and that is the experience of growing up poor in Algiers. Everything that happened subsequently is drenched in this early experience of poverty and sunlight.

What for Camus was a source of strength is, for me, a source of neurosis. He grew up rich in beauty; I grew up under a miserly, penny-pinching sky, in the niggardly light of England where, for three months of the year, it gets dark soon after lunch and for three more it doesn't bother getting light at all. For Camus the sky was a source of sustenance that he could draw on at will; for me it is a thwarted promise, something yearned for and glimpsed against the odds. Even in Algiers, on this autumn morning, I open the shutters with trepidation and find . . . an allotment sky, a sky catarrhed with cloud. A shadowless day of loitering rain.

Too late in the century because nothing of the culture celebrated by Camus survives.

Early in the Algerian War Camus tried to achieve a truce that would spare the civilian populations of both sides (a ludicrous proposal, De Beauvoir felt, since this was a war between civilian communities). After the failure of this initiative, and the disappearance of any middle ground between the FLN-led Muslims and the French *pieds noir* Camus maintained a besieged neutrality. With the FLN victory of 1962 – two years after Camus's death – there was an immediate exodus of French Algerians and, as I walk the streets, it seems ridiculous to have expected to find any trace of Camus's Algiers – like an American travelling to England in the hope of finding Dickens's London. But still, with no other guide, I drift around the city, following the very precise advice he offered in 1947:

The traveller who is still young will also notice that the women there are beautiful. The best place to take full note of this is the Café des Facultes, in the Rue Michelet, in Algiers, on a Sunday morning in April. You can admire them without inhibitions: that is why they are there.

Ten years later the smart cafés of Rue Michelet became prime targets of the FLN's bombing campaign; now, more than forty years later, on a drizzly Friday morning (the Muslim Sunday) in October, I seek out the Rue Didouche Mourad as it is now called. The café itself is crowded with smoke so I sit outside on a bench. Men in jeans and leather jackets go by, men limping, lighting cigarettes, veiled women, women in flesh-coloured tights, lugging shopping, men in leather jackets. And then, at night, the women disappear completely.

For Camus the beauty of the women was just part of his rapturous celebration of the wealth heaped on the senses here. Nowadays, struggling on in the name of Islamic socialism, Algeria is a place of austerity, one of the few countries on earth where you can't get Coca-Cola. Instead there is a vile soda, so sweet that drinking a couple of glasses is probably only slightly less bad for your teeth than getting hit in the mouth with a bottle of the stuff. In a restaurant that night – womanless, smoky – I order a beer. It comes in a green bottle and that is the major pleasure it affords. The food – chicken, brochettes, couscous – comes on a plate and half of it stays there.

Back in my hotel – disoriented, bloated with starch, tired – I lie in bed and read Camus's journal: 'There is no pleasure in travelling. It is more an occasion for spiritual testing. If we understand by culture the exercise of our most intimate sense – that of eternity – then we travel for culture.' In the morning tattered clouds are flung across the sky; the bay is flooded with sun. Even wind seems a species of light. My balcony rail casts shadows of Arabic script. Even the ants out on the balcony drag a little side-car of shadow.

Below is a road where cars crawl along on mats of shadow; further off are two long ranks of primrose-yellow taxis. Standing around, leaning on fenders, smoking and talking, tossing dog-ends into the gutter: this is the real business of a taxi-driver's life; ferrying people around the city is a leisure-consuming distraction. Behind the taxis is a crowded railway station and, beyond that, the port. Still further off, the bay curls round and vanishes in mist. A few steamers lounge in the blue water. The sea seems vertical, the ships form a pattern as if on wallpaper.

'Nothing of the culture celebrated by Camus survives' – except, I add now, stepping out into the sun-drenched streets, the light. All over the city are huge building sites where the sun pours into vast craters. It is tempting to think that what is being attempted is some sort of solar-containment, trapping the power of the sun and storing it. In fact, slowly and systematically, Algiers is being transformed: from Paris into Stockwell. Necessity is ousting beauty. Indifferent to what it falls on, the light, here and there, snags on the crumbling paintwork of the old French apartment blocks.

Shunting through the blazing streets, a taxi takes me to Belcourt, the area of Algiers where Camus grew up. I get out on the main street and ask a friendly postman – from now on the adjective will be assumed rather than written, everyone here is exhaustingly friendly – if he knows the street which, before the revolution, was called Rue de Lyon.

'*Ici*,' he says, pointing to the ground. 'Rue Belouizdad Mohamad.'

'*Ici?*'

'*Si.*'

I look up at the numbers and find that I am right outside No. 93. Camus's father was killed in the Great War when Albert was less than a year old and he grew up here with his mother and grandmother. There is no sign or plaque. I ask someone if this is where Albert Camus lived and they do not know who I am talking about.

It is a one-storey place with a small balcony overlooking the street, exactly as described in *The Outsider* when Mersault whiles away the Sunday after his mother's funeral. Below are a dry-cleaners and a watch-makers. Fig trees line the street. Clothes shops. Boys selling packs of cigarettes. People waiting for buses that stream by, looking and not looking. The sky cross-hatched by phone and tramlines.

t seventy years ago someone else turned up at this
nt, a teacher from Albert's school, to ask the boy's
mother if he could try for a scholarship to attend high school.
This was a turning-point in Camus's life and, as for many
working-class children to whom the world of books is suddenly
revealed, he never forgot the debt he owed his teacher.

The course of my own life was changed, similarly and irrevo-
cably, by one of my teachers. The first author I came across who
expressed the sense of class-displacement that ensued was D.H.
Lawrence in *Sons and Lovers*. A little later I could be heard recit-
ing Jimmy Porter's tirades from *Look Back in Anger* by John
Osborne. Then, from Raymond Williams, I learned the political
and moral consequences and obligations of being educated away
from the life you are born into. Finally, in Camus, who made the
most immense journey from his origins, I found someone who
stated, in the most affirmative and human terms, the ways in
which he remained dependent on them. This understanding did
not come painlessly but eventually, in a sentiment that is wholly
alien to the likes of Osborne, he achieved 'something priceless:
a heart free of bitterness'.

That is why I came here: to claim kin with him, to be guided
by him.

I walk towards the sea and never quite come to it. Always you
are separated from the sea by an expanse of one thing or
another: docks or roads. No trace of the *plage de l'Arsenal* where
Camus glimpsed for the first time the beauty of the
Mediterranean. Now there are only the all-consuming docks.
Gradually the sky becomes stained with clouds. The call to
prayer comes over a loudspeaker, distorted and mechanical, like
a factory whistle ordering the next shift to work.

'Eventually I come to a stretch of land – I don't know what else
to call it – by the sea. It is not part of the port but, although the

sea laps against an area of sand, it is not a beach. This is sand in the building-site sense of the world. There is rubble and rubbish everywhere. Rush-hour clouds are queuing across the sky.

Matthew Arnold, staring out at the Channel, thought of Sophocles and the sea of faith that had since receded. I think of Camus and the beauty that each year is pushed further and further out into the oil-filmed sea. As the waves lap in I detect a note of weariness in the endlessly repeated motion. Perhaps the sea never crashed vigorously here but it is difficult not to think some vital force has been sucked from it.

Camus concludes his famous study of absurdity by saying we must imagine Sisyphus happy. Easier to imagine him here, thinking 'Is it worth it?', for if he rolled his rock up this slope he would come to a heap of rubbish – and when it rolled back it would end up in another even bigger heap. Easier to imagine Sisyphus looking forward to the cigarette that will make his lungs heave under the effort of work and which, when he has tossed away the butt, will add to the rubbish below. But perhaps there is consolation even in this: the higher the mound of rubbish the less distance to heave his rock – until there is no hill to climb, just a level expanse of trash.

As I continue walking the sun bursts out again, making the bank of cloud smoulder green-black, luminous over the sea. Perched between the road and the sea, between sun and cloud, some boys are playing football in a prairie blaze of light. The pitch glows the colour of rust. The ball is kicked high and all the potential of these young lives is concentrated on it. As the ball hangs there, moon-white against the wall of cloud, everything in the world seems briefly up for grabs and I am seized by two contradictory feelings: there is so much beauty in the world it is incredible that we are ever miserable for a moment; there is so much shit in the world that it is incredible we are ever happy for a moment.

*

For Camus, Oran, the city of *The Plague*, 'capital of boredom besieged by innocence and beauty', was the mirror-image of Algiers: 'a city of dust and stone' that had 'turned its back on the sea'. After independence 200,000 Europeans fled the city and for some time it appeared to be uninhabited, a city decimated by plague. Now, even the dust has gone, but here and there you detect a strange smell: like dry damp or damp dust. Perhaps this persistent whiff of the past is why it actually seems more European – more like the Algiers of Camus's essays – than Algiers itself. Not that Europeans are actually in evidence but there are shops with things in them: clothes, records. There is even that most Parisian of institutions: a lingerie shop.

I take a room on the Rue Larbi Ben M'Hidi, formerly the Rue d'Arzew, a street of arcades and white buildings with yellow ornamentation. Camus lived here for a while – at number 67, above what is now an optician and a record shop that plays music so thin and tinny it sounds like it is coming from the headphones of a Walkman. From there I walk down to one of the main boulevards. It looks like a typical Mediterranean promenade – tiled pavements, palm trees, white buildings to the left, blue sky to the right. Everything tells you that the sea is just below to your right – but you look over and find two expressways, acres of docks and refineries and, beyond all of this, a massive breakwater. 'The apparent aim, is to transform the brightest of bays into an enormous port,' he wrote in 1939 and that has now been achieved. The sea has been forced out to sea.

A few minutes' walk away, the Boulevard Gallieni has been renamed the Boulevard Soummam, but it is still an architectural wedding cake of a street, so wide that the sun congregates here for most of the day, not simply dropping in for an hour as it has to in the canyon streets of Manhattan. Camus watched the young men and women stroll here in the fashions and style of Hollywood stars, but now it is a place where people pace quickly along, not to display themselves but simply to get somewhere else. Women hurry by and then night comes and they vanish: no final blazing sunset of the feminine, just a slow fade into the masculine night.

On my next-to-last day I take a taxi to the Roman ruins at Tipasa, fifty miles along the coast from Algiers. As we begin the long curve and haul out of the city the weather is in the balance, then rain spots the windshield. It is difficult not to take the weather personally and on this day, when it is so important that the sun shines, I think of Camus returning to Tipasa, 'walking through the lonely and rain-soaked countryside', trying to find that strength 'which helps me to accept what exists once I have recognised that I cannot change it'. For me, accepting the fact that it will rain today seems as difficult as coming to terms with the amputation of an arm or leg.

We drive through mountains and then out along a dull coast road. We pass half-finished buildings, the inverted roots of reinforcing rods sprouting from concrete columns: the opposite of ruins. Then, ten minutes from Tipasa, the clouds are rinsed blue and the sky begins to clear. Shadows cast by thin trees yawn and stretch themselves into existence. By the time I enter the ruins the sky is blue-gold, stretched taut over the crouched hump of the Chenoua mountain. The ruins are perched right on the edge of the sea: truncated columns, dusty blueprints of vanished buildings. The sea is sea-coloured, the heat is autumnal: heat that has a cold edge to it. I walk through the remnants of ancientness until, close to the cliffs, I come to a brown headstone: shoulder high, two feet wide. On it, in thin letters is scratched:

JE COMPRENDS ICI CE
QU'ON APPELLE GLOIRE
LE DROIT D'AIMER SANS
MESURE ALBERT CAMUS.

The monument was erected by friends of Camus's after his death. Since then his name has been defaced with a knife or chisel and the weather-worn inscription from 'Nuptials at Tipasa' is already difficult to read. Thirty years from now the words will have been wiped clean by the sun and the sea that inspired them.

If my trip had a goal then I have reached it. Every now and again there is a hollow boom of surf as if some massive object has just been chucked into the sea. Flies, impossible to ignore, tickle my face. Waves surf in on themselves. The horizon is a blue extinction of clouds. More than anything else it was the two essays Camus wrote evoking 'the great free love of nature and the sea' at Tipasa that made me come to Algeria. Now that I am here I am conscious of straining towards an intensity of response that I do not feel. The fact that it has been written about so perfectly inhibits my response to the place. What there is to discover here, Camus has already discovered (*re*-discovered in the second essay, 'Return to Tipasa'). There is nothing left to feel, except *this is the place Camus wrote about in his great essays*; that and the peculiar intimacy of reader and writer.

We read books and sometimes recommend them to friends. Occasionally we may even write to – or about – the author to say what his or her books mean to us. Still more rarely we go to a place simply because of what has been written about it and that journey becomes both an expression of gratitude and a way of filling a need within ourselves. Coming here and sitting by this monument, rereading these great essays, testaments to all that is best in us, is a way of delivering personally my letter of thanks.

*

On my last morning in Algiers I make my way to the Martyrs' Monument. On a hill overlooking city and bay, the monument – to the million Algerians who lost their lives in the war for independence – takes the form of three gigantic palm fronds leaning against each other. Beneath the apex formed by these fronds is the eternal flame, guarded by two soldiers who stand as if carved from flesh and blood, ripply and dream-like through the heat haze of the flame. At the base of these fronds are massive statues of guerrillas of the FLN.

If ever a monument aspired to the condition of the tower block, it is here. Of all the war memorials I have visited none has affected me less strongly, more impersonally, than this one. It demands that we become martyrs to an aesthetic edict based solely on scale. It orders us to respond to the scale of the undertaking and we obey – with all the sullenness that obedience compels. What it gives to the memory is not a sense of individual sacrifice but of its own insistent might – the might of engineering, the collective strength of concrete, its imperviousness to the passage of time. It will out-survive everything else in the city, except – and this is all it shares with that other, fading monument in the ruins of Tipasa – the sky that frames it.

Rebellion

Albert Camus means something very different to us today than he did at the time of his death thirty years ago. Lesser works like the 'Lyrical Essays' speak more intimately to us now than texts like *The Myth of Sisyphus* on which his reputation was based. Two recent books attempt, in very different ways, to relate him to the needs of the present.

Jeffrey C. Isaac's intention in *Arendt, Camus and Modern Rebellion* is to bring the two writers into dialogue, to read them against each other. The somewhat arbitrary nature of this pairing – Orwell and Simone Weil might just as usefully have been brought into the frame – is unimportant, for Albert Camus and Hannah Arendt are, for Isaac, representative of that loose configuration of 'resistance intellectuals' whose thought was shaped by – and sought to engage with – totalitarianism and the unparalleled horrors of twentieth-century warfare. Both were incessantly active in politics but essentially non-aligned; both developed a highly personal metaphysics of the human condition which was grounded in the political realities of the day. Both paid a high price for setting themselves in opposition to erstwhile allies: Camus for his stance on the Algerian war; Arendt for her insistence, in *Eichmann in Jerusalem*, on the part played by 'Jewish leaders in the destruction of their own people'. Anticipating the postmodernist suspicion of grand ideological narratives, both retained, in spite of everything, a steadfast faith in the human subject that is alien to the characteristic discourse of postmodernity. Hence the need, suggests Isaac, to retrieve their political vision.

In *Culture and Imperialism*, Edward Said positions Camus in such a way as to see how his work 'reproduces the pattern of an earlier imperial history'. Acknowledging that Conor Cruise O'Brien has shown Camus's work to represent 'either a surreptitious or unconscious justification of French rule or an ideological attempt to prettify it,' Said purports to go further. He does this by going further *back*, by looking in detail at 'earlier and more overtly imperial French narratives' which Camus's books 'are connected to, and derive advantages from'. This run-up is more impressive than the actual jump. O'Brien is berated for letting Camus 'off the hook', but Said's analysis of Camus's texts (as opposed to those that preceded him) falls far short of O'Brien's own persuasive and precise analysis of *The Plague*, for example. The plague in Oran, as we all know, is a symbol of Nazi occupation but, from the point of view of the Arab population, as O'Brien points out, the French who resist this plague are also an occupying force: a symptom of pestilence.

In Said, by contrast, Camus's writings barely feature; he is simply the terminus of a historical process, 'an extraordinarily belated, in some ways incapacitated colonial sensibility'. Although the purpose of this restorative interpretation is intended neither 'vindictively' nor to '*blame*' Camus, Said soon comes to the conclusion that his 'limitations seem unacceptably paralysing'. And while Said disavows any suggestion of authors being mechanically determined by history or ideology, the relative lack of emphasis placed on Camus *vis-à-vis* his predecessors cannot but suggest exactly this.

Let us be clear: there is no refuting the claim that in Camus's fiction the indigenous population of Algeria is, through a sleight of the imagination as casual as Mersault's murder of a nameless, faceless Arab, conveniently disposed of. By situating Camus in a history of imperial strategy while studiously ignoring all the details of his life, however, Said similarly and conveniently disposes of Camus as an individual. With his personal anguish over the fate of Algeria thereby rendered irrelevant he becomes, in Sartre's deliberately vindictive phrase, simply an 'accomplice of colonialism'. In Camus's terms, Said admits sin but refuses grace.

Isaac, on the other hand, is acutely sensitive to Camus's predicament. He judiciously plots his interventions in the Algerian crisis from his doomed attempt at organising a civilian truce in January 1956 (while a mob of *pied noir* militants bayed for his blood) to his eventual 'defensive and hollow' opposition to Algerian independence. Neutrality was impossible: his condemnation of FLN terrorism – 'which operates blindly' and which 'one day might strike my mother or my family' – was seen as implicitly supporting the French army of pacification.

Hence Isaac's exasperated reminder that Camus *was* a *pied noir*. As Said would have it, we see Camus either accurately – as the confluence of a history of imperial dominion – or vaguely, inadequately and ahistorically as a philosopher of the human condition. My own response is to locate him more precisely and more personally.

Camus's father died in the Great War; raised by his illiterate mother and grand mother, he grew up in a working-class district of Algiers where poverty was redeemed by the wealth heaped on his senses by sea and sun.

He recorded these early experiences in three volumes of 'Lyrical Essays' which contain some of his best writing. They also make clear why the Camus presented by Isaac is, for all the diligent range of reference, too abstract a figure. 'If I can be said to have come from anywhere, it is from the tradition of German philosophy,' said Arendt, thereby lending herself perfectly to the kind of academic exegesis at which Isaac excels. But Camus is not at his best in the philosophical works on which Isaac relies. Camus had to stifle himself in order to think his way through *The Rebel*. His, above all, is a *sensual* intelligence. The enduring power of *The Outsider* lies less in the sense of existential absurdity than in the glare and heat of the beach and – even more strongly in the 'draft version', *A Happy Death* – Camus's evocation of sensual happiness.

In this respect Isaac's contention that the 'sentimental vision of the Mediterranean is an important lacuna in Camus's writing' is an important lacuna in his analysis. Camus, whose gaze was always directed from Africa to Europe, from desert to sea, was both formed by this vision of the Mediterranean and gave it its most powerful expression. This vision could only have been articulated by someone in exactly Camus's position, with his peculiar sensibility and with exactly the cultural-imperial legacy of French Algeria to draw on.

Although Camus's vision depends on and is rooted in specific geo-historical circumstances – those of the *pied noir* – he in no sense *lays claim to* that which he celebrates. On the contrary: 'All I know is that this sky will last longer than I shall,' he wrote in a characteristic passage. 'And what can I call eternity except what will last longer than I shall?'

Of course Camus's claim to greatness cannot rest solely on a kind of *pied noir* pantheism. It resides in the manifold ways in which this sensualism was allied with the cause of human solidarity. But this commitment never involved – because it was inextricably bound up with – a renunciation of the sensual. 'If man needs bread and justice, and if we have to do everything essential to serve this need, he also needs pure beauty, which is the bread of his heart.'

As we move towards the December of the century the 'unconquerable summer' that Camus found within himself offers more warmth and light than ever before.

The First Man*

In 1958, the year after he won the Nobel Prize, Albert Camus wrote a preface for a new edition of his first book, *Betwixt and Between*. Re-reading these early essays persuaded him that a writer's work was nothing but a 'slow trek to rediscover through the detours of art those two or three great and simple images in whose presence his heart first opened'. His own writing was nourished by 'a single stream', Camus went on, and this stream was 'the world of poverty and sunlight' in which he grew up in Algiers.

After years of creative sterility Camus had resolved to trace this stream back to its source in the novel which he was still

---

*Translated by David Hapgood.

g on at the time of his death in 1960. According to
ɪɪeɪbert Lottman in his excellent biography, Camus referred to
the work in progress, in all seriousness, as his *War and Peace*.
Even in unfinished form it is a wonderful book. As Camus re-
drafted and completed it, *The First Man* would have become
more of a novel and less of an autobiography; as it stands it is a
great attempt to fulfil the ambition announced by Nietzsche's
Ecce Homo: 'how one becomes what one is.' Seen in this light it
doesn't even matter particularly that the novel is incomplete.
'The book *must* be unfinished,' Camus noted to himself, conscious that such a project could be realised, definitively, only
with the death that curtails its completion.

In the opening pages a husband ('he wore a three-button twill
jacket, fastened at the neck in the style of that time') and pregnant wife are travelling in a wagon, 'creaking over a road that
was fairly well marked but had scarcely any surfacing'. Tone and
scene are surprisingly Hardyesque but the setting is Algeria, the
edge of Africa, and the soon-to-be-born son is not a Jude but a
Jacques who, years later, like Camus himself, will try to understand how he emerged from the obscurity to which his family
had been condemned by history.

Camus's father was killed at the Battle of the Marne when
Albert was less than a year old. Exactly like Camus, Jacques
Cormery is raised by his mother and grandmother in extreme
poverty. He is a gifted pupil and one of his teachers persuades
the mother to let her son try for a scholarship. As the *lycée*
reveals the possibility of a life beyond the poverty and ignorance
he was born into, so 'the silence grew between him and his
family'. It's a familiar theme but no account of this process is
more moving than Camus's. His mother was illiterate (a neigh-
bour had to read the telegram announcing that Albert had won
the Nobel Prize) and the profound feeling aroused by the book
comes, partly, from the sense that it is written for the one person

who cannot read it. 'What he wanted most in the world,' Camus noted, 'was for his mother to read everything that was his life and his being, that was impossible. His love, his only love, would be forever speechless.'

The urge to bring his past to life, to offer his family the gift of speech, of words, is therefore inseparable from the desire to achieve a clarity, a sensual immediacy and intensity that will, as far as possible, transcend the verbal. The sky, the light, offer supreme, silent expression of this hope. Words yearn to *be* the light they celebrate. Drenched in the sun and smells of Algiers, Camus's last novel cries out with the same 'famished ardour' that characterised crucial early essays like 'Nuptials at Tipasa'. These essays make clear how profoundly Camus's sensibility was shaped by growing up in Algiers, but *The First Man* aims beyond the lyrical evocation of times past. In the essays the Sahara is, if you like, a vast beach; in them Camus is looking north, to the sea. In this book he looks to the interior, to the heart of a problem skirted in his earlier books. The Arabs, who, in *The Plague*, were invisible or, in *The Outsider*, killed unthinkingly, crowd in on *The First Man*. The mere fact of their visibility is enough to claim the place as their own; by 'their sheer numbers' they offer an 'invisible menace', an outcome that is premonitory but not yet inevitable. 'We'll kill each other for a little longer and cut off each other's balls,' says one character. 'And then we'll go back to living as men together.' A forlorn hope, it turned out, but, as a novelist seeking to delineate his historical predicament, Camus is less concerned with the question of who can lay claim to the land than the more profound one: *what claim does the land make on the people born there?* Early in the book a farmer complains that Parisians understand nothing of the situation of the French Algerians. 'You know who're the only ones who can understand?' he asks. 'The Arabs,' says Jacques.

s has a blood-understanding of this psychological bond.
natically embodied – to take just one example – in the
scene describing the way a crowd would gather if a fight broke
out between a Frenchman and an Arab:

> the Frenchman who was fighting would in backing up find
> himself confronting both his antagonist and a crowd of
> sombre impenetrable faces, which would have deprived
> him of what courage he possessed had he not been raised
> in this country and therefore knew that only with courage
> could you live here; and so he would face up to the threat-
> ening crowd that nonetheless was making no threat except
> by its presence.

What a book it would have been, what a book it already is! I
have itemised some of its themes but the remarkable thing is
how, even at so early a stage, these disparate concerns are so intimately entwined. Thirty-five years after their author's death,
these draft pages answer the two needs that, as Camus wrote in
his 'Return to Tipasa', 'cannot be long neglected if all our being
is not to dry up: I mean loving and admiring.'

1991/1992/1995

The Life of Roland Barthes

In the preface to *Sade/Fourier/Loyola* Roland Barthes remarked that he would love it if, when he died, his life, 'through the pains of some friendly and detached biographer, were to reduce itself to a few details, a few preferences, a few inflections, let us say to "biographemes".' He actually accomplished a version of this task himself – by compiling 'a few tenuous details' and 'vivid novelistic glimmerings' – in *Roland Barthes by Roland Barthes*, a book he also reviewed. This autobiography is one of Barthes's greatest books and Louis-Jean Calvet, after a little preliminary flirting, wisely avoids trying to emulate the master by fulfilling his wishes.*

Barthes has been fortunate in another way, for Calvet is an unfashionably courteous biographer. In the course of trawling through the facts of Barthes's life he tramples on no one's feet and does not attempt to wedge so much as a toe of his own in anyone's door. In a way this is appropriate: Barthes was a writer and man of infinite discretion and his biographer is nothing if not discreet. To a fault perhaps. 'Because I have respected their [Barthes's heirs] wishes,' he observes, 'at times, the narrative may seem a little vague. I hope the reader will bear with me.' It

---

Roland Barthes: A Biography, translated by Sarah Wykes.

rlish not to bear with a writer whose implicitly
im for his book is that it 'is the result of a great deal
aking inquiries, searching in archives, interviewing
people, tracking down references, reading'. But that, one wants
to respond churlishly, is the *easy* part of doing a book: it's the
writing that's hard.

Still, as a preliminary survey it is a lot better than Didier
Eribon's skim through the life of Michel Foucault, for example.
Partly this is a fluke of subject. In the wake of Eribon, James
Miller's *The Passion of Michel Foucault* stresses the intimate con-
nection between Foucault's sexual proclivities and his work;
Barthes compartmentalised his life so successfully that while
there may be intellectual justification for boning up on
Foucault's comings and goings in the S and M clubs of the
Castro, it doesn't matter that we don't learn what Barthes got up
to on his various trips to Morocco.

What we *do* learn is, unfortunately, sometimes a tad dull: a
third person, analytically enhanced CV tracing R.B.'s progress
from ward of the state (his father was killed in the First
World War when Roland was less than a year old) to celebrity-
intellectual. The war years, which Barthes spent in a sanatorium
('at the time', he wrote, 'tuberculosis was truly a way of life, I
would almost say an election') were especially important, removing him from the mainstream of academic advancement and
allowing him to begin developing his own highly subjective version of theory (as Calvet rightly points out, Barthes's 'theories'
were often just elaborations of mood).

In 1955, when he was writing the articles later collected in
Mythologies, Roland and his mother bought their apartment on
the Rue Servandoni with money left by his grandmother. Roland
had his study upstairs while his mother lived below; if he chose
not to come down, food and mail were hoisted up to him in a
basket. The closeness of Barthes's relationship to his mother will

come as no surprise to readers of *Camera Lucida*, a book inspired by her death, but Calvet illustrates this with some delicately chosen anecdotes. Julia Kristeva recalls how, if she called while the middle-aged Barthes was absent, his mother would explain, 'he's gone to Vincennes and he's going to come back to me with his shoes all muddy and his trousers too'.

The years following his mother's death in 1977, when Barthes was ostensibly free to be more frank about his homosexuality, became increasingly lonely. With characteristic insight John Berger has written that what he responds to is the *pain* in Barthes – a remark that brings us closer to what is essential in his writing than any number of seminars at the ICA. An article in the *New Statesman* assessing Barthes's importance ten years after his death dwelt almost exclusively on his contribution to semiotics, on works like *Image, Music, Text* and *Mythologies*, while dismissing the later, more personal works as 'marginal, lacking the satisfying stamp of authority'. In fact, it is precisely on these more personal books, specifically *Camera Lucida*, *A Lover's Discourse* and the autobiography, that Barthes's claims as an author – his claims to author-ity – rest. In them Barthes mastered all the most difficult forms of writing – the colon, ellipses, the semi-colon, italics and parentheses – and evolved a style of punctuation so uniquely his own that, even while holding the printed books in our hands, it feels as if we are reading his handwriting. *Camera Lucida*, obviously, is a great book about photographs – but it is also a book that makes you cry (the most poignant line in the book concerns an ivory powder box of his mother's: 'I loved the sound of its lid,' Barthes notes in an exquisite, heart-rending parenthesis).

Simultaneously cherishing his fame and frustrated by the claims it made on his time, Barthes in his last years often resembles a suavely Parisian Larkin. His characteristic idiom, it turns out, was to *moan*: 'that he had a headache, that he felt sick, that he had a cold or a sore throat . . . It was always the first thing he talked about whenever he met you.' For Larkin life was first boredom and then fear. For Barthes ('as a child I was often and intensely bored') it was first boredom and then boredom. His was that peculiarly French boredom which is engendered by and all but indistinguishable from hedonism. In this respect a photograph published a few months ago in *Le Monde* is extraordinarily revealing. It was taken in 1938, when Barthes was twenty-three,

on the balcony of a Paris apartment. By today's standards as well as those of the time, his hair is cut fashionably. He looks down, his eyes in shadow. His right hand is in the pocket of thick, pleated trousers; his left is resting on the buckle of a belt which is not threaded through the loops of the trousers but tied rather casually beneath them, sloping almost like a cowboy's gunbelt. The casualness is as deliberate as the slightly effeminate pose. Loneliness and ennui in this image are not only presented but *experienced* aesthetically; both, in other words, are a species of vanity. There are many photographs of Barthes in his silver-haired, sophisticated middle-age. Here, though, we see him aspiring to the style of the writer he was eventually to become. The camera is an ideal mirror in which to present the cultivated solitude of the aesthete but, such is the prophetic force of the photograph, that affectation acquires the force of destiny. The photo offers a double reflection of Barthes's later life. Firstly, because the boredom assumed for the camera will become unavoidable; secondly, and more importantly, because the young Roland pictured here is like the ideal image of 'the boys' who, in a fragment written in 1979 and published posthumously in *Incidents*, bring the middle-aged Barthes to an unavoidable acceptance of the fundamental melancholy of his life:

> Yesterday, Sunday, Olivier G came for lunch; waiting for him, welcoming him, I had manifested the solicitude that usually indicates that I am in love. But as soon as lunch began, his timidity or his remoteness intimidated me; no euphoria of relation – far from it. I asked him to come and sit beside me on the bed during my nap; he came willingly enough, sat on the edge of the bed, looked at an art book; his body was very far away – if I stretched out an arm toward him, he didn't move, uncommunicative: no obligingness; moreover he soon went in to the other room. A

sort of despair overcame me, I felt like crying. How clearly I saw that I would have to give up boys, because none of them felt any desire for me, and I was either too scrupulous or too clumsy to impose my desire on them; that this is an unavoidable fact, averred by all my efforts at flirting, that I have a melancholy life, that, finally, I'm bored to death by it . . .

1994

Louis Althusser

People like me are always complaining about the parochialism of British cultural life. Yet the original publication of *L'Avenir Dure Longtemps* immediately generated considerable debate in Britain; so did the publication earlier this year of two new studies (both written in English) of Michel Foucault. By contrast, our own homegrown controversy, the Larkin Affair, made barely a murmur in France. This can be taken – mistakenly, I think – as a sign of English insularity: the great national poet turns out to be irrelevant on the larger stage of Europe. At the risk of echoing that famous imperial report about the fog-bound channel – 'continent still cut off' – I would see it the opposite way, as an indication of continental parochialism. As an insight into the personality and mind of a figure at once famous and reclusive, who lived out his life in suburban *extremis*, Larkin's letters are considerably more revealing; as literature they are immeasurably superior to Althusser's confession.

The gist of which – and the events that led to its composition – is by now fairly familiar. On 16 November 1980 Louis Althusser ran into the courtyard of the Ecole Normale Superieure where he had studied and taught for over thirty years, screaming that he had killed his wife, Helene. By the time the police arrived *le grand philosophe* had already been whisked away to a mental hospital, where he was declared to be in a state of total collapse and therefore unfit to plead. Deemed not to be responsible for his own actions, Althusser avoided criminal prosecution at the price of surrendering control of his own life. The next ten years were spent in hospitals or living alone in the north of Paris. Attempting to shift the 'tombstone of silence' that lay on him, *The Future Lasts a Long Time** is not so much a plea in mitigation as in abnegation.

Born in Algeria in 1918, he was named after the man his mother loved: his father's brother who was killed in a plane over Verdun. From the start, then, the child Louis was a non-person, a mere cipher – *lui* – for a dead man. When, as an adolescent, his mother discovered the evidence of his first wet dreams, he felt she had raped and castrated him. When he and Helene – eight years his senior, ex-*résistant*, Communist Party activist – consummated their relationship the experience was so devastating that it initiated the cycle of breakdown, hospitalisation and recovery that was to characterise his career.

Sensational though these revelations were, they caused less of a stir in France than the admission that the author of *Pour Marx* and co-author of *Lire 'Le Capital'* was actually 'a trickster and a deceiver . . . who knew almost nothing about the history of philosophy or about Marx'.

He exaggerates, of course, but these self-flagellating boasts actually served to re-focus attention on a figure whose posthumous existence began ten years before his death and whose reputation seemed set to perish on the fringes of limbo. Earlier this year Verso published *The Althusserian Legacy*, a collection of papers from a 1988 conference in New York whose unintentioned effect was to suggest that this legacy did not extend far beyond the handful of initiates invited to speak there.

---

*Translated by Richard Veasey.

With *The Future Lasts a Long Time* we move from the academic to the *sales* conference and a large potential readership for whom Althusser's name is vaguely associated with a few well-thumbed phrases: ideological state apparatuses, Marxism as 'class struggle in the realm of theory', history as 'a process without a subject' . . .

So, what kind of book is it? How will it be read? With a lot less enthusiasm, I suspect, than the articles about it. Some hearsay testimonies can be thrown out of critical court immediately. As someone writing about madness Althusser had the advantage of first-hand experience but renders it less evocatively than, for example, Tennyson in 'Maud' or Sylvia Plath in *The Bell Jar*. The suggestion that remarkable insights are yielded by the fact that the author is both a philosopher and a murderer proves similarly ill-advised. As a piece of writing, in fact, *The Future Lasts a Long Time* is surprisingly poor. One rounds initially on the translator as the person responsible for the clumps of clichés and homely colloquialisms (always indicated by inverted commas) but these turn out to be reasonably faithful renditions of the original French. Part of Althusser's original appeal lay in the unyielding cerebration of his formulations; that he succumbed eventually to the idiom of the concierge – 'I shall leave that to those clever people who like to indulge in "analytic theory"' – alerts us to how much that was human was sacrificed for the purity of theoreticism.

Other ironies loom huge if the book is considered in relation to Althusserian theory as a whole. It has often been remarked that ideology, for Althusser, works somewhat like the unconscious in Freud. In his hands it became, in two striking phrases of Perry Anderson's, 'an unconscious system of determinations', 'a lived medium of delusions' from which there is no escape. In seeking to understand and explain himself Althusser relies on psychoanalytic probings which keep locating the cause of his actions further and further back in his psychic formation. Douglas Johnson, in the introduction, may not be literally correct in suggesting that Althusser murdered Helene in his sleep but he is metaphorically accurate; for while Althusser seeks to reclaim responsibility for his actions the terms by which he seeks to do so ensure that he can never be more than the passive instrument of them. On several occasions he speaks of 'Helene's murder' as if he had played no active part in it and, psychogrammatically, as it were, the book is all the time tending towards the passive. In his famous polemic *The Poverty of Theory*, E.P. Thompson pointed out that Althusserianism, the latest form of Marxism, turned out to be 'a very ancient mode of thought: process is fate'. If nothing else, this strangely undisturbing text proves Thompson right.

1993

The Life of Graham Greene

These days literary biography is not just a form but an institution whose high standards of literariness are so assured that they can sometimes be waived with impunity. The first volume of Norman Sherry's *The Life of Graham Greene* was hailed as exemplary – and so it was. Here were infelicities of style and forays into critical and psychological analysis that would be inadmissable in a less venerable context. It is as if the high reputation of the subject grants his appointed biographer immunity from critical attack.

In a sense the biographer does not have to be a writer in that the final product is not expected to be a work of art in itself so much as confirmation and proof of the art – of which Sherry is a master – of doggedly pursuing letters, lovers and lost contacts. 'Risking disease and death as [Greene] had done,' Sherry goes to the places Greene went, in pursuit of the people Greene met.

This time* his travels take him to Sierre Leone (where Greene worked for MI6 during the war), Malaya, Kenya and Vietnam, where Greene again fell under suspicion of spying. Greene was back in England for the last two years of the war, still working

---

*The Life of Graham Greene Volume 2:1939–1955.

for MI6 (under Kim Philby), before doing a brief stint in publishing. Physically, his marriage to first wife Vivien had all but ended before the war (their house in Clapham was conveniently trashed by the Luftwaffe) and he was spending most of his time with his lover, Dorothy Glover. Both women were sidelined in 1946 when he fell in love with Catherine Walston: rich, Catholic, beautiful – and married. Within two years Greene became world famous for *The Heart of the Matter* and *The Third Man* but he could never persuade Catherine to leave her husband for him. Hence the passionate, anguished letters that punctuate Greene's peregrinations in the remaining years recounted here.

Recounted, it has to be said, in the kind of style that emerges when concerted editorial attention irons badly wrinkled prose into something presentably bland. Taken off guard on one occasion, Sherry tells us, Greene 'fell back on cliché'. His biographer *reaches* for clichés at moments of high drama – 'there is a serpent wriggling in the love nest' – and makes do, much of the time, with the sloppily workaday: 'he sought ways of getting his family from under his feet. His mother took them off his hands for a holiday . . .'

Issues of style are less distracting when dealing with event-intensive periods abroad. Sherry is at his best when Greene is on the move, jogging along after him and providing useful historical-political context for the novels. He is at his worst when the trail of evidence dies out and he has to hack a speculative path through the conditional thickets of the possible: 'it seems likely that [Greene] wrote to Vivien . . . just as Fowler [in *The Quiet American*] wrote to Helen. If Greene did write to Vivien she would have responded by letter . . . Helen's response to Fowler's letters seems to be the kind of letter Vivien could have written.' There are several occasions like this when it is difficult to tell the trees from the would.

Then there is the paradoxical problem of thoroughness. Sherry begins with a six-page resumé of the previous volume: such a good resumé, in fact, that one wonders if the best way to read this volume (where the weight of information is always threatening to drag the story below the reader's Plimsoll line of attentiveness) might not be to wait for the synopsis in the next one. Except one never knows when there will be a oblique insight from an unimportant bystander. With this in mind biographers have to dredge up everything they can, leaving the reader to hurtle through the material and use it as a source to be consulted at will.

Eager to be more than a mere compiler of semi-processed material, however, Sherry is also at pains 'to come to an understanding of [Greene's] inner vulnerabilities'. To do this he shows how passages in *The End of the Affair*, for example, were derived from Catherine's journals. The mystery – the central preoccupation of the book – remains: how was it that at the time of his extraordinary success Greene could yet be so despairing? Why was he so often on the brink of suicide? To answer that we need look no further than Nietzsche: because the thought of it got him through many a bad night.

But why were the nights so bad?

There is a Buddhist saying that despair is the last refuge of the ego. That is to say, it can be a stage to be passed through. In Catholicism, by contrast, to despair – like Scobie in *The Heart of the Matter* – is to be damned. It is a dead-end. As a Catholic Greene had constantly to resist his own propensity to despair. It held Greene in its thrall only because he could never surrender to it. Similarly, it should be remembered that it is the atheist and not the person of faith who is denied the possibility of doubt; Greene's Catholicism effectively underwrote his capacity and need for doubt.

The strange thing about photos of Greene in the first volume of Sherry's biography is that his face, even as a child, is all the time waiting to grow old. In this volume the waiting is over: even when smiling or drinking he has the look that we begin to notice in other photographs from this period (of Orwell, for example). This look, which one sees only rarely before the Second World War, shows the face of a man who is inconsolable. A similar look – a similar condition – found expression in the work of several writers of this period: in France, for example, through existentialism. In Greene's case, through a convergence of temperament, theology and history, inconsolability became an article of faith.

In his best writing a personal predisposition tests itself as a viable measure of – and is itself tested by – the lot of men and women in precise historical circumstances. The characteristic movement is usually towards a confrontation with brutality or despair. As often as not the outcome is a gesture of affirmation so sodden and futile that it is indistinguishable from collapse or resignation – but it is also a recognition that to keep alive the tormenting possibility of consolation is the final curse of the inconsolable.

1994

Milan Kundera

1.

'All of us are mysteriously affected by our names,' says Paul, the hero of *Immortality**. Would Kundera's writing have the same qualities if he had been called Ray Duffy? Milan Kundera: a Kunderan name (in the same way that Kafka is Kafkaesque; Calvino, Calvinoesque). Speculative etymology: Kundera: from the Latin to conjure: a name to conjure with.

2.

Immortality is his seventh work of fiction, all of which, except for *The Farewell Party*, are made up of seven parts. Like *The Book of Laughter and Forgetting* it is 'a novel in the form of variations'. Though set mainly in Paris its technique, concerns and situations are essentially the same as in his previous books: speculative digressions on heterogeneous matter counterpointing the sexual and existential dilemmas of a handful of

---

*Translated by Peter Kussi.

characters. (Does it suggest a diminution of creative energy that in form the new novel is the same as the previous ones? No: by its nature the variation form is self-replenishing; he does not need variations on the variations form, only variations within it.)

In each of his books Kundera refers back to words or situations in earlier sections and, through ingenious 'meditative interrogations', proceeds to define them more precisely. In *Immortality*, similarly, he refers back to his earlier books (Paul reminds him of Jaromil in *Life is Elsewhere*, a copy of which Kundera, a character in his own creation, gives to his friend Avenarius halfway through the new novel). *Immortality*, then, is not only his seventh novel but also part seven of a huge novel which we can call something like 'The Incomparable Delightedness of Reading Kundera'. In commenting on *Immortality*, then, we are also commenting on the larger work of which it is the concluding part.

3.

'Many people, few gestures,' writes Kundera in the opening pages of *Immortality* and, later: 'many people, few ideas.' I had a similar thought – many writers, few ideas – when I read of his heroine wearing dark glasses not just as a way of hiding her sorrow but also as an emblem of it; Roland Barthes makes exactly the same observation in *A Lover's Discourse*. Am I suggesting that Kundera lacks originality? Not at all. 'The value of coincidence equals the degree of its improbability,' says Avenarius. But is there not a beautiful *inevitability* about some of the most unlikely coincidences? Like Barthes and Kundera, both wearing dark glasses, as it were, bumping into each other like this?

4.

In his list of sixty-three words (*The Art of the Novel*) that he loves, that are crucial to his work, there is a surprising omission: panties. No author loves panties more than Kundera and they are very much in evidence in the new novel. 'This revealed her bare legs and green panties (an excellent match for the green skirt)'; 'Then they led her (she was dressed only in panties) to a mirror . . .' I imagine him smiling slightly to himself every time he writes it, quietly looking forward to the next time his pen will get a glimpse of a pair. (I sometimes think that it is only treats like this that keep writers at their desks.) In Kundera the perpetual promise of panties (inversely proportionate to their size) is always counterposed to the episode in *Life is Underwear* – sorry, I mean *Life is Elsewhere*, when Jaromil flees from a desirable woman because he suddenly realises he is wearing a pair of vast, shapeless grey underpants. Possible paper: Kundera and the lingerie of the novel.

5.

'If a reader skips a single sentence of my novel he won't be able to understand it, and yet where in the world will you find a reader who never skips a line?' In 'bicycle race' narrative, as Kundera calls it, you can skip confidently because it is easy to guess what is happening in the gaps. The variation form mitigates against skipping because you never know what is going to happen next (in his way Kundera is a master of suspense, of suspended narration) but skip we do. One way of combatting skipping might be to insert into a novel a few passages that are there in order to be skipped so that the longing to skip is assuaged without real damage being done to the text. Would this enhance or detract from the perfection of the text as experienced by the skipping reader? Of course it is possible that s/he will skim the other bits and plod dutifully through the passages designed to be skimmed.

For example: in his notes on *The Sleepwalkers* by Hermann Broch, Kundera talks of a need for 'the specifically novelistic essay'. *Immortality* is full of these 'inquiring, hypothetical' aphoristic essays. Compared with these, my favourite passages, I find I don't much care about Kundera's characters in their Rohmeresque environment. I love Kundera speculating about his characters but when the characters are on their own, when he is not around, in other words, *when he is not looking*, I skip. Why not, *à la* Barthes, a novel composed entirely of essays, stripped of the last rind of novelisation?*

6.

'Modern stupidity means the non-thought of received ideas.' Yes, and isn't there, in precisely this sense, something stupid about the English admiration for Kundera? Is he admired simply because he is a great writer or, if we think it through, does this admiration not function somewhat like the racist's proverbial best friend, leaving us free to admire writers who (and to legitimise tenets of admiration which) are profoundly unKunderan? Genuine though it may be, the English admiration for Kundera reminds me of Graham Taylor's attitude to Turkey after a recent international: lots of fancy footwork but, when it came to it, they couldn't stick the ball in the net. When push comes to shove all Kundera's ball skills somehow reinforce

---

*Kundera effectively obliged with his next book, *Testaments Betrayed*.

our preference for literary kick and rush. Admiring Kundera with his foreign chatter of high ideas somehow leaves us free to build our national squad around the native worth of Kingsley Amis and his ilk. We admire Kundera as an exotic continental import rather than internalising his influence. If we admired less, might we absorb more?

7.

What is the highest compliment we can pay Kundera? None of his books will ever be used to swear oaths on.

Or perhaps not: they are the perfect books on which to swear oaths – they allow you to lie with impunity.

1991

Jayne Anne Phillips

This is one of those novels you start reading again from the beginning as soon as you finish the last page. Not because you enjoyed it, necessarily, but because of the near impossibility of making up your mind about it. Come to that, it is difficult to make up your mind about Jayne Anne Phillips's work as a whole.

After the snazzy, vacuous promise of *Black Tickets*, her debut collection of fictive bits and pieces, came *Machine Dreams*, a sustained, densely impressive chronicle of pre- and post-Vietnam America. Another collection of stories, *Fast Lanes*, which included off-cuts from the previous novel, felt like something to keep publishers and public going while she got on with another big novel. A decade after *Machine Dreams*, here it is, a novel so dense with its own impressiveness as to make you wonder about the foundations of that impressiveness.

Shelter is set in a girls' summer camp in West Virginia in the summer of the early 60s. More accurately, it is set in July 1963; in late July to be exact. The precise temporal anchoring is stressed at the outset, but the novel floats free of historical circumstance except in so far as the girls at camp are in the midst of a pre-permissive adolescence. Phillips's concerns are anthropological rather than historical; tribal, almost. The swelling sexual urges on the brink of being unleashed are felt more powerfully by being historically corseted by knee socks and wool berets.

Hideous, beast-like, an ex-con called Carmody slouches towards this Eden. Parson, a drifter who shared a jail cell with Carmody, has followed him into the area. His aura is scarcely less menacing than Carmody's as he watches over a group of four girls, whether to protect them against Carmody or to abet in the universal degradation associated with him remains unclear until the novel's disturbing apotheosis.

The landscape heaving under the camp and crouching round it is snake-infested, shot through with religious gleamings, ominous, heat-drenched, almost a jungle. The same is true of the prose. It writhes and exults and crams your nose with the feel of surfaces and depths, touches your eyes with the reek of light. The air is sentient with nouns become verbs; even in motion a tranced stillness holds sway as verbs stall into adjectives. You don't read this prose; you peer into it. The narrative unfolds and coils through the murk and glare of writing in which even half-tones inflame the eye. Everything is heightened, nervy, lyrical, jagged.

The weakest passages read like writing programme exercises in stream of consciousness. There is a tendency, too, for metaphors to become overblown (someone tastes 'the night in his mouth like a wish, a night so big, so warm and wet and full of air, falling away forever like the sky falls with its stars') or to blow themselves out ('silent, like a scream too high-pitched to hear').

These are quibbles. Critical energies are better deployed in articulating the overall effect of reading and re-reading this obviously important novel. Here is a representative passage, chosen at random:

> It all looks empty in the dim light, swept with a broom
> maybe, but there is no broom, and the inside has a hay

smell like clean dust even in the rain. In the splintering pour of the storm there is such a silence, like a church or a cell, a cloister, empty, and rain courses down the broken glass of the block-paned windows. Some of the jagged glass juts up like tongues, other panes are shattered intact, jewelled in their panes.

Even as you admire stuff like this, it seems to me, part of you is thinking what a pain in the neck it is, this *strain* of writing that is so saturated in its own effects. Lenny, one of the main characters, finds that she 'can't believe in any prayer made of words: she understands now that she doesn't believe in words at all'. Even in context this sentiment has a false ring to it. As far as Jayne Anne Phillips is concerned – bear with me if this sounds a ludicrous charge to level at any writer – there is nothing but words, nothing but writing. At one point, tellingly, a fish jumps, 'flashing like a comma'. A few pages later Lenny, swimming, moves 'through stripes of cold'. Perfect images, absolutely perfect, but after 250 pages even moments like these, where sensation is rendered so precisely, seem simply part of a pattern, an inevitable consequence of a verbal heightening that is largely rhetorical and therefore flattening.

'Concede the heat of noon in summer camps', the novel begins, beautifully, hypnotically. Concede also that while saying a novel is imagined entirely at the level of writing sounds like the highest praise imaginable, it can also suggest a forestalling of the imagination, a falling short.

1995

Richard Ford

Richard Ford's narrator, Frank Boscombe, quit serious writing to become a sportswriter. This was the making of Ford. It wasn't until *he* became Boscombe, the sportswriter, that Ford turned himself into a major writer.

At odd moments in *The Sportswriter*, Frank looks back on his abandoned literary career. He had published a 'promising' collection of stories, *Blue Autumn*, and had then started in on a novel he never finished. It was going to be about an ex-Marine in Tangiers, a place Frank had never visited but which he 'assumed was like Mexico'. In his late thirties, with the abandoned manuscript in a drawer, Frank looks back with bemusement at these efforts to sound 'hard-nosed and old-eyed about things'.

This is an accurate enough diagnosis of what was wrong with Ford's first two books, *A Piece of my Heart* (1976) and *The Ultimate Good Luck* (1981), both of which were published in Britain only in the wake of the success of *The Sportswriter* (1986), his third. *A Piece of My Heart* was swamped by low-lit contrivances, by loading the banal with a freight of what Frank comes to call 'hard emptinesses':

'I ain't hot,' he said, keeping his head sealed against his wrist and spitting in the dust.

She got quiet, and he decided to let things be quiet awhile.

'I'm waitin,' she said.

'What're you waitin on?' he said . . .

She sat staring straight out at the long curve in the road, breathing deeply.

Set in Oaxaca – a place like Tangiers? – *The Ultimate Good Luck* is harder – 'Quinn wanted the money put away fast' – and emptier: 'Money gave him nerves. It was too important to fuck with'. Quinn is a Vietnam vet (naturally) who, in the opening pages, takes a girl he's just met to a boxing match ('He wanted this fight to be over and better fighters to come in, and so did the Mexicans'). The boxer has an eye put out but Quinn doesn't even blink. After the fight the girl sucks him off in his room, and after that there's a lot of bad-ass chat and some shooting. In both these two early novels, incidentally, cigarettes are not 'put out' or 'stubbed' but 'mashed'.

According to Frank Boscombe, the problem with his earlier stories was that he could always 'see around the sides' of what he was writing, just as we can see around the sides of what Ford was doing in his first books: when male American writers take us to a boxing match, it's generally so we can watch them squaring up to Hemingway. Writing about sports, though, Frank hit upon a style that was entirely his own, 'a no-frills voice that hopes to uncover simple truths by a straight-on application of the facts'. For Ford, you might say, the breakthrough was writing *Frankly*. If anything of Hemingway survives into this phase of Ford's writing it is the quality John Cheever claimed you could taste in all of Hemingway's work: the taste of loneliness.

Ford had always been a writer with a message in the sense that there was always a mood, a resolution his fiction was drawn towards, a generalised sense of the way things tended. But he had sought to realise this through people (like the hero of Boscombe's unfinished novel) on the edge. With Frank Boscombe he was able to realise this ambition through a man who was in the *middle* of everything: born in the middle of the century, middle-class (his earlier protagonists were drifters), suburban, stalled in the middle of the journey. Born into 'an ordinary modern existence in 1945', he is now 'an ordinary citizen' living the 'normal applauseless life of us all'. Years ago, in the Marine cadets, he was 'somewhat more than average' – and still is in the sense that his is an *achieved* ordinariness, an ordinariness rendered with extraordinary precision.

Emptiness, here in the suburbs, is not hard but delicate, manageable even. When the novel opens on Good Friday, Frank and his ex-wife meet at the grave of their dead child. The whole book circles around loss (of child, of wife, of literary ambition) and the 'terrible searing regret' that underwrites – but is all the time threatening to undermine – Frank's accommodation with the everyday. Not least among the novel's remarkable achievements is the way that, for Frank, acknowledgement and evasion are indistinguishable from each other. For close on 400 pages Ford sustains a tone in which numbness, comfort, desolation and contentment are there in equal measure, not just in every scene but in every sentence, every *word*. This complex of antinomies generates tremendous, unrelieved suspense – we never know where the consequences of the smallest actions will end – which leaves the reader of this awful almost-comedy in an appropriately compounded state of relaxed and exhausted admiration.

The sequel, *Independence Day*, finds Frank in his so-called 'Existence Period'. Having abandoned serious writing for sports journalism, he has now given up sportswriting to sell real estate. He's in his forties, still living in Haddam, New Jersey (in his ex-wife's house), going about his unremarkable business: collecting rent – or trying to – on a house he owns, showing properties to a couple of increasingly wretched clients, and preparing, as in *The Sportswriter*, for a holiday weekend away. Not, this time, with a 'lady friend' but with Paul, his troubled teenage son.

Since Ford locates the novel so precisely, on a 4th July weekend in 1988 with elections looming, you think initially that Frank, like John Updike's Rabbit, will serve as some kind of litmus for America's larger historico-political fortunes. This turns out not to be his intention, or only a tangential one at least. Ford battens everything down, anchors the action to a particular historical moment, because he needs to hold his novel tightly in place while simultaneously allowing Frank's monologue to drift where it will. A digressive novel by most standards, *The Sportswriter* was, by comparison, wire-taut. It hummed. Ford's version of suspense in *Independence Day* is *to leave things hanging*. He pays out the narrative willy-nilly, carelessly, haphazardly it seems. When calamity strikes and the novel *snaps*, the wrench is even harder because of all the excess that has been piling up unnoticed in harmless coils and loops. Only then do you realise that the narrative rope has actually been measured out inch by inch.

It's a risky business though. At times *Independence Day* nudges too close to the ordinariness it depicts. When Frank advises us of every twist and turn of his itinerary –

up to 80, where untold cars are all flooding eastward, then west to Hackensack, up 17 past Paramus, onto the Garden State north (again!), though eerily enough there's little traffic; through River Edge and Oradell and Westwood, and two tolls to the New York line, then east to Nyack and the Tappan Zee, down over Tarrytown . . .

– we switch off, let it all wash over us without registering *where* he's going. Whisking us off on a 'bystander's cruise' through town he succumbs to what is either an exhaustive short- or a highly abbreviated long-hand:

> past the closed PO, the closed Frenchy's Gulf, the nearly empty August Inn, the Coffee Spot, around the Square, past the Press Box Bar, the closed Lauren-Schwindell office, Garden State S & L, the somnolent Institute itself and the always officially open but actually profoundly closed First Presbyterian, where the WELCOME sign out front says, *Happy Birthday America! * 5K Race * HE Can Help You At The Finish Line!*

As narrator, in other words, Frank is carrying some extra weight these days, suffering a little middle-page spread. Not that it bothers him. In his semi-resigned way he's actually pretty chipper, 'larrupping' down the ole highway, heart going 'ker-whonk' as he notices a girl sway '*waaaay* back' on her heels. When prose is as easy on the ear as this you have to attend carefully lest, lulled by the lope of Frank's voice, you miss important turns (of phrase). In the itinerary passage quoted earlier, it turns out, there *were* none but it is by tail-gating the quotidian like this that Ford captures those interludes, too vague and drifting even to be termed states of mind, the aggregate of which gives the Existence Period its characterless character.

Frank's voice also proves – and this was the breakthrough of *The Sportswriter* – surprisingly flexible. With no perceptible change of gear it can – at the risk of sounding ludicrous – cry out like Rilke before gliding back into the humdrum:

> My heart has begun whompeting again at the antiseptic hospital colours, frigid surfaces and the strict, odorless, traffic flow yin-yang of everything within sight and

hearing . . . And *everything's* lugubriously, despairingly *for* something; nothing's just for itself or, better, for nothing. A basket of red geraniums would be yanked, a copy of *American Cage Birds* magazine tossed like an apple core. A realty guide, a stack of *Annie Get Your Gun* tickets – neither would last five minutes before somebody had it in the trash.

Lucky American writers for whom the dominant narrative voice of literature is so close to the lives of the people *within* the narrative! 'Every time I talk to you I feel everything's being written by you,' complains Frank's ex-wife at one point. 'That's awful. Isn't it?' Skew things round a little, though – everything Frank writes sounds like it could have been *said* by someone in the book – and it becomes anything but awful. Think of the hoops James Kelman has had to wedge himself through to close the gap between narrative and dialogue; then think of Ford and that all-accommodating, middle-of-the road voice that is equally at home either side of inverted commas.

As in *The Sportswriter* much of the action of *Independence Day* is made up of Frank chatting with people he bumps into. Characters – even those with walk-on parts like Mr Tanks, the removal man with the wristwatch 'sunk into his great arm', or Char, the cook Frank almost gets something going with – step into the book and are instantly, vividly *there*. They don't even have to *be* there to be there: when Frank phones through to check messages on his answering machine, a deserted motel lobby is suddenly jostling with six or seven people at once, all breathing down his neck. (I may be wrong but Ford, as far as I know, is the first writer to have tapped the novelistic potential of this relatively recent technological innovation; I'm surprised Nicholson Baker hasn't made a whole book out of it.)

I mention these messages because they show, in the most

concentrated form imaginable, how adept Ford has become at conveying entire lives in a few words. Nothing in *The Sportswriter* is more suggestive of the gulf-bond between Frank and the world than the exchanges with his near-suicidal acquaintance Walter Luckett, each of them finishing everything they say with the other's Christian name. Ford also has that uncanny knack of making what characters say somehow *contain* the light or weather that surrounds them. A gesture is implied by a voice, a state of mind by a gesture. The instance that sticks in my mind occurs in *Wildlife*, the near-faultless short novel published in 1990, between the two Boscombe books: the teenage narrator sees his mother on the phone to her lover, 'winding the phone cord around her finger and looking at me through the door as she talked to him'. (The American arts of writing and acting are probably more closely related than we think.) The new book is dense with moments like this, where the psychological dynamics of a scene are actualised by a few simple movements – as when Frank is ferrying around a couple of increasingly desperate house-buyers who are close to 'realty meltdown':

'Maybe we *should* think about renting,' Phyllis says vacantly. I have her in my mirror, keeping to herself like a bereaved widow. She has been staring at the hubcap bazaar next door, where no one's visible in the rain-soaked yard, though the hubcaps sparkle and clank in the breeze. She may be seeing something as a metaphor for something else.

Unexpectedly, though, she sits forward and lays a consolidating mitt on Joe's bare, hairy shoulder, which causes him to jump like he'd been stabbed. Though he quickly detects this as a gesture of solidarity and tenderness, and lumpily reaches round and grubs her hand with his . . . It is the bedrock gesture of marriage, something I have somehow missed out on, and rue.

Passages like this remind us that although he was imported into England wrapped in *Granta*'s modish 'Dirty Realism' packaging, his virtues are primarily those that have always been associated with quality fiction. Indeed, the journey made by Frank and his son Paul both locates *Independence Day* quite consciously within the tradition of the American novel *and* implicitly tugs that tradition towards Ford's own preferred territory.

From Haddam they head to Cooperstown, to the dawn, as it were, of the American novel, where James Fenimore Cooper is preserved in dozens of variants of the Leatherstocking Giftshop, or the Deerslayer Inn where Frank and Paul spend the night. Frank is struck by the geography involved in their journey from Haddam, by the way that:

> in three hours you can stand on the lapping shores of Long Island Sound, staring like Jay Gatz at a beacon light that lures you to, or away from, your fate; yet in three hours you can be heading for cocktails damn near where old Natty drew first blood – the two locales as unalike as Seattle is to Waco.

And in the middle of these two literary poles, of course, is Haddam, New Jersey, where Ford stakes his own claim to literary greatness. It's tantamount to saying that he is *right up there* – and it is a claim I would not dispute. It is not just that Ford deploys these traditional tools and qualities of the writer's art so abundantly; also, and perhaps more importantly, he reminds us that these qualities are themselves difficult to surpass. You can go beyond them (as Joyce, Faulkner and their progeny have tried to) but you cannot better them.

1995

Michael Ondaatje

In Michael Ondaatje's books the poet and the novelist hold each other in risky equilibrium. His last and most ambitious novel, *In the Skin of a Lion*, stitched the lyric intensity and damaged grace of *The Collected Works of Billy the Kid* and *Coming through Slaughter* into a narrative that was historic and delicate, momentous and humane. Understandably, then, *The English Patient* is less an advance than an extension – geographical, historical – of the imaginative possibilities inherent in that last book: a sequel of sorts.

Two of the new novel's four central characters will be familiar to readers of *In the Skin of a Lion*. As the Second World War is ending, Caravaggio, the thief, makes his way to a ruined villa north of Florence. Hana, daughter of his friend Patrick, hero of the earlier book, has stayed on there to nurse the English patient. Bed-ridden, charred, he came into the hands of the allied authorities after falling burning from the sky over the Sahara. Aside from that his identity is a mystery – 'a vacuum on their charts' – which deepens as we discover more about him.

This war-scarred trio – Hana is shell-shocked; tortured, his thumbs removed, Caravaggio's nimble hands are now 'terrible paws' – are joined by a young sapper, Kip, part of a unit clearing mines left by the retreating German army. Late summer. Electrical storms. 'A villa romance.'

Everything around the villa has been shattered by war and the stories unfolding within it are, to make a neatly predictable point, torn, fragmented. The war-time adventures of Kip and Caravaggio vie for our attention with the English patient's disturbed, chaotic memories of the great pre-war era of desert exploration. Through everything he has kept with him an old edition of Herodotus, adding to it, 'cutting and gluing in pages from other books or writing in his own observations'. Ondaatje's books usually carry within them a guide to their internal workings and *The English Patient* is a mirror image of this volume of Herodotus. Pasted into Ondaatje's own writing are journal entries, lines from Milton, quotations from a book about bomb disposal.

This last field of expertise offers another dramatised diagram of the book's circuitry: the wires of narrative are deliberately tangled and the reader unravels them like a sapper, carefully, gingerly. Defusing a bomb, Kip re-creates the thought-process of the bomb-maker, and reading this book brings us close to the intricate graft of its construction. To hurry through it is fatal. Ondaatje relies not on narrative suspense – the outcome of the various stories concerns us less than the brief contingency of their entanglement – but on suspended narration. Taken at speed his writing is merely frustrating. 'Read him slowly,' the English patient says of Kipling. 'He is a writer who used pen and ink. He looked up from the page a lot, I believe . . . Think about the speed of his pen.'

And, one should add of Ondaatje, the frequent use he makes of scissors. Razors, scissors, instruments of excision, of maiming and mending, are as crucial to the action of the book as the jump cut is to its composition. Elements of a single scene are dispersed – and thereby concentrated – into spatially isolated sections of text. Like the books in the villa's ruined library, Ondaatje's depends on 'missing incidents' and 'gaps of plot like sections of road washed out by storms'. The individual sentences are similarly lack-enhanced. 'In any of Patrick's sentences,' Hana remembers her mother complaining, 'you lost two or three crucial words' and Ondaatje's is a prose whose power derives from what is omitted. 'In the apartment there is light only from the river and the desert beyond it. It falls upon her neck her feet the vaccination scar he loves on her right arm. She sits on the bed hugging nakedness.'

This elaborately abbreviated immediacy becomes irritating when the sentences seem deliberately self-highlighting, when verbs crouch conspicuously in the surrounding silence of white space. Or when the characters' reactions and perceptions are tuned to a pitch that is automatically feverish: 'He is a survivor of his fears, will step around anything suspicious, acknowledging her look in this panorama as if claiming he can deal with it all.'

Occasional 'ghosting' like this, a tendency to twist the brightness control too far (the word 'terrible' is terribly over-used), is inevitable in a book where binoculars, magnifying lenses and telescopic sights are key thematic props. Every detail is amplified and magnified. Even the English patient's hearing aid is turned up so that he is 'alive to everything in the house'. Ondaatje's interest in character, in other words, is not psychological but forensic. In the slow strobe of his prose, action is broken down into its gestural increments. Any motion leaves a slow blur of intention in its wake. A character's movement across a room is registered by the disturbance of light angling through a window.

This point is anything but incidental. For if the internal workings of the book are glimpsed in the ways noted, it is *light* that frames and sustains Ondaatje's unique imaginative vision. The bleached glare of the desert, trees making 'a sieve of moonlight', 'pink late daylight', lightning that 'drops towards any metal or spire that rises up out of the landscape', the *chiaroscuro* of candlelit meals in the ruined villa, the blinding flash of news that brings the novel to an end . . . To cite every mention and inflection of light would be, in effect, to transcribe the entire novel, for light is its shaping force, its valency.

> The long Cairo evenings. The sea of night sky, hawks in rows until they are released at dusk, arcing towards the last colour of the desert. A unison of performance like a handful of thrown seed.

1992

Cormac McCarthy

All the Pretty Horses

> They said that it was no accident of circumstance that a
> man be born in a certain country and not some other and
> they said that the weathers and seasons that form a land
> form also the inner fortunes of men in their generations
> and are passed on to their children and are not so easily
> come by otherwise.

'They' are Mexican ranch-hands and it was after returning from
Mexico that D.H. Lawrence described England as a country the
size of someone's backyard. Back in the 1950s there were com-
plaints about the way so much British fiction was preoccupied
with the Hampstead middle class; the same gripe is still heard
today when there is an impressive literature of the housing-
estate working class. The real, underlying grievance, I think, is
that we seem condemned to fiction that takes place *indoors*. To
that extent James Kelman is as much the heir of Jane Austen as
Anita Brookner. Hemmed in by the size and restricted by the cli-
mate of our cloud-shrouded little rock we are all – even
imaginatively – confined to quarters. Hence the stifled longing

for a fiction of the outdoors, a fiction of travel that – sea yarns excepted – has been virtually extinct since Fielding.

America, by contrast, has a vast tradition of wilderness literature. Step out of your front door in an English novel and you're on your way to the newsagent; in an American novel you're heading off, heading out. Updike is hardly an apostle of the wilderness but, in the final volume of the tetralogy, even the ageing Rabbit has the imaginative opportunity to cut loose and take off. For his part Cormac McCarthy in this, the first volume of an intended trilogy, waits only thirty pages before starting a paragraph with the three words which, for him, are synonymous with the act of writing itself: 'They rode out . . .'

John Grady Cole and Lacey Rawlins are only in their teens when they ride out from Texas in the late 1940s. At first their way is barred by wire fences but soon the land opens up and they head towards Mexico. Crossing the border they meet up with a third boy, Blevins, who is even younger than they are. Cole and Rawlins come from ranching families; the skill and knowledge of generations of cowboys is in their blood, their hands; Blevins is the lost, stunted heir of the even older culture of the outlaw whose genealogy McCarthy traced in *Blood Meridian*.

In Mexico they steal back Blevins's horse after it becomes lost in a storm. With riders in pursuit the two friends separate from him and head off on their own. Later, when they come upon a *hacienda* and are taken on as ranch-hands and horse-breakers the boys find the vanished life of their dreams perfectly preserved.

Up until this point the novel has been as engrossing as any you have ever read; now, as they settle into the routine of work and Cole meets and falls for the owner's daughter, it moves into the realms of rapture. 'How long do you think you'd like to stay here?' asks Rawlins as they talk one night. 'About a hundred years,' says Cole. 'Go to sleep.'

You can't, though: you are already lost in the dream-time of the novel, immersed in the wonder of it all. Anyone prone to skip descriptive passages will find that impossible too: in McCarthy landscape is a verb, a part of the action that courses through it. Earth and sky, horses and work, male friendship and Cole's evolving, dangerous relationship with Alejandra are all rendered with such force and beauty that you want this interlude to continue for hundreds of pages.

It actually lasts for less than fifty: Blevins has been caught and Rawlins and Cole, too, are hauled off to jail. The ensuing prison scenes are no less impressive, no less vivid than those on the plains.

Underpinning everything in the jail is a 'bedrock of depravity and violence where in an egalitarian absolute every man is judged by a single standard and that is his readiness to kill'. The same ethic underlay the Homeric Western, *Blood Meridian*. 'Whatever in creation exists without my knowledge exists without my consent,' claims a character known as the judge – who duly slays every living thing he sees. *Child of God*, an earlier novel also predicated on slaughter, delves even deeper – ludicrously so, in my opinion – into an abyss of violence.

The great strength of the new novel is that the simmering pathology of McCarthy's world is itself defined by a morality that survives – and derives strength from – every assault upon it. While emerging from prison as a man capable of forcing himself to do and endure almost anything, Cole never forsakes his credo of down-home loyalty: 'You either stick or quit,' he says to Rawlins, 'and I wouldnt quit you I dont care what you done. And that's about all I got to say.' Indeed it is this quality that gives Cole the strength to survive the savagery of prison and the betrayals that lie beyond it.

As a result of what happens to him in Mexico, Cole (like earlier McCarthy protagonists Lester Ballard and Cornelius

Suttree) is set apart 'from the common enterprise of man' but never falls or strays from the book's moral meridian: 'all courage was a form of constancy . . . it was always himself that the coward abandoned first. After this all other betrayals came easily.'

McCarthy has always been a courageous writer but mastering his own ideal of artistic constancy has proved an even harder trek for him than most novelists. There are still gouts of Faulkner (whose influence swamps *Suttree*) and hanks of Hemingway but his prose also has a visionary richness and imaginative rhythm that is entirely his own. Combine this with the inherent narrative pull of his subject matter and you have, in *All the Pretty Horses*, one of the greatest American novels of this or any other time: one that persuades you that, really, there is nothing on earth more pleasurable, no adventure greater than sitting indoors, reading.

The Crossing

'Always the teller must be at pains to devise against his listener's claim,' declares one of the *meseta* visionaries encountered here, 'that he has heard the tale before.' This tale, the second in Cormac McCarthy's Border Trilogy, seems, in outline, very like one we've heard before. Two teenage boys cross from the southwest of America into Mexico, on horseback. In doing so they cross a temporal frontier and find themselves in the world of the vanished American West, where blood, violence and dying are conditions of living. That it's set in the late 1930s rather than the late 1940s, and that the boys are brothers rather than friends and come from New Mexico rather than Texas is incidental: the terrain crossed in the new novel is very similar to that roamed by *All the Pretty Horses*.

Once again McCarthy sets off on those vista sentences – parascapes – that warp and shimmer and acknowledge no grammatical horizon other than their own eventual resolution. Between the bleached bones of punctuation, there are yet resilient ligaments of dialogue; in the demotic Spanish of many such exchanges can still be heard the gristle of a Godly rhetoric. In summary – 'He said that as the memory of the world must fade so must it fade in his dreams until soon or late he feared that he would have darkness absolute and no shadow of the world that was' – this becomes the arcane testament of the Border, 'that place where acts of God and those of man are of a piece.'

The ostensible similarities between the two published parts of the trilogy actually emphasise the differences. Everything about *All the Pretty Horses* impelled us to proclaim its qualities immediately and without qualification; if our response to *The Crossing* is more muted that is because the book demands that its measure be taken in a different way. A brooding, haunting novel, it forces us to be halting, hesitant in our judgement because even its uncertainties seem the issue of unerring authorial command. To take the tiniest of examples: there are dozens of occasions when, for the sake of clarity, a character should be referred to by name but McCarthy insists, confusingly, on the third person pronoun. Now, this is fifth-form criticism, obviously, but in the face of McCarthy's implacable imaginative conviction other, larger reservations – about the book's structure, for example – are rendered similarly inauthoritative, petty.

The Crossing does not afford the sweep or narrative engulfment of its predecessor. The wordscape is deeply faulted, criss-crossed by parables and broken by outcrops of wisdom whose glare darkens all around. Again and again, as Billy and Boyd track their parents' killers, the trail dies out and the brothers find themselves lost, stranded. They ride on. A vast purposelessness accompanies their most determined endeavours. But, equally, even the most inconsequential of actions seems like increments of fate. 'While men may meet their deaths in strange places which they might have avoided,' says a rider encountered near the end of the book, 'it was more correct to say that no matter how hidden or crooked the path to their destruction yet they would seek it out.'

This is the path followed by McCarthy's protagonists in all his novels. Like all of these earlier protagonists Billy Parham finds himself 'elected out of the common lot of men'. In many of the previous books, especially *Blood Meridian* and *Child of God*, it was their propensity for violence which set them apart; what *The Crossing* demonstrates most powerfully, however – especially in the scenes where a doctor treats a gunshot wound, or a gypsy tends an injured horse – is the opposite point: the long reach of human kindness. This is not to prefer a sentimental to a savage view but to affirm the greater inclusiveness and depth of McCarthy's vision in his more recent works.

For many years McCarthy's path took him beyond the edges of the American literary map. That map has had to be redrawn and extended to include him, but McCarthy remains in many ways the perpetual stranger, a self-elected outcast, what an old man in the book calls a 'huerfano' (literally, orphan): 'He said that . . . he contained within him a largeness of spirit which men could see and that men would wish to know him and that the world would need him even as he needed the world for they were one.'

Cities of the Plain

Compared with the terrain covered in the first volumes of the Border Trilogy, the narrative of *Cities of the Plain* is considerably geographically restricted. The journey traced in these pages is that of two men inching towards a fate already looming over them. Excepting the very weird epilogue – a dream-parable in which McCarthy maps out his (to my mind) incomprehensible metaphysics of destiny – all the action takes place on or close to a ranch in New Mexico, or in the whorehouses and bars just across the border.

It's 1952 and the protagonists of the earlier books – John Grady Cole from *All the Pretty Horses*, Billy Parham from *The Crossing* – have ended up working as cowboys for an old rancher whose values – hard work, loyalty, taciturn honesty, courage – have endured into an era which threatens their extinction. These are the qualities that sustained Billy and John Grady through the often atrocious events of the earlier volumes. Both have suffered terrible loss, but, on the ranch, among men whose memories stretch back to the West of legend, they find a community of equals. Bound by their love and understanding of horses – it's a shame, really, that so much cornball horse whispering is going on in territory adjacent to McCarthy's – and possessed by the same unswerving moral rectitude, Billy and John Grady become as close as kin: as close, in fact, as Billy was to his brother, Boyd, who died during *The Crossing*.

Life on the ranch is arduously idyllic, as beautiful in its celibate masculinity – or, sceptics might claim, as thoroughly sentimentalised – as the Mexican prostitute with whom John Grady falls helplessly in love. They speak to each other in *el corazón* Spanish, a language of the heart. She is epileptic, damaged, ill-used, but, to John Grady, as worthy of devotion as the Virgin ('In Mexico there is no God. Just her.'). Her pimp, too, regards her with sadistic veneration and, after failing to negotiate her release, John Grady arranges instead for her to escape. He repairs a tumble-down old shack for them to live in, plans their marriage. To what extent he believes in their future as a practical reality is uncertain since even her beauty is ominous: McCarthy's world is predicated on – and the tension of the book derives from – 'a knowing deep in the bone that beauty and loss are one'.

There are times when McCarthy seems in danger of over-egging this characteristically black pudding. *Blood Meridian*, had, as an alternative title, 'The Evening Redness in the West', and, in the new book, the colour is invariably prefixed by the substance: sky, bar lights, even carpet are all 'blood red'. McCarthy's unrelenting verbal insistence is, of course, an intrinsic part of the narrative-trance his work induces in the reader. Scenes unfold in tight incremental detail ('Billy spooned the eggs and set the bowl down and reached for the sausage') and roll on through a grammatical landscape stripped of all features – apostrophes, inverted commas – that might distract from the elemental force of the language. This language lulls you, so to speak, into a unique state of matchless linguistic and visual receptivity. Quotable instances – like the view of ponies 'across the creek where they stood footed to their darkening shapes in the ford', or the terrified horse with 'its eyes like eggs in its head' – do not really convey the quality of prose that achieves its effects cumulatively, hypnotically.

'They rode out . . .'; 'They rode all morning . . .'; 'They set out across the broad creosote flats of the valley . . .' The trilogy is strewn with paragraph openers like these. The circuitry accessed by variants of such lines is simultaneously ancient, vast, mythic *and* – because of the pervasiveness of Westerns in the movies – instantly generically familiar. One of the reasons McCarthy's words work on the reader so intensely is because the cinema has provided a visual template for what we encounter in print. The pimp, for example, comes grinning out of Sergio Leone: 'A match flared and Eduardo's face leaned in the flame with one of his little cigarillos in his teeth.' As a mode of imagining this borders on cliché and *eh-gringo* stereotype, but it is, precisely, in such dangerous proximity that the trilogy's greatness and originality lie. McCarthy's world-view is that of the down-home prophet or huckster visionary; stylistically, he is the self-conscious, blood-boltered heir of Hemingway and Faulkner. But his books are also haunted by Zane Grey (who, in *Wanderer of the Wasteland* – later made into Hollywood's first all-colour film – wrote of a proto-McCarthyite breed of 'men who go forth to seek and to find and to face their souls') and a posse of pulp Western writers whose names are long forgotten (if they were ever known). Out of this combination – febrile, feral and immensely sophisticated – the completed trilogy emerges clearly as a landmark in American literature.

1993/1994/1998

Jay McInerney

As the allusive title suggests, *The Last of the Savages* is a novel addressing itself to big themes. Grappling with race, the legacies of slavery and the Civil War, it is 'about the past's implacable claims on the present', about – as a character accents it with some incredulity – *hi*story. It is also, tacitly, a novel about the confrontation with a frontier: a demonstration of a writer coming up against his limitations. In the end it is less the work itself that compels admiration than the author's willingness to extend himself beyond his undoubted strengths.

Jay McInerney has always been most at home within narrow alleys of narrative: a few blitzed-out days in *Bright Lights, Big City*, a few more in *Story of My Life*. We enjoy Nicholson Baker for the way he notices little things the rest of us have overlooked; McInerney offers the pleasure of recognition, of providing a narrative inventory – at once definitive and highly contingent – of situations his constituency of readers have already glimpsed for themselves (this was explicit in the second person narration of *Bright Lights*). His last novel, *Brightness Falls*, was broader, more ambitious, but it relied on that same ability to furnish a catalogue of the lifestyles that under-wrote a particular moment – Black Monday – of historical convergence. In this novel, though, he has not just to cut across history but to become its chronicler.

The story begins in familiar, rites of passage territory when narrator Patrick Keane meets his prep school roommate, the rebellious Southern aristo, Will Savage. In galvanic reaction against a family history that has included the brutal suppression of a slave rebellion, Will's self-proclaimed mission in life is to 'free the slaves'. As an adult this means recording blues musicians and becoming a music mogul; as an adolescent it involved inviting Patrick down to the family home in Memphis and getting him stoned at a blues club. At that club Will makes his first advances on Taleesha, the young black singer he later marries, partly out of love, partly to cause maximum offence to his family, partly, according to Patrick, as a way of 'healing the jagged rift across the face of our land'. While Will becomes a prime mover in 1960s and 70s counter-culture, Patrick beavers his way into law school and the comforts of corporate life. By middle-age the friends' lives exemplify the ways in which a generation defines the era by which it is shaped.

As even this resumé makes clear, there is a lot of story-telling, of *history* – close on three decades – to get through. Conscious of the scale of his allotted task, McInerney resorts on occasion to summary. Dramatically, material is contrived so that it can be dealt with economically. Fortunately for the author, his narrator is in a taxi when Will and Taleesha's house goes up in flames: by the time he arrives on the scene the fire has only a paragraph left to burn. A key moment in Patrick's sexual evolution is likewise dealt with retrospectively, in a paragraph. The reason for this postponement is to maintain suspense about 'the darkest enigma of [his] being' – but the suspense is proclaimed by lines like that rather than by self-generating increments: if the novel was working McInerney wouldn't need Patrick to persuade us that there was an enigma.

As a way of summarising some of the problems of authorial summary let's look at a characteristic passage from the middle of the book.

It was spring, [Will] was in love and the scent of marijuana
was in the air. The slaves were growing their hair out and
marching on Washington. The Pentagon would shortly be
levitated. Robert Kennedy and Martin Luther King and
Jimi Hendrix were still amongst us.

Now that might be OK as commentary on a TV documentary
where the on-screen images are doing nine-tenths of the work,
but in a novel we need something happening in the foreground.
The author duly obliges: 'We wandered the downtown streets for
hours, pausing in front of various night clubs which Will considered hallowed . . .' That 'various' is a little slack (a few pages
later, incidentally, we learn that Patrick chose to study history
'for a variety of reasons') and so, conscious that he has fallen
below the minimum amount of writerly effort needed to *fix* the
scene, McInerney makes sure that, by the end of the sentence,
his characters do wind up somewhere precise, namely 'the Cedar
Tavern'. But that's all it is: a name. As soon as they are inside, it
melts away entirely, ceases to exist. The characters could be anywhere. A quick establishing shot has been used as a buffer
between stock exterior footage and generic interior.

Throughout, this kind of problem is exacerbated by the way
that the dialogue has to do more narrative load-bearing than in
the previous novels. Since the characters drift apart from each
other a given snippet of dialogue has to provide us with a couple
of years' worth of character development. Meeting Patrick at
the Harvard club – another example of generic site-specifica-
tion – for the first time in three years Taleesha explains that:
'Everybody at the company's fascinated that I quit singing. But I
never really had that hunger. I'd rather be backstage, thanks.' As
with a suitcase crammed too full of luggage, chunks of dialogue
like this are all the time threatening to burst out of the inverted
commas that have been stretched around them.

A lack of concentration is also apparent at a simple, linguistic level. When Patrick goes to his first blues club he falls into 'a kind of hypnotic rapture'; a little later someone shakes his head 'with a kind of fetal languor'. Like burglars, writers leave their prints on everything they touch and there is an invisible, implicit 'kind of' before many of the phrases in *The Last of the Savages*, a tacit admission that McInerney has not focused sharply enough, has not immersed himself sufficiently deeply in his writing. The protagonist of *Bright Lights* contemplates a life of writing, of losing himself in 'the imperatives of words in the correct and surprising sequence'. There are odd felicitous touches – like the view of 'the expensive Pacific' – but what is surprising about the prose of the new novel is the lack of surprises. Will drives Patrick through Memphis at 'terrifying speed'; later on, we hear, 'they roared out into the night'; later still the car comes 'screeching to a halt'. These, it might be argued, are not very significant instances but this tendency to reach for the nearest phrase to hand – to write, as it were, without due care and attention – turns out to be endemic. It might also be argued that these locutions are those of McInerney's narrator, and there are occasions when a low-intensity irony is wrung from Patrick's heartfelt conviction that others 'couldn't possibly imagine the sheer vivacity of my being, the poetry of my fierce yearnings and fears'. When Patrick writes that he 'threw [himself] into academic life with a vengeance', on the other hand, McInerney is reclining into the writing life with a lack of vengeance. In a crucial scene Patrick lets Will take the blame for a serious breach of school rules: we should not make the mistake of letting Patrick take the rap for his creator's shortcomings.

These are most significantly exposed in the character of Will Savage himself. It is important for the novel's success not only that Will embraces the causes of the counter-culture but that he embodies them. As a physical presence he is understandably felt most strongly early in the book. Thereafter the lack of linguistic toning that we have observed begins to imaginatively sap him. Drawn to a language that seems expressive of the novel's grander ambitions, McInerney yields to an idiom that radically undermines it. 'The benevolent glaze in his eyes had suddenly given way to a menacing intensity.' No character can survive these kinds of ministrations from an author who is applying the glaze to something that is still only half-baked. 'The gaunt beauty of his youth had dissipated': that, likewise, is less a response to Will's *appearance* than a seductive appeal to a vault of sentiment patented by Fitzgerald and coveted by McInerney.

Will believes there is a curse on him and his family but the eagerness to elide this taint with the 'curse that came over to the New World with the first black slave' and which has 'been here ever since' is accomplished at the level of authorial declaration rather than convincingly manifested in his characters' actions. *The Last of the Savages* is an engaging, complex character but we are not persuaded that his story is *history*. We are left with the statement of great purpose rather than its achieved substance and form.

1996

Martin Amis

Night Train is, so to speak, a nominal title. It's really The New Amis. The new McEwan, the new Byatt, the new Barnes: they're just books to be read or not read according to your taste. The New Amis, though, is not just an exciting prospect, it's an event to be reckoned with – even if you don't read it. The old New Amis, *The Information*, took this to extremes, the text itself becoming a postscript to the overwhelming experience of its publication. Everyone wanted to know what it was like. Nobody really cared to find out because everybody already knew all about it. There was no mystery. There was too much information.

The new New Amis is all mystery. It's an American *noir*, narrated by Detective Hoolihan – a woman – who's investigating an apparently blatant suicide. The suicidee is Jennifer Rockwell, beautiful daughter of the Chief of Police, who's leaning on Hoolihan to somehow change -cides, from 'sui-' to 'homi-'. The fact that Jennifer has *three* bullets in her head certainly lends credence to such a possibility.

That's enough plot. No one reads Chandler for the plots – Chandler didn't *write* Chandlers for the plots – and certainly no one reads Amis for the plot. The genre's allure is stylistic. *Night Train* is set in a city of words, a textual city ('Whitman Avenue', 'Yeats's Bar'). That the book is to be largely an investigation of rhetoric is announced in the opening pages. 'Compared to what you guys give me to read,' says one of Hoolihan's superiors about her reports, 'this is fucking oratory.' Amis had mastered 'the most exalted villainspeak' – as he puts it in *The Information* – several times over; this time he was going to have a bash at American copspeak. Which he does brilliantly, naturally. Amongst other things *Night Train* is a virtuoso display of night-stick poetry and cop oratory. There are nice soft-boiled touches too: the house on 'a slow drip' after a downpour ('Drip, drop, said the rain').

If on occasions we think that Hoolihan sounds a bit too like a man, Amis wipes away his prints by having other characters mistake her for a man also. Especially on the phone: everyone thinks she sounds like a man. Specifically, her voice is like her creator's, her liver is like John Self's: 'If I bought a new liver, I'd just trash that one too.' It's not about doing the police in different voices, then, it's about doing them in the *same* voice, the *Amis* voice. This voice has given him an undisputed claim to a stylistic terrain so pervasive that you're in danger of encroaching on it before you've even set foot in it. (We youngish male writers consequently expend a lot of our energy accusing each other of imitating him. I've been accused of it myself. I've convicted other people of doing it. Will Self received a stiff sentence for it in the *Guardian* only a couple of weeks ago. A few years ago myself and another reviewer were quick to pounce on D.J. Taylor for using Amisian italics. *Italics.* What will he do next? Patent the question mark?) In this sense Amis is a genuine star as opposed to a very successful writer. The main attraction of seeing De Niro act in recent years has not been to see him play a character but to see him doing his De Niro riff. It's the same with Amis: we want him to do his Amis riff and – *The Information* again – it's 'quite a riff by now'. Some of the verbal chord sequences are, as he has remarked of old Rolling Stones songs, already embossed on the senses – 'when a pair of slobs shack up together you don't get slob times two – you get slob squared. You get slob cubed,' – but there are other kinds of Amisisms, recognisable as such less by syntactical familiarity than by stunning imaginative conceit: 'Take away the bodies, and the autopsy room is like the kitchen of a restaurant that has yet to open.'

As expected, there is much to admire. The ongoing investigation of Amis's career, after all, has been the search for a form that facilitates the maximum concentration of Amisisms. It was not long ago that Q and As with Amis concentrated entirely on this kind of thing, on his ability to mint phrases like 'rug re-think' and 'sock'. Then, somewhere along the line, his stylistic signature imperceptibly acquired the weight and substance of a world-view. No, a *universe*-view. The thermo-nuclear jag in *Einstein's Monsters* marked the beginning of an ongoing fascination with astronomy and astro physics. Here, too, there's plenty of 'Dark Matter', a phrase which, in its non-technical usage, alerts us to a deeper continuity, stretching back to *Other People*. According to her egghead boss, Jennifer's work as a theoretical physicist offered her a glimpse of a universe so vast as to bring us to the brink of a 'revolution in consciousness'. Such a revolution, he concedes, would not be without casualties. If Jennifer *did* commit suicide, was she impelled to do so by her awareness of 'just how fragile and isolated our situation really is'? Though later disavowed, this idea forms a vast backdrop – or *black*drop, rather – to Hoolihan's investigation.

Novelists are under no compulsion to think through the ideas behind their work. But if *Night Train* is to be an investigation of a condition rather than of a freak incident – remember how much store Amis set by the idea of the Universal in *The Information*? – then the value of the ideas it dramatises needs to be examined. So let's compare the egghead's hard-boiled suggestion that 'human beings are not sufficiently evolved to understand the place they're living in', that 'we live on a planet of retards', with something similarly thought-provocative. Suppose, writes John Berger in an essay on Leopardi, that all the utopian dreams of the past will come to nothing, that the condition of the world will always be closer to hell than to heaven. What difference would it make to our actions? The answer: none. 'All that would have changed would be the enormity of our hopes and finally the bitterness of our disappointments.' In comparison with this earthy determination the millennial hysterics of *London Fields* and the astro babble of *The Information* seem simultaneously spectacular and derisory. In *Night Train*, too, it is difficult to shake off the impression of someone bedazzled by astronomically big numbers – all those billions of light years! – in the way that Keith Talent was carried away by the idea of Boadicea playing darts in AD 61 ('AD 61! thought Keith'). Not for the first time, then, there is an electric tension between Amis's massive incidental intelligence and matchless linguistic power and the relative banality of his thought; between what he starts out with in each book and where he ends up.

Like the three big novels – *Money*, *London Fields*, *The Information* – *Night Train* comes apart towards the end. It dissolves. The only one of his books that ends well is *Time's Arrow*, which ends with the beginning (Amis is far better at beginnings than he is bad at endings). So we wait for the next New Amis, for a book it would be unreasonable to expect from anyone else: one that keeps beginning right up until the last page.

1997

Pounding Print

Boxers, traditionally, have shown little interest in the ignoble art of writing, but writers have long been fascinated by the noble art of fighting. Joyce Carol Oates considers the first and third Ali–Frazier fights to be 'boxing's analogues to *King Lear* – ordeals of unfathomable human courage and resilience raised to the level of classical tragedy'. Norman Mailer (whose best book is probably not *The Naked and the Dead* but his report on the Ali–Foreman encounter in Zaire, called, in homage – presumably – to Hazlitt, *The Fight*) reckons the great heavyweight champions can 'begin to have inner lives like Hemingway or Dostoyevsky, Tolstoy or Faulkner, Joyce or Melville or Conrad or Lawrence or Proust'. If that is the case then their inner lives, according to one of those invoked by Mailer, turn out to be very like those of, er, the great heavyweights: 'I started off very quietly and I had Mr Turgenev; then I tried hard and I beat Mr Maupassant,' bragged Hemingway. 'I fought two draws with Mr Stendhal, and I think I had an edge in the last one. But nobody's going to get me in a ring with Mr Tolstoy unless I'm crazy or I keep getting better.'

When Mike Tyson embarked on an eclectic programme of reading and study at a prison in Indiana his appreciation of Hemingway – to square the circle yet again – was expressed in exactly the pugilistic terms that Papa liked: 'he uses those short, sharp words, just like hooks and upper cuts'. With Tyson's newly awakened literary interests very much in the news, it is worth taking a highly selective look at the way the boxer has figured in American fiction. In the process we will confront some of the central preoccupations of some modern American writers.

The major landmark is Hemingway's story 'The Battler', from in *In Our Time* (1926). Shaken up after getting chucked off a freight train, Nick Adams encounters a man whose face is 'queerly formed and mutilated . . . like putty in colour'. Seeing Nick watching him, the man asks 'Don't you like my pan?', and urges him to take a closer look.

He had only one ear. It was thickened and tight against the side of his head.

Where the other ear should have been there was a stump.

'Ever see one like that?'

'No,' said Nick. It made him a little sick.

'I could take it,' the man said. 'Don't you think I could take it, kid?'

'You bet!'

'They all bust their hands on me,' the little man said. 'They couldn't hurt me.'

He's Ad Francis, it turns out, a famous prize-fighter. Later, when Ad is ranting and raving, about to give Nick a pasting, his companion shows up, a black guy called Bugs who, to calm him down, lays Ad out cold. What's made him so crazy? Nick wants to know. 'He took too many beatings,' Bugs explains.

Taking beatings is not just a major theme of Hemingway's; it's a vivid, bloody thread in the pattern of American fiction. In a culture predicated on the idea of everybody having the potential for getting on – for winning – much of the best American writing has pledged itself to the idea that it is by following the down-trodden, the losers, the beaten, that we find, to adapt a title of Raymond Carver's, the path to the waterfall of truth. In the title story of *The Pugilist at Rest* (1994) by Thom Jones, the narrator meditates on a picture of Theogenes. 'Then, as now,' he reflects, 'violence, suffering, and the cheapness of life were the rule.'

For Jones, a conscious heir of Hemingway, taking a beating is not only subject and theme, it's an *ethic*: 'I had seen enough of them on my own in boxing to know that sometimes a bad beating could do a fellow a world of good.' Like Wordsworth coming across the leech-gatherer, Nick meets the battler accidentally and emerges from his chance encounter enlightened, changed, but physically unscathed. In Jones we hear the real thing: the voice of the scathed. ('I suffered three broken ribs, a broken nose, and a broken eye-socket. I pissed blood for two weeks, developed a fever, and went into a delirium. I thought I was going to die. You take a beating like that and it puts the fear of God into you.') A development of considerable significance is contained in this simple distinction.

Since Hemingway, and especially since Faulkner, one of the main projects of American fiction has been to forge the authentic literary register of illiteracy. This ambition has been achieved so thoroughly and so successfully that some of the most eloquent voices are those which approach the condition of dumbness. For some time now the ideal of timeless elegance has been worn down by the no-less-demanding idea of the permanently defected ('Don't you like my pan?'). A highly wrought inarticulacy is the goal.

For such an undertaking, the type, encountered in Hemingway's story, of the punchy boxer is obviously, as they say in the fight game, pretty useful. The fighter becomes the dramatic projection of the writer's own enterprise.

The Pugilist at Rest demonstrates this nakedly. The protagonist in most of Jones's stories is a Vietnam vet and prize-fighter. He comes through Vietnam without a scratch only to get 'tagged' in the ring: 'It felt like he was hitting me in the face with a ball-peen hammer. It felt like he was busting light bulbs in my face.' He goes on to win this fight but, as a result of the beating he's taken, he now suffers 'a form of left-temporal-lobe seizures which is sometimes called Dostoyevsky's epilepsy'. Boxing messed him up but it was getting his brains smashed around like this that put him in the same league (epileptically speaking at least) as Dostoyevsky.

The critical conundrum posed by *The Pugilist at Rest* is exemplary, also, in that the distinction between very fine and totally dumb writing in these pages has collapsed to the point where the two hold each other in a mutually supporting clinch. In vain, the critic-referee shouts 'Break!' for the dumbness is a guarantee of the authenticity which is the hallmark of its quality. Taking a beating: not only subject, theme and ethic, but an aesthetic alibi and principle to boot.

The importance of Jones is that he allows us to extrapolate and delineate the quandary of a contemporary American literary ideal: if only it were possible to not be able to write at all – *and still be able to write*.

Pinckney Benedict *can* write, no doubt about that. His novel *Dogs of God* (1994), raises the lesson of 'The Battler' to the level of a violent metaphysics. In a hallucinatory prologue, the protagonist, Goody, finds himself in a fight that is endless. It goes on and on, even after both boxers have blinded each other:

We stand arm's length apart, lashing out, not even trying to duck or block. The blows have taken the place of our eyes, of the light. And each lick of the gloves, mine on him, his on me . . . tells us all we need to know: that we are still alive.

But it is a bare-knuckle fight at the end of the book that is most revealing. Goody has plenty of technique but has to use his big shots sparingly because his hands break up easily. He hits his opponent with a right and knocks him out: 'The stroke was a strong, clean one, and Goody felt elation sweep through him just as his hand broke.' Miraculously, his opponent manages to come out for the third round and Goody has to soak up some quality literary punishment: 'One of his eyes was closed now, and he could feel the other beginning to swell. There was no one in his corner to slit the puffed flesh of the eyelids and give him some relief'. Goody finally puts his opponent away with a murderous left that breaks that hand too.

He wins the fight but in so doing wrecks both his hands. Afterwards he can't even hold a beer can – let alone a pen. He's also blind in one eye, a detached retina, he thinks. We could hardly wish for a more dramatic metaphor for the writer's predicament. The goal for writers like Benedict is, I have suggested, to achieve a prose, so to speak, so thoroughly worked over that it is slurred to perfection. To succeed, to score points, language has to break itself up. Its clarity and precision are synonymous with its propensity for self-maiming. Its power is inextricably bound up with and dependent on its capacity to damage itself.

Most telling of all is that in both Benedict and Jones, the main characters are up against bigger, stronger opponents, opponents they have no right to be in the ring with. 'I shouldn't have fought him,' one of Jones's battlers says of the guy who gave him the beating 'that was the beginning of the end.' Goody, in his fight, is giving away something like forty pounds. Both fight anyway. They win against all odds, but sustain irremediable damage in the process. Harold Bloom's handy notion of the anxiety of influence has alerted us to the ways writers work through and overcome their dominant influences. It is perhaps not too fanciful, then, to suggest that Hemingway's boxing metaphor for literary ambition has been unconsciously absorbed to the extent that the opponents, in both cases, are those undefeated heavyweights Hemingway and Faulkner. One way or another American writers – white male ones at any rate – are still busting their hands on them.

1994

Muhammad Ali

Just as people remember, proverbially, where they were when President Kennedy was assassinated, so I remember what I was doing on the nights of many of Muhammad Ali's greatest fights: listening to them on the radio in the kitchen while my dad shaved. More striking than the vivid contingency of such memories is the suspicion that they are not genuine, that they have been created retrospectively. Actual events have become so encrusted with significance that the subsequent elaborations of memory are impossible to detach from the incidents in which they have their origin. In thinking of Ali, in other words, we are in the realm of *myth as lived experience*.

The recent documentary *When We Were Kings* exemplifies this process: even if the 1975 Rumble in the Jungle passed you by *at the time* the film creates a space in which the fight with George Foreman – barely glimpsed on screen – can be not so much replayed as belatedly accommodated in memory. This is partly a quirk of available technology: the peculiar colour saturation of the footage – especially the blurred luminescence of the fighters' shorts – creates the impression that what has been captured on film is not a historical moment but memory itself.

In *The Fight*, his book about that encounter, Norman Mailer suggested, correctly, that being a Black Muslim might 'be the core of Ali's existence and the centre of his strength'. Conversion to the Nation of Islam was crucial to the transformation of Cassius Clay from exquisitely unorthodox athlete and proto-rapper – the Louisville Lip – to a figure of world-historical importance. If he had not become a disciple of Elijah Muhammad, then Ali would not have possessed the proud discipline of principle to resist the draft ('I got no quarrel with them Viet Cong'), would not have become such an important symbol and example of the liberating potential of Black consciousness. E.M. Cioran has remarked that the further one advances in life the less there is to convert to. As was also the case with Malcolm X, Ali's conversion to this cult with its mumbo-jumbo theology and its formidably impressive imperatives to self-improvement was both a revolutionary step forward and a sign of how little he had advanced in life *up to that point*. It also set a limit to how far he could continue to advance afterwards without in some measure falling foul – as happened to Malcolm X – of what he had converted to.

In an introduction that provides an excellent context for the articles he has assembled,* editor Gerald Early delineates issues like these in such a way as to celebrate Ali's extraordinary power without being dazzled by it. Commenting on Ali's low score in an army IQ test, Early observes:

I think the score was an honest reflection of Ali's mental abilities . . . When he was younger he could successfully debate with those who were much smarter . . . because he had the zealot's set of answers to life's questions. His mind worked through formulas and clichés. His personality gave them a life and vibrancy that they would otherwise

---

*I'm A Little Special: A Muhammad Ali Reader.

have lacked. He was intuitive, glib, richly gregarious a___
intensely creative, like an artist.

Specifically, as Mailer claimed, he was the fighter who managed to 'demonstrate that boxing was a twentieth-century art'.

The pieces in *I'm A Little Special* offer variously interesting
takes and out-takes on that artistry, providing either commentary to accompany mental re-runs of the canonical fight
sequences, or more privileged speculation as to what was going
on off-screen, in Ali's mind. If even the hottest sports reporting
goes quickly cold once removed from the narrow-columned
oven of the back pages, then the so-called new journalism of the
1960s and 70s now seems as archaic as Smollett. What Fredric
Jameson calls 'the obligatory camp sarcasm' of Tom Wolfe and
the hectic excess of Hunter Thompson look, on the evidence
presented here, increasingly like individualised instances of
some saggy default rhetoric. Even a heavy hitter like Mailer
sometimes edges dangerously close to this kind of thing, but his
piece on Ali and Frazier is marked by a sustained clarity of
engagement. Less grandly, several pieces offer poignant glimpses
of Ali in private, especially in the last few years when just keeping his hands steady enough to sign autographs – which he
never tires of doing – requires the single-mindedness of a concert pianist. Gay Talese's account of Ali gazing 'stagnantly' at
Fidel Castro during a recent, quasi-ambassadorial trip to Cuba is
a masterpiece of agnostic reportage.

According to Angelo Dundee, however, the saddest thing is
not that Ali ended up, in Frazier's unforgiving phrase, as 'damaged goods' but that we never saw him at his peak. When Ali lost
his licence in 1967 he was still improving, adding strength to his
speed. When he began his comeback in the autumn of 1970, his
legs had begun to go and he had to change style: from avoiding
being hit to coping with being hit.

Other things had changed too. Ali's rise to fame was part of a larger tidal surge of Black American advancement. More exactly, the emergence of his revolutionary approach was both contemporaneous with and a stylistic equivalent of Free Jazz or the New Music that was itself intricately related to (and a profound expression of) a militant flowering of Black American identity. Malcolm X was killed in 1965, Martin Luther King in 1968. John Coltrane died in 1967; having announced the Shape of Jazz to Come in 1959, Ornette Coleman, a decade later, was performing only rarely. If we had to specify a symbolic moment when the liberationist promise of the New Music came to an end that would be November 1970, when the body of Albert Ayler was found floating in the East River. When Ali began fighting again, then, it was not just a personal physical peak that had been missed: a wider cultural movement that had run in tandem with his own progress had also pretty well exhausted itself. Symbolically, his wresting the title from Foreman in 1975 was a belated reclamation of the highest aspirations of Black Unity (to borrow the title of a representative Pharoah Sanders album of the period).

These days Ali is wheeled on to the world stage like a zombie from a superior era of African-American achievement. You look at him and ask, like Wilfred Owen in 'Futility', 'Was it for this the Clay grew tall?'

1998

John Carey

Modernism, it turns out, was a conspiracy. Confronted with the rise of mass culture, early twentieth-century intellectuals consciously attempted to prevent the masses 'reading literature by making it too difficult for them to understand'. The principle around which modernist culture and literature fashioned themselves 'was the exclusion of the masses, the defeat of their power, the removal of their literacy, the denial of their humanity'. Following Raymond Williams – though the debt is not acknowledged – John Carey points out that 'masses do not exist' except as a metaphor which 'serves the purpose of individual self-assertion because it turns other people into a conglomerate. It denies people the individuality which we ascribe to ourselves and the people we know.'*

Although Carey goes on to examine H.G. Wells, George Gissing and Arnold Bennett in depth – for all of whom he has a certain fondness – it is the writers cited in the opening sections who embody these attitudes most nakedly. With evident relish Carey details Virginia Woolf's snobbery, Clive Bell's etiolated idiocy, T.S. Eliot's priggishness, Yeats's endorsement of eugenicist principles.

The Intellectuals and the Masses: Pride and Prejudice among the Literary Intelligentsia, 1880–1939.

Some of Carey's observations are incisive and lacerating, as when he notes how Virginia Woolf overhears the conversation of some women in a lavatory and instinctively re-imagines it through the idiom – 'If you don't give it him, there's others will I said' – of *The Waste Land*. Commenting on a 1926 poem by Graham Greene, Carey notes that mention of the unemployed 'attests [Greene's] proper leftist sympathies. Their function is, in effect, to vouch for the intellectual who observes them': an insight that applies also to many of the 'honorary proletarians' of the Auden generation. With equal and opposite perspicacity he notes that Sherlock Holmes's 'redemptive genius as a detective lies in rescuing individuals from the mass'. The main force of Carey's intelligence, however, is brought to bear on works where the mass is feared and loathed rather than redeemed.

Now, I'm as fond of toff-bashing and Bloomsbury-baiting as the next man but Carey's case is radically undermined by the combined effects of tone, intellectual manipulation and the strange political vacuum in which, for all his professed allegiance with the common person, he operates.

This is most apparent in his treating of figures who have a complex relation to their class origins. With scant regard for how they distort the overall picture of the author concerned, Carey goes through his sources in search of incriminating passages. D.H. Lawrence is presented, quite unashamedly, as though he is nothing more than a raving racial supremacist. That he actually wrote one of the great novels of working-class life is seemingly irrelevant. And even if, like Carey, we concentrate on the expressed opinions of the essays rather than the fiction it is dishonest to isolate one aspect of a writer whose life was predicated on the notion of ceaseless flux. The same man who wrote 'three cheers for poison gas' also believed that the purpose of any state was 'to make proper facilities for every man's clothing, feeding, housing himself . . .' More broadly, Lawrence, as Carey

unintentionally concedes with his crack about the novel
coming across Nietzsche's writings 'in Croydon Public Library in
1908', was a *product* of mass literacy. As the first great English
working-class novelist – and one who expended a good deal of
spleen on the life-denying cerebration of the intelligentsia – he
might even be seen as its flag-bearer.

Carey's consideration of Orwell is more sympathetic but here,
too, he distorts. Discussing Orwell's time in the Spanish Civil
War he points out how Orwell was appalled by the way the soldiers defecated in their trenches. But, Orwell goes on, 'the dirt
never worried me. Dirt is a thing people make too much fuss
about.' 'The contradiction is glaring,' says Carey, 'astonishing.'
Assuming, that is, you don't see any difference between shit and
dirt. A few pages later, in a slip with considerable ramifications
for the book as a whole, he talks of Orwell's 'intellectual isolation' from the workers when what is crucially at issue is the
class-bred isolation he sought to overcome. Intellectual isolation
was never a problem for Orwell – it was concomitant with intellectual and political integrity. Throughout, Carey prefers to
ignore the complex, underlying social relations *within* the loose
grouping – and apparently unproblematic term – intellectuals.

Avoiding a definition of the term is very convenient for Carey
since it can then be used to denote anyone who articulates the
attitudes he is attacking. Thus the populist J.B. Priestley *was*
one (because of his assaults on 'Admass') while art historian
and novelist Anita Brookner (because she is attacked by critics
'for being middle-brow and unexperimental') somehow is not.
People like Edwin Muir, who reinforce Carey's position, stop
being intellectuals and become reliable witnesses.

The elisions and sleights that litter the book come to a head in
Carey's last chapter where any vestige of scholarly fair-play is
swept aside by polemical vehemence. He begins by pointing out
there are similarities between Hitler's 'ideas' and those of the

intellectuals cited earlier. Then, by a slight syntactical shift, Hitler actually *becomes* an intellectual – 'like other intellectuals, Hitler . . .' – and before we know it they are all in the dock at Nuremberg together. Once this has been done the net can be cast sufficiently widely to make even the flimsiest coincidence of ideas incriminating: 'Like [Wyndham] Lewis, [George] Steiner and many other intellectuals, Hitler believes that it is the presence of a divine spark that makes great art great.' Like Lewis's dismissal of Hitler's anti-Semitism, Carey's argument in this chapter 'has the appearance of deliberate misrepresentation'. The fact that Hitler, in terms almost as sweeping as Carey's (two can play at this game), denounced all modernist art as degenerate is not mentioned. This is insulting. Not just to Steiner, but to me, to *us*, because Carey assumes his readers won't recognise, for example, when they are being fed a travesty of Nietzsche's ideas. The Nietzsche we are offered is his sister Elizabeth's notoriously corrupt, ideologically manipulated version. In his eagerness to play up the influence of Nietzsche on Hitler, Carey passes over the philosopher's abhorrence of the 'accursed anti-Semitism' that, in Nietzsche's own words, was 'the cause of a radical breach between me and my sister'. (One gets tired of making this point in the pub; it makes a change to have to emphasise it in such scholarly surroundings.) Carey, presumably, thinks he can get away with this kind of thing because he assumes his readers won't know any better. In other words, we are being talked down to, patronised.

This is part of the larger irony whereby Carey embodies many of the qualities he deplores. The blurb alerts us to this, praising his 'scornful eloquence'. As an encapsulation of the pride and prejudice Carey has in his sights, it might even have made an alternative title for the book. More importantly, even while denying that there is such a thing as the masses Carey constantly re-invents or appeals to them to validate and vouch for his prejudices (a different version of the thing he saw happening in the Graham Greene poem). 'This contradiction,' as he says of Orwell, 'leads to further muddles.' While conceding that we know Leopold Bloom 'more thoroughly than any character in fiction has ever been known before' he claims that Bloom 'would never and could never have read *Ulysses* . . . More than almost any other twentieth-century novel, it is for intellectuals only.' Like E.M. Forster – criticised by Carey on exactly this score – he is saying that the poor Leonard Basts of this world are better off not trying to get to grips with the big books on the shelf. Moreover, the fact that we know Bloom so well suggests that Joyce might be a better writer than Arnold Bennett. Carey has necessarily to skirt this dilemma because it threatens to bring his whole case crashing in on itself. (The 'hero of this book', incidentally, is Arnold Bennett, whose 'contribution to narrowing the abyss' between the intellectuals and the masses 'was book-reviewing, which educated the taste of the English public'; put like this, Bennett is a vicarious portrait of the man one suspects is the *real* hero of this book: its author.)

Of Rayner Heppenstall's *Two Moons*, Carey notes that 'the avant-garde technique of the novel excludes ordinary readers'. Which ordinary readers? Readers who aren't Merton professors of English? If you can't subsume an individual's identity in the idea of the mass then you can't very well subsume it in the ordinary either. Besides, the idea carries with it the implication that once you've achieved a certain degree of education you become *extra*ordinary – which is a mirror-image of the outlook Carey deplores.

This is crucial for it enables us to see where Carey's purported championship of the ordinary reader leads. Contemporary intellectuals – TV producers, newspaper editors, publishers – are all the time making decisions about what to print or broadcast according to what *they* think the public is ready for. Ideas or proposals are rarely rejected because they are of no interest to the producer/editor concerned; instead, typically, the response is, effectively: *Yes, of course it's of interest to you and me but not to the poor dimwits out there in TV-land.*

The only appropriate response to this position, to Carey's position, is, to adopt the style of Tony Harrison's skinhead in *V*: *Listen cunt, we'll make up uz own minds thanks. We want all the riches of civilisation. Don't try to palm uz off with Coro-fuckin'- ation Street.*

Ultimately, though, this book saddens rather than angers; reading it you are haunted constantly by the memory of Raymond Williams, who covered similar territory so differently. Williams had little eloquence as a writer but his long qualifications, his refusal to shirk anything that didn't fit conveniently into his preferred vision of things, his refusal to simplify – all these were ways of addressing his reader as an equal. His eloquence consisted in a tireless unravelling of complexities while appealing constantly to what was best in us rather than what is vengeful. There is a world of difference between Carey's advocacy of the middle-ground and Williams's insistence that we 'must emphasise not the ladder but the common highway, for every man's ignorance diminishes me, and every man's skill is a common gain of breath'.

1992

Artificial Stupidity

Five years ago a friend of mine began researching into artificial intelligence. When I bumped into him a few months ago he told me it had all been a mistake, he was giving it up. Artificial intelligence was a dead-end; the really exciting field, these days, was artificial stupidity.

I was reminded of this recently when I came across an essay by Jon Bird in the catalogue for the 1988 Michael Sandle show at the Whitechapel Gallery. I say essay but, taking his cue from Barthes's *S/Z*, Bird proposes a series of 'divagations' on Sandle's work rather than a boring old essay. Aided and abetted by the obligatory citations from Benjamin – 'The Work of Art in the Age of Mechanical Reproduction' *and* 'Theses on the Philosophy of History' – Bird's formidable achievement in these divagations is to cram virtually all the clichés of postmodern discourse into less than ten pages: 'topology of fragmentation', 'commodified social space', 'transgressive', 'dialectic of desire', 'relations of power/knowledge', and (my personal favourite) 'mnemonic'. Lest this froth obscure the underlying political issues, however, Bird reminds us that 'within the culture of late capitalism, dirt accumulates at points of production and consumption threatening the structure of economic and social relations'.

Clever stuff. Too clever by half. Or is it?

It's worth pausing over this, since to dismiss it on the grounds of its complexity is tantamount to affirming the author's intellectual and analytic prowess, thereby conceding the meagreness of our own powers of comprehension and concentration: playing into his hands, in short. Following Nietzsche's dictum – 'Those who know that they are profound strive for clarity; those who would like to seem profound . . . strive for obscurity' – I would argue the opposite: that this is stupid writing and stupid thought. But it's not *just* stupid: it's *artificial* stupidity. Every phrase – even the syntax and rhythm of that sentence quoted above – reads as if it is the Xerox of a Xerox of a copy of a long-lost original.

In fairness, Bird is no worse than fellow theorists like Griselda Pollock. Bear in mind, also, that this was 1988 when synoptic books by second-rate Eagletons were flooding from the cutting-edge imprints of the academic presses. The self-proclaimed status of these texts as radical and challenging has withstood the test of time except in two minor details: they are not radical and they're not challenging. In the process of assaulting the citadels of traditional academic exegesis – so-called bourgeois art history, for example – the discourse merchants built one of their own. By the time Eagleton published *Against the Grain*, a selection of his essays, *Going with the Flow* would have been a much more appropriate title. Either that or *Running out of Steam*, for Eagleton was rapidly getting to the point where he had exhausted every permutation of the three or four words he used in his titles: Ideology, Criticism, Theory and Marxism. In the visual arts, meanwhile, the net gain of the rise of discoursese – as in journalese – to a position of alternative academic orthodoxy was to formalise a way of looking at art with your eyes closed.

Now, few reading experiences can compare with the rush of Foucault, the sensual intimacy of Barthes, the relentless dialectical probing of Adorno. But *Discipline and Punish*, *Camera*

Lucida and *Minima Moralia* are the works of dazzlingly original minds and great *writers*. What became of their legacy in lesser, academic hands was best expressed, two centuries ago, by a famous jibe at Pope, who, according to William Cowper,

> Made poetry a mere mechanic art
> And ev'ry warbler has his tune by heart . . .

Cowper's words are especially relevant to Bird-like warblers since one of the peculiarities of ICA-speak is that you can become fluent in it without understanding it. Recently I happened to see a thesis submitted for one of the more fashionable post-graduate courses. Complete with epigraph from Bataille and citations from Bachelard, there was much discussion of the dialectic of the image (or was it the image of the dialectic?). Above the epigraph was the name of the 'Colledge' – Goldsmith's, naturally – to which it had been submitted. Strangely unsurprising and wholly appropriate, that: a text that would fail GCSE English but which was quite good enough for an MA. I was reminded of an old *Beryl the Peril* annual that included some of Beryl's answers to difficult exam questions. Asked to construct a sentence using the word 'discourse' she wrote '"Discourse is too hard for me," said the golfer.' How quaint! Twenty years on she would probably have no trouble coming up with a whole paper on 'The Self and its Others' or 'Dis-Ease in the works of Kathy Acker and William Burroughs'.

My own waning fascination with this stuff finally came to an end in New York in 1990, in circumstances I can locate very precisely. My girlfriend gave me a book to read on the long flight back to England. She'd bought it at the St Mark's bookstore in the East Village (very hip) and it was published by Zone Books (even hipper) and came complete with black endpapers (her inscription, consequently, was written in white). In spite of the fact that it actually contained just two little divagations – one by Foucault on Blanchot, one by Blanchot on Foucault – generous apportioning of blank space succeeded in padding out the contents to just over a hundred pages.

People may have bought *Foucault's Pendulum* by Umberto Eco with no intention of reading it but it was still a book in the sense that its nominal purpose was to be read. *Foucault/Blanchot* was something else: the truth is that the last thing you would do with this book – which was given in order to sustain me through an eight-hour flight – would be to read it. To have read it would have been to have violated its essence. It was, if you like, pure signifier: an almost textless text whose meaning was inscribed in its virtual textlessness.

But what a potent signifier – of my own cerebral might – it was! Nowadays it would bestow about the same intellectual *gravitas* as a dunce's cap. And the whole idiom of discoursese has ossified to the extent that it is now actually insight-resistant: it is impossible to formulate interesting – let alone *original* – thought in these terms. By contrast, the sight yesterday of a student on the tube reading Christopher Ricks's *Tennyson* seemed a step forward: a radical, challenging, exhilarating step.

1993

Fred-Perry:
Jameson and Anderson

'Commentary', according to Fredric Jameson, 'makes up the special field of postmodern linguistic practice', even though 'the sacred text', the essential, commentary-generating work is absent. Into this vacuum whooshed *Postmodernism, or The Cultural Logic of Late Capitalism* (1991), the very book in which Jameson made this declaration about the primacy of commentary. Effectively, then, this pioneering work was a commentary on its own existence, or at least on how the author's thought had evolved up to the point of writing it (since the death of Peter Fuller, Jameson's claim on the *as-I-have-shown-elsewhere* or *I-have-already-argued* mode of self-promulgation has been undisputed). The conclusion of *Postmodernism* offered a series of 'secondary elaborations' on the pages that had gone before; the essays collected in *The Cultural Turn: Selected Writings on the Postmodern, 1983–1998* are addenda to – or tertiary elaborations on – the *magnum opus*.

Perry Anderson's little book, *The Origins of Postmodernity*, was initially intended as an introduction to *The Cultural Turn* but then outgrew its brief. Within Anderson's formidable *oeuvre* it takes its place as the final volume in a trilogy of synoptic works – the others being *Considerations on Western Marxism* and *In the Tracks of Historical Materialism* – in which, exactly as prescribed by Jameson, the task of commentary is raised to the level of primary intellectual exploration. Since Jameson is the central figure in Anderson's account, *The Origins of Postmodernity* is also the latest instance of the kind of sustained grapplings with writers or thinkers featured in the magisterial collection, *A Zone of Engagement*. The difference here is that whereas 'an element of resistance was in the past always an ingredient in the impulse' to write about someone, in the case of Jameson, Anderson lacks 'the safety of sufficient distance'.

Before celebrating Jameson's achievement, however, he takes us through the genealogy of the idea of the postmodern, displaying, in the process, the same breadth and depth of learning that he did in working through the pre-history of Fukuyama's influential idea of the end of history. Anderson locates the first usage of postmodern in the 'Hispanic inter-world' of the 1930s; Arnold Toynbee and Charles Olson also used the term in the 1950s, but it is not until Lyotard's *The Postmodern Condition* (1979) that we get a sense 'of postmodernity as a general change of human circumstance'. The foreword to the English edition was written by none other than Jameson who then went on, in Anderson's words, to make the crucial step of anchoring postmodernism 'in objective alterations of the economic order of capital itself, linking an emergent structure of feeling with 'the saturation of every pore of the world in the serum of capital'. This fundamental intervention was followed by 'a majestic expansion of the postmodern across virtually the whole spectrum of the arts, and much of the discourse flanking them.' It is this totalising ambition, I guess, that has led Anderson to capitulate, to write about someone without the feeling of 'significant dissent' usually 'necessary to irritate a liking into a capacity for writing'. Does this absence mean that the book itself lacks some of Anderson's customary bite?

The lack of resistance certainly exacerbates the reader's. Local objections generate more general ones: 'Is there any contemporary critic with an even distantly comparable range?' Of course there is: John Berger (how come Anderson has never got to grips with *him*?). That rhetorical claim of Anderson's comes hot on the heels of an even more extraordinary one. Having quoted Jameson's observation that, of the thinkers of Western Marxism, Adorno 'was the supreme stylist of them all', Anderson wonders 'whether the description does not better . . . apply to [Jameson] himself'. To extend this relay of refracted praise, I wonder whether the description might not better apply to Anderson himself. Anderson reckons that Jameson is 'a great writer' but it seems to me (while conscious of Jameson's own caveat that great is often simply 'an expression of enthusiasm') that it's *Anderson* who is the great writer. Jameson, on the other hand, is a writer trapped by the prison-house of his peculiar idea of virtuosity. Anderson admires 'the spacious rhythms of a complex, yet supple syntax' but, increasingly, the flamboyant baroque of Jameson's prose is an irritating impediment to what is being said. More broadly, if Jameson's influence is as extensive as Anderson suggests, then he must shoulder much of the blame for the torrent of discursive gabble that has fatally contaminated the field. The self-posturing and show-boating of Jameson's obsessive parenthesising works principally as a form of self-interruption, a written equivalent of swallowing the words you are pronouncing. Reading him I am reminded of those T-shirts on which 'Dazed and Confused' is printed deliberately indistinctly so that the more sharply you focus the more blurred the words become.

Anderson's prose, by contrast, has just the 'compelling splendour' he admires in Jameson. If the obligation to look up words like 'usufruct', 'velleity', 'annealing', 'exordium' is an inherent part of reading Anderson – you're always learning something new! – that is because he is working at the cutting edge of language. His *exacting* vocabulary is part and parcel of an impulse to present complex ideas without simplification but with the elegance of absolute clarity. In doing so he reminds us that confining the search for great stylists to the category of fiction is deeply parochial.

The densely populated world of novels, however, makes one aware of how, in both Anderson and Jameson, the phrase *lived experience* always seems to come in tacitly inverted commas whereas the world of theory, of books – the world, if you like, of inverted commas – is, so to speak, free-standing. This is not an inevitable consequence of 'theory': the Baudrillard of *America* and the various instalments of *Cool Memories* is both a theorist and a wonderful guide to the practical challenges and exhilarations of negotiating the rapids of postmodernity.* There is, by contrast, something cringe-making about Jameson citing The Clash or The Gang of Four. While a crucial component of postmodernism is the elision of the high and the popular, Jameson's style means that he cannot render the latter unless it is mediated by analytical tools appropriate to the former. Anderson points out that, while modernism unified 'after the event a wide variety of experimental forms and movements', postmodernism was 'germinated in advance of the artistic practices it came to depict'. This is part of Jameson's anticipatory achievement in the work up to and including *Postmodernism* but it comes as something of a surprise to find in *The Cultural Turn* that, despite his alleged 'range', he has remained deaf to developments in contemporary music. The definitive postmodern practice of sampling, for

---

*I am often struck by similarities between Baudrillard and Don DeLillo; if the riff on motels in DeLillo's *Americana*, for example – see p. 257 of the US Penguin edition – were pasted into Baudrillard's *America* the joins would hardly be noticed.

example, does not get even a mention. And since, to be sort of dialectical about it, virtually none of the makers of postmodern culture sample or cite Jameson, one wonders how, if his contribution is actually as vital as Anderson claims, so many people have been able to find their way around this new terrain while being oblivious to his 'cognitive mapping' of it.

1998

The Absent Woman:
Janet Malcolm

In the course of the protracted legal wrangle between Janet Malcolm and Jeffrey Masson, the aggrieved protagonist of her book *In the Freud Archives*, it was remarked that while some people (like Masson himself) had a powerful presence, Malcom had an equally palpable absence. Joan Didion has written of the reportorial advantages that can accrue from this: 'I am so physically small, so temperamentally unobtrusive, and so neurotically inarticulate that people tend to forget that my presence runs counter to their best interests.' As this passage indicates, however, the calmly frazzled Didion more than makes up for this on the page where she is always in the thick of her writing.

Malcolm is always an actor in the events she describes but this participating 'I' is recognisable principally by its lack of distinguishing traits. If you had to characterise Malcolm's prose in a word then you would do so negatively: unblemished. Or unruffled. One is tempted to add 'un-metaphorical' but this is untrue (after reading Bernard Crick's biography in manuscript, Sonia Orwell realises, in Malcolm's words, 'the worthlessness of the trinkets she had traded her territory for'). What we mean is that the ambient tone of precisely reasoned exposition is undisturbed by the metaphors gliding in and out of it. The contrivances in her writing are effaced so skilfully as to leave almost no trace (effectively this is what the Masson case hinged on).

Reading Malcolm I am often reminded of T.S. Eliot's remark that the only quality a critic needs is to be highly intelligent; the 'I' of her books is a kind of concentrate of learned, well-heeled, cosmopolitan intelligence. Her shape is delineated by the way the other participants in a given story move around her.

The same is true of the figure at the heart of her latest narrative, the silent woman, Sylvia Plath. *The Silent Woman* is less about Plath than the various biographical approaches to her. Through the brambles of this notoriously acrimonious example can be seen the dangers and temptations that beset any biographical enterprise.

The story of Plath and her biographers scarcely needs rehearsing here. Plath's literary estate is controlled by 'her husband' (as Ted Hughes refers to himself in the introduction to her posthumously published *Journals*) and administered by his sister Olwyn. Anyone wishing to quote from Plath's writings therefore has to obtain their permission – which is unlikely to be granted unless they like what they see. Anne Stevenson received unprecedented co-operation from the estate – Olwyn also acted as her agent – but this assistance became increasingly coercive, nudging her to the brink of breakdown. When *Bitter Fame* eventually appeared, Stevenson's strongly anti-Plath account was reviled as ghosted propaganda.

For his part Hughes has sought to protect his and Plath's children from the rising tide of speculation about their marriage, while simultaneously managing the literary estate in such a way as to 'earn as much income as possible'. A crucial psychological twist in *The Silent Woman* is Malcolm's discovery of Hughes's apparently mercenary motives for publishing *The Bell Jar* in America; the drama of this discovery is undermined somewhat by the fact that the above quotation is not from

Malcolm's book but from Hughes himself, in a 1971 article in the *Observer*.

Quibbles notwithstanding, as Malcolm uncovers the intricacies of the story, she demonstrates her characteristic ability to make an intellectual inquiry as gripping as a thriller (though personally, I have rarely been gripped by thrillers). In classic genre style the maverick investigator flies into a strange country to solve an apparently baffling case. In a genteel, taxi-taking way the book is also a discursive picaresque as Malcolm crisscrosses England in pursuit of witnesses (many of the incidental delights preserve her bemused reactions to the peculiarities of our little island, like the fireplaces where 'a few flames wanly flickered'). This generates suspense but it is the quality of Malcolm's musings – there is a wonderful meditation on 'the genre of the unsent letter' – that rivets the reader's attention.

That and the way the book seems drawn like a magnet from the silent woman to the silent man. If Ian Hamilton's Salinger escapade proved anything it is that the more desperately people try to remain in the shadows the more they are tugged into the glare of publicity. In trying to protect his privacy Hughes has been forced to break cover time and time again; in telling this story Malcolm also sheds some of her customary reserve.

'In all complicated feuds,' she observes, 'there tend to be small pockets of agreement between the antagonists.' Amid all the squabbling and recrimination recorded here one thing is beyond doubt: Hughes is irresistible. In a series of swooning letters home Plath recorded her first meetings with the 'man in black', the pockets of whose corduroy jacket were full (bizarrely) 'of poems, fresh trout and horoscopes'. According to a girlfriend of Al Alvarez, Hughes 'looked like Jack Palance in *Shane*'. His letters alone work on Malcolm 'as if they were the electrically attractive man himself'. This comes to a head in a faintly comic meeting with Jacqueline Rose whose *The Haunting of Sylvia Plath* particularly irked Hughes. Jacqueline shows Janet a letter from Ted, and then thinks better of it: 'You immediately felt it wrong to "give" me what Ted Hughes had "given" to you,' writes Malcolm in an unsent letter to Rose.

So there we are, or there I was, smugly congratulating myself on decoding this 'charged' exchange, only to find Malcolm plucking the words from my mouth and explaining how, for a while at least, it seemed as if 'Jacqueline Rose and I were fighting over Ted Hughes'.

A trivial example perhaps, but one that illustrates a characteristic pleasures of Malcolm's writing: her knowingness. In the same way but on a larger scale, she knows that her own book is implicated in the events it describes. In this business – as she knows only too well – witnesses give evidence from the dock. Since this particular trial can be adjourned but never completed, her record of it is already a vital exhibit within it.

1994

'My Favorite Things'

Some songs – Dylan's most obviously – have a special quality of loyalty: except on very rare occasions – as when Hendrix covered 'All Along the Watchtower', or Keith Jarrett, 'My Back Pages' – they come fully alive only when played by their composer. Others drift from performer to performer, happily, promiscuously. Sometimes, though, a song can end up being so firmly identified with a particular performer that it changes hands, becomes theirs, not the composer's. This can take time: Ornette Coleman's 'Lonely Woman' is gradually becoming a Charlie Haden song . . . But 'My Favorite Things', well, that's been a Coltrane song for over thirty years . . .

There is a long history of American musicians finding jazz in unpromising sources – as Sonny Rollins did with his swinging-in-the-saddle version of 'Wagon Wheels' – but few pieces have travelled as far from their origins as the dainty little tune 'My Favorite Things'.

It was originally manufactured by the indomitable song-writing factory of Richard Rodgers (music) and Oscar Hammerstein (lyrics) as part of their 1959 stage musical. This ignorable piece of harmless entertainment then went on to blight the lives of children the world over when, in 1965, it was made into a multi-Oscar-winning film starring Julie

Andrews as Maria, the nun-to-be who finds love and happiness as a governess in the strict household of Baron Von Trapp (Christopher Plummer). Now, the musical, as we all know, is the most worthless filmic form imaginable, and of all the irritating moments from this inherently repulsive genre none is more nauseating than when Julie Andrews, reassuring the Trapp children in the midst of a thunderstorm, bursts into a list of her favorite things: 'bright copper kettles and warm woollen mittens, brown paper packages tied up with strings, these are a few . . .'

Coltrane was drawn to these catchy tunes. He recorded 'Greensleeves' and 'Chim Chim Cheree' from *Mary Poppins* but neither of these captivated him or his listeners like 'My Favorite Things'. He first recorded it within months of establishing his own regular band, on 21 October, 1960 – *before* the film was made. Three-quarters of what would become the greatest quartet in jazz history are present on this recording. Jimmy Garrison soon replaced Steve Davis on bass but the core sound – of Trane plus Elvin Jones on drums and McCoy Tyner on piano – is already there.

Trane never tired of playing 'My Favorite Things', it became almost his signature tune. The last recording I have was made in Japan on 22 July, 1966, a year before his death. In between there are over a dozen recorded performances. In this one song, then, we can hear in microcosm the relentless journey of search, discovery and further searching that characterised Coltrane's most creative period.

Trane had made his name as a tenor player but 'My Favorite Things' was one of the first recordings on which he played soprano. From the start his soprano playing had an Eastern feel and this became even more pronounced – to the disgust of Philip Larkin who disparaged his 'cobra-coaxing cacophony' – on later recordings.

Certain characteristics that run through all subsequent recordings are there on the first one: the pretty melody gradually breaking up into squalls and coils of sound, strangled cries and piercing morse that summon back the melody. But compared with later versions, it actually lopes along pretty gently. Elvin sets up a relaxed, swinging beat; relative to its full, propulsive power, McCoy's pounding left hand sounds almost restrained here (*My Favorite Things*, Atlantic 1961).

Although Trane's quartet was a fairly stable unit there were several changes and additions in personnel over the years. In the performance recorded in Stockholm on 23 November, 1961 the quartet – with Reggie Workman substituting for Garrison – is augmented by Eric Dolphy on flute (*Coltranology*, Vol. 1, Affinity 1978). At the Newport Festival in July 1963 Roy Haynes sat in for Elvin (who was undergoing mandatory rehab following drug problems). The quartet sound came to be increasingly dominated by ferocious battles between Elvin and Trane; with Haynes behind the traps we hear Trane in a more spacious setting. I can't improve on Francis Davis's distinction in the liner notes when he says that Haynes, for all his intensity, doesn't '*surround* Coltrane with rhythm' as Jones did (*Newport '63*, Impulse 1993).

The more Coltrane played 'My Favorite Things' the further it moved from its origins. The increasing familiarity of the refrain enabled him to allude to it more and more briefly and obliquely. It also got longer and longer. At Antibes on 27 July, 1965 we hear the classic quartet – Trane, Tyner, Garrison, Jones – at the peak of their form, responding instantaneously to each other's every move, enhancing the lyricism of the tune by the ferocity of their attack on it (*Live in Antibes*, INA 1988).

By the autumn of 1965 Coltrane had pushed the quartet form to the limit. Although he had often embellished his music with extra musicians he now used younger 'free' players – like Archie

Shepp and Pharoah Sanders – to create a fundamentally different sound. In the increasing musical density – for a while he used two drummers, Elvin and Rashied Ali – Tyner was having trouble making himself heard, but it was actually Elvin who left first, in December 1965. Tyner himself quit three months later.

When Trane appears at the Village Vanguard in May 1966 it is with the band that will mark his final phase: wife Alice on piano, Pharoah, Rashied Ali on drums ('he ain't playin' *shit*,' was Elvin's comment), and Garrison, the only member of the quartet to stay with Trane till the end. The wonderful, turbulent assault on 'My Favorite Things' (*Live at the Village Vanguard Again!*, Impulse 1966) begins with a long solo by the bassist. By July, in Tokyo (*Live in Japan*, Impulse 1991), the whole piece has extended itself to an hour with Garrison's bass intro alone lasting fifteen minutes.

Asked why he tended to use white bassists (like Haden) Ornette Coleman said that 'black people haven't taken the string instrument as a part of their high ethnic expression'; strings, in other words, were too securely attached to the white European tradition. In out-chambering, out-reciting anybody who ever picked up the bass in a classical setting, then, Garrison's solo represents a discreetly important moment in the ascendancy of black music. Since then even the cello, in the hands of players like Abdul Wadud, has been able to play its part in the Coon Bid'ness (to borrow the title of a Julius Hemphill album that features Wadud to great effect) of serious black music.

In Tokyo, when the band enters after Garrison's solo, Trane is playing *alto*, an instrument he'd never played in his own bands. Yamaha had given one to both Trane and Pharoah when they arrived in the country and he thought he'd try it out. Within moments we realise it's a completely new sound: Trane's never sounded like this and nor has the alto. He wails and calls and cries for five minutes before we recognise the melody and he's off again, this time taking us even further out before swerving briefly back to the theme. Now he is flying. With Alice playing star-splash piano and Rashied on shimmering, stellar drums, he's free of what Steve Lake called the 'gravitational tug' of Elvin and McCoy. They *drove* Coltrane; Alice and Rashied *beckon*. It's pretty and then dangerous as he reaches so high the sky blues into the darkness of space before re-entering, everything burning up around him. Despite its extended length it's a masterpiece of economy, this solo: a whole career on alto compressed into just eleven minutes.

The baton changes are the moments of greatest intensity in a relay race. It's the same in jazz. When Trane ends his solo and Pharoah, twenty-six at the time, takes the stand, you sense him handing over the torch. Pharoah, after flaring full of grace for a couple of minutes, doesn't know what to do with it, loses his way – by which I mean that *I* don't know what he's doing with it, I lose *my* way. It's the same either way: Pharoah and the listener share the same dilemma.

You see, Trane was driving forward so relentlessly that his solos start from the point where, a few months previously, they would have come to a shrieking climax. The pace of his development was such that by late 1965 he was unsure where to go next. When the other band members failed to show up on time at the Newport Festival in February 1966 he went on stage with Thelonious Monk and his group. After the set the promoter expressed his relief that the band hadn't showed up and Trane confided that he sometimes doubted if he was going in the right direction. Elvin had been in no doubt: all he could hear in his last months with Trane 'was a lot of noise'. Certainly stretches of the last phase seem almost unlistenable-to. In this context 'My Favorite Things' is like a familiar path through the sometimes impenetrable jungle of this final phase. We cherish an ameliorative hope that an artist's last works will be his best but some of Coltrane's – like the duets with Rashied Ali from February 1967, released posthumously as *Inter-Stellar Space* – are frenzied, despairing testaments to the musical impasse to which he eventually drove himself.

Pharoah's problem that night in Japan, then, is the one that jazz has been grappling with ever since this heyday of the avant-garde: if you start with a scream where do you go from there? Let's put it more simply: what is there left after Trane? In a sense Pharoah's subsequent career has been dedicated to answering that question, to bearing the torch.

After Pharoah there's an inconclusive duet between Rashied and Alice, lengthy enough to leave us to wondering if, deep down, we don't wish it were still Elvin and McCoy there instead . . . Then it's Trane again, this time on soprano. He seems to be trying to put into this one solo everything he's ever done and ever will do – and he's doing it. I begin to think yes, maybe it's his greatest performance ever (this incessant ranking and judging: the critic groping for criteria of rapture) because – the idea is almost mind-blowing – along with everything else he is *swinging* harder than ever.

And perhaps he even answers the question of what will come after him. Traditionally musicians built up their solos by moving from a theme or melody outwards. Coltrane's last recordings turn this inside out: he works his way towards them just as, in the quarter century since his death, jazz has worked its way back to tighter, more traditional forms. Shepp has ended up playing the blues; Pharoah's screaming has brought him to the grandeur of what he calls his 'cathedral' sound.

And the melody, as Trane plays it for the last time, 'free through all he has given up, rejoicing in his mastery', sounds fresher, more beautiful, more full of life than ever. The words are Rilke's, from a poem written four months before his death.

Ah the ball that we hurled into infinite space,
doesn't it fill our hand differently with its return:
heavier by the weight of where it has been.

Yes, but lighter too . . .

I sometimes wonder if there is any life left in some popular jazz tunes, like Monk's 'Round Midnight' or Trane's 'Naima'. Rather than exhaust 'My Favorite Things', though, Trane suggested the opposite: its *in*exhaustibility.

That's why people still play it. Guitarist Ronny Jordan has recorded a funky acid-jazz mix; at the Jazz Café in London a few years ago, Ahmad Jamal's trio roared through a wonderful, dancing version of the piece. One of the reasons it works so effectively in a trio setting is because there is no horn player to inevitably remind us of the power and invention of the absent master.

Most recently, it crops up, sort of, on Elvis Costello's album *Brutal Youth* (WEA 1994). The song 'This is Hell' turns Rodgers and Hammerstein upside down, itemising Costello's least favorite things. It all comes to a head when

'My Favorite Things' are playing again and again
But it's by Julie Andrews and not by John Coltrane.

1994

Nusrat Fateh Ali Khan

In Islamic countries, in the desert, it sometimes seems as if the call to prayer, although issuing from the minaret, is actually summoned into being by the vastness of the sky. As if the call is itself a response to the immensity of the surrounding silence . . .

Nusrat Fateh Ali Khan, 'Shahen-shah-e-qawwali' – 'the brightest shining star of qawwali' – sits cross-legged, barefoot on the concert stage. To his left are the other members of his 'party': eight-man chorus, tabla player, two hand-pumped harmonia, and, furthest from him, the youngest member of the ensemble, his pupil. Over the drone of the harmonia the chorus set up a slow pattern of handclaps. As simple as that. The clapping initiates a rhythm of expectation, a yearning that cries out for the Voice which will become the medium of still greater yearning. As soon as we hear it – minutes into a performance that will last for hours and leave us dazed and ecstatic – we are held by the implacable power of Nusrat's voice.

In our century there have been only one or two voices like this: voices that cry out beyond the cry, that rend the soul even as they soothe it. A voice like this – like the voice of Callas or of the great Egyptian singer Om Calsoum – longs to be answered by something as beautiful as itself. And so it soars. Higher and further, until it consumes and destroys itself. Or until it finds God. That is why, on the Peter Gabriel soundtrack, it is Nusrat's voice you hear in the climactic moments of the Passion, in *The Last Temptation of Christ*.

Qawwali – literally 'utterance' – is the devotional music of Sufism, the mystical sect of Islam founded in tenth century Persia. An amalgam of classical and popular music, qawwali, in something like its present form, was established in the Indian sub-continent at the end of the thirteenth century.

Nusrat himself comes from a line of qawwals stretching back over 600 years. He was born in Lyallpur – now Faisalbad – in Pakistan in 1948 and received informal lessons from his father Ustad Fateh Ali Khan, a qawwali master. When his father died in 1964 Nusrat began training with his father's eldest brothers. By 1971, with the death of his uncle, Mubarik Ali Khan, he was already established as one of the greatest living qawwals. Since then, especially in the last eight or nine years, he has achieved a world-wide audience.

Much of the credit for the popularity of Nusrat and fellow qawwals, the Sabri Brothers, must go to Womad and Real World. Nusrat's greatest hits run to over twenty volumes and there are fine concert recordings from Paris (on Ocora) and London (on Navras) but the best-produced albums – like *Shahen-shah* (1989) and *Shahbaaz* (1991) – are all on Gabriel's label. There are dozens of re-mixes and samples of Nusrat floating around the Asian dance circuit but, again, the most sensitive of these are found on Real World's *Mustt Mustt* (1990), which crosses Nusrat's voice with a range of electronic backing tracks, including a dub-intensive Massive Attack remix of the title piece. This willingness to embrace Western electronic dance music has led to accusations from conservative elements in Pakistan that the devotional character of the music is being debased, cheapened.

There is no hint of compromise or sell-out in Nusrat's cross-over work, however, only of musical open-mindedness and boundary-pushing exploration. For many listeners Nusrat's East–West work provides a way in to the recordings of traditional work like his latest release *The Last Prophet*.

By the robust standards of qawwali, it's a relatively gentle album, consolidating the repertoire of dedications to prophets and saints, and only gradually attaining the sustained ecstatic heights of 'Jewleh Lal', a twenty-five minute chant on *Shahbaaz*. Known more simply as Rumi, the poems of Jewleh Lal offer prophetic description of the great qawwal:

> This voice seizing me is your voice
> Burning to speak to us of us.*

Intended to induce a state of religious delirium, 'Dancing to the drum of suns, these cries/Sounds of extreme love', yet have an overwhelming, transcendental effect on even the most secular ears.

Rumi's poems combine secular and sacred love, and as qawwali has developed, so the devotional and secular strains have become deeply entwined. So much so that it is difficult not to hear the high, ringing voice of Nusrat's pupil as the embodiment of the feminine beloved. But there is an element of playfulness in all of this as well, with the master (whose father, remember, died when he was just sixteen) calling across the chorus, treating his pupil with magisterial indulgence: 'So, puppy, you think you can bark?' Nietzsche warned that he is a very poor pupil who remains only a pupil and these dialogues point to the time when, one day, a pupil will begin to match his

---

*Quotations from Rumi are from Andrew Harvey's 're-creations' in *Speaking Flame*, 1989.

master, perhaps even to fly beyond his grasp. How long can Nusrat's voice last? How long will he continue to soar?

These are questions for the future. Now, as the chant settles deeper into the body, members of the audience are whirling, throwing money on to the stage. Nusrat's hands, which, initially, had been simply rising and falling, emphasizing the rhythm, are now tracing invisible dance scriptures in the air. Pitting himself against the massed power of the chorus, he flings back elaborations of the main phrases, leading them in surging, hypnotic repetitions.

Nusrat is no longer projecting his voice, he has become the physical incarnation of the Voice. Much Western religious music seems clammy with death; driven by the gallop of handclaps and the dust-swirl of tabla, qawwali exalts in and of itself: incandescent, burning . . .

> I am not a voice, I am the Fire singing
> What you hear is crackling in you.

1994

Rabih Abou-Khalil

The Sultan's Picnic

'Let our turn be now.
Our book is on the rise,
and it is not mere print
but a prophecy that grows and grows'*

Adonis

The most exciting jazz is now found on the fringes of the form, where it is scarcely jazz at all. Beyond this, in the interstices of world music, jazz is apparent as a determining trace, one element in shifting, multi-valent compounds. This is where some of the world's greatest musicians – musicians who feel at home anywhere – meet as equals (not to play second fiddle to Paul Simon). And it is in this crucible of the future that we find the oud player Rabih Abou-Khalil, born in Beirut, based in Munich and accompanied, on this album, by musicians from America, Cabada, France and Syria.

I first came across Abou-Khalil's music a few years ago, by

*From 'The Funeral of New York', translated by Samuel Hazo, *The Pages of Day and Night*, 1994.

accident. A friend told me of a new record by Charlie Mariano featuring an Arab musician I'd never heard of. The tail, it turned out, was wagging the dog. Mariano was one of a number of American and Indian musicians assembled by Abou-Khalil for his album *Blue Camel*. And this was actually his sixth record. In places on the earlier records you can hear the diverse elements struggling to cohere but on *Bukra* and *Al-Jadida* this is achieved consistently. An exemplary track from *Bukra* opens with saxophonist Sonny Fortune's call to prayer (which is also a call back into the jazz tradition, to Roland Kirk and the opening cry of 'The Inflated Tear') answered by galloping ensemble play.

The Sultan's Picnic is his best album to date even if, on paper, the choice of instrumentation seems eccentric to the point of perversity: oud, harmonica, trumpet, alto sax, tuba, serpent, electric bass, conga, frame drums.

In recent years musicians like Henry Threadgill and Arthur Blythe have tried out some unorthodox instrumentation (the tuba is enjoying something of a renaissance just now), neither of them with unqualified success. By contrast, Abou-Khalil's strange, unheard of instrumentation sounds immediately familiar, as if it is the most natural combination imaginable, as if the music itself has determined the instruments that create it. There is nothing experimental about the music. In all the arts, that laboratory word, experimental, has come to connote a procedure where novelty seeks to disguise the uncertain or arbitrary nature of the undertaking. Abou-Khalil is not experimenting; he is *searching*. It is a search driven by rhythm and drenched in tradition. Traditions rather: of Arabic music, of jazz, of the blues. So: a forward-looking music that is thoroughly steeped in the past. The musicians don't settle into a groove, they plunge into it. What's important, we realise, is not the instruments, but the *musicians*.

Especially since these instruments often don't sound as they're meant to, don't accept the limitations which have been historically associated with them.

To us the oud is a lute, OK for Camelot atmospherics and not much else: a dead instrument. Arab culture sees the oud more poetically, attributing its special resonance to the singing of the birds who once sat in the branches of the trees from which it was made. In places you would think Michel Godard was playing the trombone rather than the notoriously cumbersome tuba or the archaic serpent. On his first solo on the album, bassist Steve Swallow sounds as if he is playing calypso in a Caribbean steel band. And then there's lanky Howard Levy – '*notre grand version de Bob Dylan*', as Rabih introduced him during his debut appearance in Paris – who grants the harmonica the expressive range and depth of Mariano's saxophone or Wheeler's trumpet. At the heart of Levy's sound there is always the camp-fire or prairie thing – the prairie at night, I mean, not the prairie itself but the sky over the prairie, when the blue blazes black and the first stars blink on over Illinois, over the Louisiana swamps . . .

The landscape we associate with Abou-Khalil himself is not so much the mountains of his native Lebanon, as the emptiness of the desert. Many of the song titles on the earlier albums – 'Dusk', Dawn', 'Finally . . . the Oasis' – encouraged us to hear them visually, in terms of the desert, of journeys through it. 'So still,' says a character in Antonioni's *The Passenger*, looking out at a sea of sand. 'A kind of waiting.' A waiting that accumulates momentum with each note until drums and tuba join the caravan of sound. Like jazz but it doesn't swing, it *sways*. Lebanese flamenco. A mirage of the blues. Camp-fire waltzes.

On slow numbers on the new album it still seems as if the percussion is not just generating rhythm but measuring distances, distances so vast that even movement becomes a kind of waiting. Likewise, the dust-swirl of percussion is heard through-out the fast numbers but the topographical range has been extended. Extended as far as 'Sunrise in Montreal', albeit a Middle-Eastern Montreal, one twinned with Beirut . . .

At the New Morning, 'Dream of a Dying City', a song about Beirut, opened with Levy playing minaret harmonica: desolate, windswept, haunting, shot through with the blues – a call taken up by Abou-Khalil with a brooding solo that slowly generated its own consolation.

On similar tunes on the new album the mourning mood is underscored by a bass so deep it's subterranean. Deeper than the blues even, a call that is all the time subsiding into itself. What is it laying down that bottomless bottom? The bass-oud, an instrument which doesn't exist, or didn't exist until Abou-Khalil had one made. It's heard at its meanest on the brooding 'Solitude', a title consciously echoing Ellington's famous ballad.

The ballad is almost exhausted as a form. What remains are departures. By which I mean that all successful ballads now are departures from the idea of the ballad.

> Trees bow to say goodbye,
> Flowers open, glow, lower their leaves to say goodbye,
> Roads like pauses between the breathing and the words
>   say goodbye . . .*

The ballad, Abou-Khalil reminds us, is a form which is forever being left behind. This is why its survival is ensured. By the same logic, if *The Sultan's Picnic* is one of the best jazz albums of recent times, that is precisely because, in any kind of limiting sense, it is not a jazz album at all.

---

*Adonis, from 'The Desert: Diary of Beirut under Siege, 1982', translated by Abdullah al-Udhari, *Victims of a Map*, 1984.

Arabian Waltz

Ah, strings! The greatest jazz musicians have aspired to recording with them – often with less than spectacular results. It's as if even masters like Charlie Parker were bedevilled by some lingering insecurity about their music. Only playing alongside violin, cello and viola, with the instruments of the great European musical tradition, it seems, can afford the final confirmation and seal of classic status.

Any such misgivings vanish soon after beginning to listen to Rabih Abou-Khalil's latest venture. For a start he has chosen to record with the Balanescu Quartet, who are immediately identifiable by the distance they are willing to put between themselves and their classical training (*pace* their versions of Kraftwerk songs). For leader Alex Balanescu, in any case, the classical element was only one part of a larger musical formation which included the gypsy-folk tradition of his native Romania. More to the point, the Balanescu Quartet are not *backing* Abou-Khalil – are not, so to speak, playing second fiddle to him – but recording in collaboration with him.

Notwithstanding this there was still a lot of ground to cover if the Balanescu Quartet and Abou-Khalil's trio were to come together as a single unit, a cohesive band in its own right. The night before they began recording this album they played a gig in Karlsruhe, Germany. It was full of promise and daring but, at the same time, hesitant, tentative. You could hear the two outfits, tiptoeing around each other, in Kerouac's famous phrase, like heart-breaking new friends.

What Abou-Khalil did in the course of further rehearsals and recordings was to bind the strings more tightly round his own unique musical amalgam of occidental and oriental influences. Linking them is the element most conspicuously lacking in the history of the European string quartet: rhythm.

Which brings us to Abou-Khalil's long-time collaborator, Nabil Khaiat. The first rock groups I ever saw, in the 1970s, featured massive drum kits: if you could actually see the drummer then – or so these vast terraces of percussion seemed to imply – he couldn't be much of a drummer. Something of the spirit lives on in world music today with percussionists' fondness for flaunting their virtuosity by playing – at the same time – as many different drums and bells as there are African languages. The great percussionists, though, can coax the most intricate of rhythms from the simplest of instruments, like the frame drums played by Nabil. His fingers gallop like hooves. From a standing start – silence – he creates a rhythm that engulfs and guides.

Not that rhythm is the preserve of the percussionist alone: Abou-Khalil had written different rhythmic lines for each of the strings. In effect the members of the Balanescu Quartet were playing solos, individual fragments that make up a surging collective rhythm. Abou-Khalil wrote these parts without knowing if the quartet could play them. Michel Godard, apparently, thought not. For his part, Abou-Khalil thought that even a virtuoso like Godard would struggle to play the parts he had written for the tuba. As you can hear, they were both wrong. There are echoes of Thelonious Monk's approach here: writing the music as it would ideally be heard, with no concessions as to whether musicians would be able to realise that ideal. As far as Monk was concerned the music was there, in the instruments, and it was up to the musicians to get it out.

I want to change approaches here, to take Monk at his word, as it were, and to do this I need you not only to listen to the musicians but to *watch* – to see them, as it were, through my eyes. Look how much time Nabil, Godard and Abou-Khalil have. Whatever the tempo, however complex the time signatures, they are never hurried. Compared with what they are capable of, their fingers are surrounded by deserts of time. Notice, too, their stillness. I remember rock drummers throwing themselves round their kits but Nabil, in particular, is all but motionless. This is a residue of the etiquette of performance in Syria, where the drummer must do nothing to distract attention from the featured singer. Still, one wonders if holding the body like this is a way of ensuring that none of the rhythm is dissipated. Unable to escape, to *leak* via the head or feet, its only egress is the hands and fingers through which it pours. Such is the musicians' stillness, in fact, that they seem less to be *producing* music than to be listening, waiting. To what? For what? Perhaps the answer becomes clear when I say that their attitude reminds me, above all, of people *fishing*.

Musicians arrive in a recording studio. They assemble their instruments, engineers arrange recording equipment and then, together, they record various takes until they have enough music for an album. This is literally what happens. Watching these musicians, however, a different process – or a different way of evoking the process – suggests itself.

As the moment to record a piece of music draws near everyone in the studio becomes quiet. The air itself seems to become more silent, as if something were about to take shape within it, as if the music were about to *appear*. Imagine, then, that instead of music being made by musicians they have, instead, to *catch* it. More precisely still, imagine that the music on this record was in the world, was – to borrow Eric Dolphy's enigmatic invocation – in the air. It offered itself to the musicians in the form of a rendezvous which would be kept only if certain very elaborate and highly contingent conditions were met. These conditions were historical, geographical and individual. Historically, the period of jazz advancing *as jazz* had to have come close to exhausting itself. Geographically, there had to be some kind of meeting point – somewhere akin in spirit to 'neutral' Switzerland in the

Second World War – where the musicians could meet not as equals but on equal terms. Individually, the musicians had to have advanced to a very high degree in their technical development; ideally, like Michel Godard, they would be at home anywhere, in any setting. If all these conditions were met then, in the studio, the chances were that if the participants were attentive and patient, this elusive music could be not so much made as called into being or – to revert to that fishing metaphor – reeled in.

I have left out the single most important condition for the distillation of the music preserved on *Arabian Waltz*, namely that Abou-Khalil himself had to have arrived at the point where his own musical achievement – as composer, arranger and instrumentalist – was substantial enough to constitute *its own tradition*. That is to say, the point where the greatest influence on his music is his own work. Having created a considerable body of music that is unlike anyone else's, Abou-Khalil is now able to draw sustenance from a tradition that did not exist before he invented it. We can hear clearly on this album how two songs from his own back catalogue ('Dreams of a Dying City' and 'Ornette Never Sleeps') serve the same function as standards, as Ellington's 'Caravan' did on his own earlier *Roots and Sprouts*, for example: not to be re-recorded but re-invented, re-invoked.

But it is actually one of the new pieces whose title, 'No Visa', comes closest to summing up Abou-Khalil's ambition and achievement. Its appropriateness to his work becomes especially clear if a distinction between borders and frontiers is kept in mind. A characteristic of the modern state is that it is defined by established borders that are precise and readily identifiable. A common characteristic of classical musicians is, likewise, a reluctance to venture beyond the borders of their elected form. Abou-Khalil, though, is drawn to *frontiers* which – in contrast to borders – are not settled or definitively fixed but shifting, contestable. More exactly, he is preoccupied by a single frontier, the one that has attracted all great artists and pioneers: the frontier of the possible.

1994/1995

Nils Petter Molvær

A little less than a decade ago, going to hear McCoy Tyner or Elvin Jones at Ronnie Scott's seemed to me a pleasure supreme. I didn't just love jazz, I pitied anyone who didn't, especially those poor souls who wasted their time on dross like House or Techno or whatever it was called.

Now, on the rare occasions that I go to a jazz gig, I feel like I'm in an improvised mausoleum. As a form, jazz, especially since the death of Don Cherry in 1995, has come to seem curiously obituary driven. Reviews of new releases – most of which are re-releases – read like memorials even when the featured artist is alive and blowing in some post-bop (i.e. neo-trad) time-warp. Jazzy jazz – drums, sax, piano and all that – is close to creative exhaustion. With world- and dance-music developing astonishingly quickly, jazz, if it is advancing at all, does so at a glacial pace. It is only on the outskirts of the form that significant strides – if not the Giant Steps announced by Coltrane – are still being made. In this uncertain region the invocation of Cherry, by name (as on 'Don' or 'Cherry Town', from Trilok Gurtu's recent album, *The Glimpse*) or in spirit, is an invariable sign of vitality.

It's not just the allusive trumpet floating through the title track of Nils Petter Molvær's *Khmer* that signals its *livingness*: everything about Molvær's conception of music-making exudes a Cherry-like willingness to advance beyond the given. The release of that album already looks like a historic moment: the moment when ECM, synonymous with the highest ideals of musical purity, accepted the importance, and embraced the liberating potential, of dance-music. (Who could have foreseen the day when an ECM release would begin to merit that least exalted term of approval, 'bangin''?) This was a sign of massive open-mindedness on the part of ECM's head honcho, Manfred Eicher, an open-mindedness that will be shared, hopefully, not just by jazzers but by those approaching this stylistic collision from the other direction, from dance-music.

Molvær was born in 1963 on the north-west coast of Norway. The first trumpeter he got into was Miles Davis – not the Miles of *Kind of Blue* but the Miles of the electro-murk phase, from *Bitches Brew* to *Agharta*: a radical break with jazz tradition that has since become part of that tradition. You can hear Miles everywhere in Molvær's own trumpet-style, specifically his middle register loneliness. Actually, 'reserve' would be a more accurate evocation of Molvær's playing, a never-quite-letting-go that generates tremendous longing on the part of the listener. More generally, Molvær is doing what Miles did throughout his career: helping himself to whatever is happening in contemporary popular music. Sadly, what Miles helped himself to in his last years was usually a kind of generically decrepit funk. Molvær, though, has plugged into and sampled from the best of Drum'n'bass, Trip-hop (the essential dreariness of which lends itself well to the Nordic melancholy of his trumpet), Jungle and Techno. Nothing if not versatile, guitarists Eivind Aarset and Morten Molster fling shards of heavyish metal and exquisitely glinting tracery into a surging, increasingly turbulent mix.

Since a good part of this mix is based on programming and sound treatment, hearing Molvær live does not represent a categorically different experience to listening to the music on disc.

He hails, evidently, from the Kenny Wheeler school of profound inexpressiveness. Plus there is the unwieldy problem of dancing in a jazz club: standing there, in other words, and doing the lager shuffle. Tables and chairs had been cleared from the area in front of the stage at the Jazz Café, but a jazz audience standing doth not a dance crowd make. Which is a shame because this is music to listen to with your whole body, not just your head and ears. I found myself looking forward to the day when Molvær and his crew would play one of the chill-out rooms at Pendragon, surrounded by glowing fluoro mayhem.

It might yet happen. On a special remix CD, material from the *Khmer* sessions is, quite literally, given the treatment by The Herbaliser, Mental Overdrive, Rockers Hi-Fi and others. The result is a relentlessly subtle texture of sound in which the lyrical trumpet barely manages to lift clear of the rhythms that are always threatening to engulf it. This is crucial to the emotional tension of the music because, historically, the improvising instrument *has* been engulfed. That is to say, jazz has been buried beneath the landslide advance of Techno and its myriad related sub-genres. This is why Molvær's music is so prescient, so important and, above all, so poignant: he locates and accepts jazz as a *glimmer* in the millennial twilight.

1998

Ramamani

Ever since I first heard her voice I have been in love with Ramamani.

I've never actually set eyes on her – let alone met her – though on one occasion, a few years ago, I came pretty close. I was in Karlsruhe, in Germany, to see Rabih Abou-Khalil; two days later – two days after I left – she was playing there with the Karnataka College of Percussion.

I first heard her sing on a record by saxophonist Charlie Mariano, featuring the Karnataka College. A subsequent, even better album recorded the same three-way collaboration during a live performance. As far as I know she has not recorded a solo album of classical Indian vocal, but now there's another chance to hear her, on the new Mariano CD, *Bangalore*. In truth it's not a great record. Whereas their previous collaborations were forward-looking, ground-breaking, some of the 'jazzy' elements in the new material – especially the intrusively obsolete electric bass – drag the project back to the woeful days of fusion. All that is best about the record derives from Ramamani who, as Mariano says in the liner notes, is her usual exquisite self. Less happily, from my point of view, it turns out that Rama is married to T.A.S. Mani, principal of the Karnataka College!

Perhaps, then, I should re-phrase my claim to be in love with his wife. To do this – to convey the sound of a voice in words – I need, as it were, to be *objectively personal*. I love Ramamani's voice because it is beautiful. And her voice is beautiful because in it, I hear, vividly, everything about the woman I love. So: Ramamani's is the voice of the beloved in all her specialness.

Her voice is especially beautiful because she is trained in Indian – specifically Karnatak or south Indian – classical music, and it is in Indian classical that the female voice *as an instrument of music* (rather than as a vehicle of verbal intent) has found supreme expression. I hear an objection: 'What about Callas?'

Lear recalls Cordelia's voice as being ever 'soft, gentle and low, an excellent thing in woman'. Callas furiously disputes this claim, usurping the sovereign role for herself. Even when she is giddy with happiness, spiralling away in one of those *bel canto* equivalents of the 'Pretty, I'm so pretty' ditty from *West Side Story*, there is an implicit ambition to surpass all previous claims to happiness, an over-vaulting urge to tragic supremacy; Callas wants to overwhelm, to conquer. This is what made her a great singer and gave her performances their vertiginous intensity. There is, consequently, nothing *girlish* about her.

One of the sad things about British life is that women, after a certain age, are almost obliged to wear their hair short. Among the audiences at Indian concerts and recitals, by contrast, there are many sixty- and seventy-year-old women with lovely, long grey hair. Their hair is a visual equivalent of the inherent gaiety that can be heard in all the great Indian female singers (who, as the devastated, wonder-struck Othello says of Desdemona, 'can sing the savageness out of a bear'). Lakshmi Shankar, for example, was born in 1926; when she performed in London a few years ago she looked, at first, somewhat grand, stern, but, as she sang, the years fell from her. Her voice was skipping, girly, light-footed.

William Gedney articulated the music he heard on the sub-continent in similarly visual terms. For him, Thumri, one of the styles of light classical singing at which Lakshmi Shankar excels, was 'the swinging gait of young girls in saris'. And so it is: even when sung by a woman in her seventies. In the otherwise stupidly contrived film *Things To Do in Denver When You're Dead*, there is a nice moment when Andy Garcia hits on Gabrielle Anwar by complimenting her on the way she walks: 'Most girls simply plod along, you, on the other hand, you glide.' That is how Ramamani walks. Nietzsche – who believed that 'what is good is light; whatever is divine moves on tender feet' – would have loved her.

At the very least her voice could have diminished his terrible loneliness. During long periods of being single, girlfriend-less, Ramamani persuades you that there is a woman, somewhere in the world, who you will come to love. Thus one speaks not only of the charm but the *promise* of her voice. (Again, a comparison with Callas is instructive: her voice was like a promise so great it could only be broken.) The importance of faithfulness and constancy in relationships is often debated. But there is another, far rarer kind of constancy: to remain faithful to your deepest longing, to the idea that there exists someone who will be everything to you. Ramamani's voice enables you to keep faith with this ideal.

In *Notes of a Jazz Survivor*, a documentary about his drug- and jail-ravaged life, Art Pepper and his wife Laurie listen to his recording of 'Our Song'. The entry of the saxophone, Pepper explains, is 'like the most subtle hello'. Ramamani's voice is the response to this call; it is Laurie's hand reaching for her husband's as they listen. Ramamani tells us not only what it is like to love, but what it is like to *be* loved.

When I hear her voice, darling, I feel your hand in mine.

(for Vesna)
1999

The Guidebook

For the last two hours we have been trying to get a bus out of
Madrid to the Valle de Los Caidos. I am sitting on a long
wooden bench while Sue is bending over to talk through a
hole in the cardboard that serves as a partition between staff
and customers. She speaks a language that no one can understand, a combination of French, Italian and Spanish inflections.
No one can understand her because the only Spanish words
she knows are the names of fish or seafood: gambas, calamari,
trucha, pescadillo. But we don't want fish. What we want is a
bus to the Valle de Los Caidos. Apparently there aren't any.

Eventually someone in the queue says 'Escorial' and 'Valle de
Los Caidos' and holds up his hands close together.

'They are close together?'

'Si.'

'We get a bus to Escorial?'

'Si.'

We buy the tickets to Escorial, relieved to be going somewhere.

The monument of the Holy Cross of the Valley of the
Fallen . . . is 58 kms from Madrid . . . It is reached by the
Coruna highroad. A fine autobahn leads to Las Rozas,

where it divides on the left to the Escorial and on the right to Segovia by the Lion's Pass. The whole landscape is typical Velasquez.*

We are out of Madrid very quickly and heading up into the mountains. There are drops of rain on the windscreen and the pavement and road are dark with damp.

The bus climbs steadily into Escorial, a village with narrow streets and lots of coaches. At the office we book seats on the next bus to Valle de Los Caidos and everything is very straight-forward. Escorial is beautiful: steeply rising streets looking down on an old monastery, old men moving up the streets slowly.

The bus is full of young students or school-children and I'm reminded of a school trip to Stratford to see *Henry IV Pt II*. After the first act most of us went to a pub called the Dirty Duck and swilled beer instead of watching Shakespeare, whom we didn't understand anyway.

Up, winding up through trees, the valley falling away beneath us. The road ahead is bending and twisting back on itself now instead of winding on ahead. Behind us the sky hangs over Madrid, like a curtain.

A romantic, rocky valley opens out before us. The only vegetation consists of pines, brooms, oaks, ebony trees and poplars, just a few of the latter in a sheltered corner. There are also some holm-oaks and holly, together with brambles, thyme, marjoram and other aromatic herbs, which give an austerity to the landscape . . .

---

*Extracts are from the English version of the guidebook to Santa Cruz del Los Caidos (Editorial Patrimonio Nacional, 1983).

At large ornate gates the driver stops and hands a slip of paper to a grey-uniformed guard. In Spain it is difficult to tell the difference between police and soldiers because there are so many different kinds of each. The most threatening are the 'Nacional Police', who wear brown anoraks and carry sub-machine guns. They look like vigilantes.

Policemen walk towards you very slowly. Soldiers stand still, move their eyes slowly.

The guard waves us on through the gates and we pass between two pairs of thick monolithic shafts, 'like sentinels guarding the way into the valley'.

We are still climbing, with a view of the valley and snow-peaked mountains on the horizon. Then looming over the whole valley: the huge cross. Against the shifting grey of the sky it is vast and precarious, rising out of convoluted rocks at the top of the valley. It dwarfs the summit that it is built from:

> The cross is the predominating feature of the whole monument. It rises to command the valley and excite the admiration of all beholders. Its beauty of line, its proportions strictly related to the size of the mountains, the way it springs out of the fine rocky crest of the massive Risco de la Nava, and the elegance of its outline against the sky, all combine to give it aesthetic as well as symbolic value.

At first all you can take in is the cross and the huge figures at its base, straining against the rock in which they are cast.

We make our way past a grey arcade to a vast esplanade jutting out from the mountain. From the edge we look down and see the valley stretching below, trees, flowers, trees. Looking back to the monument there is the cross and, below it, the sweeping arcades and entrance to the crypt. Above the entrance is a massive sculpture of Christ, dying in the arms of the Virgin

Mary, cast in dark stone: 'enough to stir the emotions of even the most hardened unbeliever.'

The cross is not just a monument. Beneath it a church has been carved out of the solid rock of a mountain.

I take some photos and ask Sue to pose for them, in front of the entrance. She refuses but offers to take one of me.

On the bronze doors is an injunction to be silent. Children are swarming all around the entrance, shouting and tripping each other up.

Inside it is like a massive sacred cave. Its size is unbelievable. I walk in – past two statues towering above and leaning out into the aisle on huge swords – and daylight and noise fade away. It is almost dark; the only light is from dim yellow lamps on the walls. Everywhere there are arches, the simplest expression of power, the most powerful expression of simplicity. And more statues.

The nave of this subterranean church is (I am told) one of the longest in the world. It leads deeper and deeper into the mountain, past dim tapestries of the apocalypse, past tombs and shrines, until the tunnel gives way to a massive dome blazing with gentle light overhead. It depicts Christ seated. Far below, rising from the floor is a statue of Christ crucified.

> There is a certain primitive look about the whole crypt, which is neither forced nor mannered but the result of an unparalleled struggle to overcome technical difficulties without precedent in the history of architecture . . . Hence the air of simplicity and strength which faithfully reflects the nobility and high moral purpose of the builders' efforts.

The awe inspired by the cross and the darkness of the crypt is certainly primitive: it excites rather than moves, overwhelms rather than inspires. Everywhere, it is the scale that works on you, if not the physical scale of dimensions then the scale of the undertaking. It is a place of power and ambition rather than contemplation; your gaze is led constantly upwards, like Faust's. Its greatness is entirely vertical, its emotion is vertiginous.

The pictures in the guidebook give no sense of this nor of the size of the monument. They are too bright; shot on days when the sky is postcard blue and birds are singing in leafy trees. Today the sky is thick grey, on the edge of a storm. The air is full of rain.

The text of the guidebook is also curious. There is much talk of the size of everything: the cross is 150 metres high, its arms are 'wide enough inside for two average-sized motorcars to pass each other', the sculptures at its base are each eighteen yards high. The adjectives of the text insist on 'unity', 'high moral purpose' and 'simplicity'. The monument is 'stark', 'austere', 'harmonious', 'ascetic'. Beyond this it speaks of the symbolic power of the monument without saying of what it is symbolic. There is a silence at the edge of the page.

Why is this?

Each year the Valle de Los Caidos is visited by tens of thousands of tourists: Americans, Europeans, children, students, lovers. They all take photographs and play the electronic games in the cafeteria and read the guidebook for information on the architecture and origins of the monument.

The previous Head of State conceived the monument and chose the site for it . . .

A decree issued on 1st April 1940 ordered the monument to be erected.

The previous Head of State was Franco. The decree of 1940 was more explicit than the guidebook: 'It is necessary that the rocks from which it will be built will have the size of the ancient monuments which defy time and forgetting and which will constitute a place of meditation in which the future generations pay a tribute of admiration to those who led to a better Spain.'

Franco himself tramped around the mountains of Madrid for seven weeks looking for a suitable site. Work on the monument lasted nineteen years. It was built by Republican prisoners from the civil war. Many of them died in the massive labour.

Franco is buried here. For the seven years between 1975 and 1982, Leopoldo Calvo Sotelo, a minister in the first government after Franco's death, came here to pray at Franco's tomb every day.

None of this is mentioned in the guidebook.

The next day.

I am outside the Prado, the museum in the centre of Madrid that houses a daunting collection of paintings by Goya, Velasquez and others. I wave a printed ticket stub under the eyes of armed policemen, who direct me away from the Prado into smaller streets. A couple of minutes later I show the ticket to another policeman, who directs me still further away.

Eventually I find the entrance to a much smaller museum. I have to check-in my bag and go through an airport-type metal detector even though there is only one painting here. There are several guards, none of them armed.

The security precautions are necessary because fascists said that if ever this painting were returned to Madrid they would blow it up. The painting now hangs behind an elaborate construction of bullet-proof glass.

The painting is *Guernica*, begun by Picasso within a week of the town being bombed flat by German bombers flying for Franco. Until 1981 the painting hung in New York but was returned to Spain, as the artist requested, when democracy was restored.

It is a huge canvas, dwarfed by the security construction in front of it. Looking at the painting under the harsh lights and behind the bullet-proof glass you are reminded of how flimsy is the canvas, how easily it can be torn.

1984

Oradour-sur-Glane

The day after the wedding of Jean-François and Elisa I took a train from Chateauroux, a town in the dead centre of France, to Limoges, 120 kilometres to the south and west. From there it is only another twenty kilometres to Oradour-sur-Glane. Several of the wedding guests knew of this village but none had visited it. Certainly, there is no need to hurry to Oradour. It is enough to know it is there; after that, like a telephone number safely recorded on paper – or a face preserved on film – it can be forgotten.

The sign at the gate admonishes SOUVIENS-TOI: REMEMBER. Beyond the gate you can see the ruined walls of a few houses. Propped against one of these, a large sign admonishes SILENCE. Rusty tram-lines follow the main road as it curves up into the village. The sky is scored by tram and telegraph wires, powerless to transmit. A small sign on one of the posts warns: DEFENSE ABSOLUT DE TOUCHER — DANGER DE MORT.

For fifty years the whole village has been in ruins. Skeletal walls. Rubble-strewn rooms. Rusting girders. Gaping windows. Some walls have remained relatively intact but there are no ceilings or floors. This is small consolation: the vertical may last better than the horizontal but it will always lose out in the end.

Every house looks the same but there are usually some details to remind you that this was a butcher's, this was a home, this was a shop. The things people used: at the Café Chez Marie there are rusted scales, pots and pans hanging on the wall. In another house there is an old sewing machine. A rusted bedstead. The remains of a tiled floor. A bucket. Bicycle frames. On the wall of the garage is a red advertising sign for HUILES – RENAULT. In the market square is the rusted hull of a car.

The sky gets in everywhere. Framed by broken walls it sits in the middle of rooms, pours in through collapsed roofs, stares out of window frames. Shades of grey. Smoke-drift clouds. In the distance are the lungs of winter trees that have long outgrown the village. Birds perch in them, wade through the damp air.

There is a consistency to the ruins because they all date from the same day. The elements have worked equally on all buildings but within each house there are gradations of ruination. The relative longevity of building materials: glass and cloth are always the first to go; walls become clumps of brick and then rubble; metal – bicycle frames, saws, water pumps, railings – turns rapidly to rust but it endures, after a fashion. Eventually everything becomes rust or rubble. Ultimately it becomes part of the landscape. Walls are turning green with moss. Rubble is becoming soiled. Which is why, from a distance, the ruins already seem to be merging into the surrounding countryside. One kind of time stopped here on an afternoon in 1944 but a different, slower kind – that sculpts hills and silts rivers – has taken over.

It was at 2.15pm on 10 June, 1944 when the trucks and half-tracks of a contingent of the Der Fuhrer Regiment of the 2nd SS (Das Reich) Panzer Division rolled into Oradour. Transferred from the Eastern front they were en route to Normandy to reinforce the German defences against the allied invasion. The journey had to be made by road because the French rail network had been severely damaged by allied bombing and sabotage. Continued resistance action inflicted few casualties on the battle-hardened Das Reich, but the cumulative effect of this campaign of harassment led to all-important delays in the Division's progress through France. To counter these 'terrorist acts' the Germans wasted still more time (strategically speaking) attempting to subdue the population by a series of ruthless reprisals. At Tulle, some sixty kilometres south of Limoges, ninety-nine civilians were hanged from lamp posts in retaliation for the *résistants*' assault and brief liberation of the town.

Why the SS should have hit Oradour is more difficult, if not impossible to establish. Theories abound but the most likely explanation is the one offered by Max Hastings in his book *Das Reich*. Information reached Major Otto Dickmann (who commanded a battalion of the Der Fuhrer regiment) that *maquisards* were either hiding in the village or, at least, using it as a hiding place for weapons. Whether this rumour was true or false was irrelevant: it provided Dickmann with the pretext to unleash his troops and make of Oradour an example that would spread terror throughout the region of the Limousin.

Refugees had almost doubled the village's normal population to 650 in June 1944. Within half an hour of arriving the SS herded everyone into the market square. Women and children were then taken to the church, the men to five separate sites in the village. At about 3.30pm the Germans embarked on the systematic slaughter of everyone in the village, firing machine guns, throwing grenades and setting fire to the church that held the women and children. By 5.00pm the whole village was ablaze. Only five men and one woman escaped.

When the SS pulled out the following morning they left in their wake over 640 dead in the smouldering ruins of the village. Over the following days, charred bodies were recovered and buried in the cemetery at the far edge of the shattered village. The ruins were left as we find them today.

With its busy jumble of graves the cemetery looks like any other in provincial France. On many of the headstones there are photos of the dead. Husbands and wives. Young and old. Smiling. Dressed for weddings or christenings in their Sunday best. On one headstone, designed to look like the pages of an open book and arranged around a photograph, the inscription reads:

> A La Memoire De Notre Fille Cherie
> Bernadette Cordeau
> Brullée Par Les Allemands
> Le 10 Juin 1944
> Dans le 16e Année
> Regrets Eternels.

Who was she? She was someone who looked like this.

A few days earlier I had looked at another photograph which showed a line of ten dirty, dishevelled men in overcoats. They were prisoners of war, obviously, and most looked as if they had been beaten. The caption explained that they were SS troopers who had been identified by *Wermacht* soldiers as guilty of war crimes. They are humble and defiant, resigned, exhausted . . . The more accurately you try to pin down their expressions, however, the more difficult it becomes. You peer into their faces as if listening to depositions in court. You strain your eyes looking at this photograph, trying to ascertain innocence or guilt, but the only thing it proves – the only thing any photograph ever proves – is what it shows: these men looked like this.

You can walk round the village in twenty minutes. It is doubtful if anyone stays more than an hour, but to understand these ruins properly it is necessary to read them quite carefully. Oradour is not just a monument to German brutality, nor to the apocalyptic destruction of the Second World War. The question 'Why Oradour?' is two-fold, referring not simply to why the village became the target of such ferocity but why the French have memorialised *this* place in *this* way. The two answers are linked, for Oradour weaves together two almost contradictory strands of meaning.

Between the cemetery and the ruins, stone steps take you down into a dimly lit crypt. Dozens of domestic items salvaged from the ashes of Oradour are diligently preserved here. Fragments of ration books and letters. Pen knives. Scissors. Bowls and spoons. Spectacles. A propelling pencil. Glasses and bottles, melted in the fire, twisted. Watches, clockfaces without hands: bits and pieces of dead time. These display cases put you in mind of both archaeological museums and certain holocaust museum-memorials where odd possessions of the victims are cherished and preserved. Memorials to a nation's military dead are stark, unadorned: these personal effects emphasise that the dead of Oradour were not soldiers but innocent victims.

This is a crucial component of the meaning of Oradour: there was no justification for the massacre, there were, in fact, no *maquisards* or arms hidden here. (When the SS announced that any arms must be declared, one man stepped forward and said, 'I have a 6mm. carbine which has authorisation from the council.' The German replied, 'That's of no interest to us.') The villagers of Oradour were simply people going about their business. They had played no part in sabotage or 'terrorist acts'. This means that the massacre at Oradour is exempt from controversy – for the presence of even one *maquisard* would have implicated the village in its fate.

Faced with 'terrorist acts' the Germans often established a reprisal-ratio, declaring, for example, that for every German soldier injured by *résistants*, ten civilians would be killed. But however it is reckoned, the essence of a reprisal is that it must be so far in excess of the original offence as to annihilate the possibility of counter-retaliation. By its nature, then, the reprisal is always consuming the logic, the arithmetic, that engendered it. The result will inevitably be an act of violence that defies understanding or calculation: a massacre.

From the point of view of the SS, events in Oradour were the consequence of an accumulation of frustration and delay occasioned by acts of resistance elsewhere. The innocent victims of Oradour, however, were simply engulfed by a volcanic eruption of violence.

But it is not enough for the dead of Oradour to be simply victims. If this were the case then they would be symbols of the fall of France, of capitulation, of defeat. They have to be not simply victims but martyrs. This is where the second strand of meaning comes into effect, a strand represented by a plaque, near the exit from the crypt, that reads: MORTS POUR LA FRANCE.

Since the arbitrary choice of victims is part of the logic of reprisal, any victims of German violence *were* implicated in the overall campaign of resistance. The passivity and innocence of the people of Oradour in no way precludes them from the history and memorialisation of the struggle of France to liberate itself from Nazi occupation. Indeed, thanks to the logic of reprisal, the passive victim becomes an active component in the myth of French Resistance.

In this way Oradour is exempted from the whole vexed question of resistance-collaboration and the ideological turmoil surrounding it. At the wedding reception the day before my visit to Oradour I sat next to a Frenchman who remembered his father and uncle arguing about a second uncle who was alleged to have collaborated with the Germans. The father was a Communist and had been active in the resistance; his brother, the uncle with whom he was arguing, had concentrated on his business and the well-being of his family, hardly concerning himself with the war. Arguments like this have raged in France for the last fifty years. In Oradour all shades of opinion were subsumed and united by the tragedy of 10 June, 1944. It is not just time that stopped; the whole aggrieved discussion is arrested and *resolved* by the massacre and its memorialisation.

One of the few things to have survived the fire of June 1944 is a roll of honour dedicated

A NOS MORTS GLORIEUX
GUERRE 1914–18

Located in the church where the women and children were later burned, it is inscribed with the names of one hundred men from Oradour. Memorials like this are found in every French village. Similar memorials can be seen throughout Britain but the War had been fought on French soil and, in both absolute terms and relative to its population, France suffered far more heavily than Britain. Over a million and a half Frenchmen lost their lives, more than 160,000 of them in the ten-month battle of Verdun. It had been General Falkenhayn's intention to 'bleed the French white' at Verdun, and though France emerged victorious from the War it was a victory all but indistinguishable from defeat. The ashen memory of the carnage of the First World War, especially of the meat-grinder of Verdun, lay behind France's surrender in the first months of the Second. For the next four years France crouched under the German occupation.

Whatever the practical achievements of the resistance in June 1944, its chief contribution was, in Max Hastings' words, 'towards the restoration of the soul of France'. Like all monuments, the ruins at Oradour were intended not simply to preserve the past but to address the future. To that extent they are like a bid at prophecy, an attempt *to call into being*. And what is called into being by these ruins is – in a final paradoxical resolution – the moment when this process of *restoration* is complete. Only then can they be forgotten.

1994

Parting Shots

1.

A noiseless blizzard is blowing outside my window. A few cars, figures trudging through the grey snow of Belgrade. Cocooned from the world, the only noise is the ambient hum of hotel luxury. Already half-drunk, I open a beer from the mini-bar, flick through the channels on TV. Basketball, CNN (blizzards over Croatia and Bosnia), skiing, films dubbed into German and Italian, a couple of scrambled channels, basketball again. You could waste eternity itself doing this and still never watch anything. I float in the bath for half an hour, drink another beer and resume channel-hopping. This time I linger over what turns out to be a porno movie.

At first I think it is a low-budget romance but an extended bout of kissing gradually gives way to a love scene, which looms, suddenly, into pubic close-up. I am struck by how like real sex it is – then I realise it's not like real sex – it *is* real sex.

As the sex intensifies and escalates so the nominal plot dissolves – but never entirely disappears. In the closing scene the couple from the first act say an emotional farewell to each other, exactly as in any soap opera: it's just that here she has to speak her lines while writhing on the brink of an orgasm induced by another woman who happens to be lying on the sofa between her legs. Perhaps this is why the leave-taking is so unconvincing: in the porno world people come rather than go.

It may not be pretty but there is something idyllic, paradisiacal about this world where everyone has wonderful sex with everyone else, regardless of gender or any obligations they are meant to fulfil (even a helicopter pilot manages to have cramped mid-flight sex in his aptly named cockpit).

The film ends. Slightly stunned by it all I scroll through the channels again. Basketball, snow over Bosnia and Croatia . . . It is still snowing here in Serbia, too. Beyond my wide-screen window Belgrade hunkers down, waiting for the blizzard to pass.

2.

Relative to the scale of the slaughter, very few pictures of the British dead survived the First World War. The pictures that have been preserved tend to show isolated or small groups of dead soldiers. They give no sense of death on the scale recorded by John Masefield, for example, who, four months after the Battle of the Somme had ended, wrote of how the dead still 'lay three or four deep and the bluebottles made their faces black'.

During the Spanish Civil War Robert Capa took the most famous war photograph of all time which showed – or purported to – the precise moment of a Republican soldier's death in action. In his photographs of the Second World War we come across the dead almost casually, in houses and streets. A photograph from December 1944 shows a frozen winter scene with bare trees, cattle and huts in the background. A GI advances across the photo towards a body lying in the middle of the field. Some way off, beyond the margins of the frame, in the next photograph, there will be another body. Through Capa's photos, in other words, we follow a trail of bodies. This trail leads, ultimately, to the photos of mass death at the core of our century: naked bodies piled up in concentration camps. Capa, personally, had no intention of photographing the concentration camps because they 'were swarming with photographers, and every new picture of horror served only to diminish the total effect'.

Theodor Adorno said famously there could be no poetry after Auschwitz. Instead, he should perhaps have added, there would be photography.

Since the concentration camps we have seen hundreds, thousands of photographs of the dead: from Cambodia, Beirut, Vietnam, Salvador, Sarajevo.

Photographs of the dead are now ten a penny. In recent months a war of escalating explicitness has been underway in the media. A South African boy with his nose shot off, blood pumping through the hole in his face. Muslim women burned in their homes. No news bulletin worthy of its name comes without a warning that some of the images in it might upset some viewers. Introducing a report from Bosnia, Peter Sissons said viewers would find many of the images very disturbing. ITN will retaliate, presumably, with a report which all viewers will find unwatchably terrible.

Not only is ours a time when anyone – from Presidents of the United States to nameless peasants – might die on film; this has been the time when, to a degree, people die *only* on film. I have seen hundreds of bodies on film and never one in real life.

3.

We head off to an art gallery in the centre of Belgrade where there is an exhibition of photographs. The ground floor of the gallery has huge windows and from a distance, without my glasses, I see only the glamorous blurs of magazine colour.

The exhibition is entitled 'Crimes against Serbs'. The pictures are of bodies with their brains splattered out, their throats cut. Strangled with wire, beaten, set on fire, shot. Bodies that have been killed three or four times over. Sometimes the blood is bright red, staining the white snow. Other times everything is turning brown or ghastly grey.

The photos of the dead are juxtaposed with pictures of the victims when they were just old people or mothers or girlfriends. Snaps like the one of you I carry, faded, in my wallet.

The inevitable question: how could people do these things to one another? The answer comes back immediately: with the greatest of ease, without batting an eyelid.

In the basement, as background to the current conflict, photos show the earlier history of atrocities inflicted on the Serbs. These, as befits an issue of history, are in black and white. One, from the camp at Jasenovac, shows a man propped up on one elbow as if modelling clothes in a catalogue. His head lies on the floor, three feet away.

In the visitors' book I transcribe Auden's lines from 'September 1, 1939':

> I and the public know
> What all schoolchildren learn,
> Those to whom evil is done
> Do evil in return.

We are about to leave when a man in his sixties looks up from the book and says,

'English?'

'Yes.'

'It is difficult for you to understand. It is different for us. They are our people.'

'They're my people too.'

'You are English.'

'They're still people.'

Unlike news reports these photographs do not provoke tears or pity any more than the film I watched a few nights ago induced love. They are too stark for that. But, outside, where the snow is turning to slush, I walk with my hand very gently round your shoulders. Not to harm anyone: simple enough, that hope seems an ambition vast enough to consume a lifetime.

Back at your apartment we make love and doze. We wake to find your period has started, smudging the white sheets.

We lie talking for hours, my hands in your hair. Your eyes. Your Serbian face. These are our last hours together and we try not to sleep again. Drifting on the edge of sleep, I think again of Auden's poem: 'We must love one another or die.' Auden eventually cut this line because, he reasoned, we're going to die anyway, whether we love one another or not. But he could, it seems, have changed the 'or' to an 'and'.

4.

My name is Milan Pavlovic. I drive the minibus that takes people from Belgrade to Budapest. Since sanctions have closed the airport at Belgrade there is a great need for this: to get anywhere you must fly from Budapest.

The first bus leaves Belgrade at five in the morning and this is the shift I like best. Five is when I pick up the last passenger; the rest are already in the bus by then.

I arrange the schedule and route for picking up my passengers. They are scattered all over the city and sometimes I have to pick up the first one as early as quarter past four. If their apartment is very difficult to find I arrange to meet them at the corner of a street that is well known. People are always waiting. No one is late. On street corners or outside their houses, girlfriends leave their boyfriends, husbands leave wives. They say goodbye, embrace, kiss: they are always the same, those last moments: their eyes are like cameras, trying to store up this memory of the other to keep by them when they are away.

They all think they have had to get up early but I have always been up before them. They are sad to leave their loved ones and never think that every morning I, too, leave my wife in bed. I wake before the alarm goes off and cuddle against her while she snores. Then into the cold. At this time of year the minibus is freezing but by the time I reach the first pick-up – today a boy leaving his girl – it is warm and nice for them.

Next a young man is leaving his family, returning to Israel. Every one kisses and says goodbye. The mother is crying. Sometimes there are people on their own and I can almost feel their happiness from a distance when they see the lights of the minibus approaching. Once the bus is full we are on our way, crossing the river and leaving the city before even the news-stands or cafés are open, before the sun is out of bed!

The return journey is not the same. I drop people off at their homes but the reunions take place invisibly. I pick people up at an exact time but because no one knows precisely when they will return their families are waiting for them inside. Life, as I see it, is all about farewells rather than reunions. That is why we have songs and photographs. It is parting that makes up our lives.

(for Vesna)
1993

Def Leppard and the
Anthropology of
Supermodernity

I'd assumed that I would spend my thirty-eighth birthday at home, watching England–Switzerland, but I somehow ended up at a Def Leppard gig in Seoul. I still hoped to see the game, though. As I understood it, the time-difference meant that if the match was broadcast live I could watch it first thing Saturday morning, eight hours before it actually took place.

The Leppards' vocalist, Joe Elliott, put me right on that score. Tomorrow's gig at Seoul's Olympic Gymnasium – the eighth date in what will turn into an eighteen-month rockathon – would be over by ten; with any luck, Joe said, we could be back at the hotel by eleven, in time for kick-off.

We'd been talking in the lobby of the Sheraton. In the band's early years, in the late 1970s, one might have written a piece called 'On the road with Def Leppard'. Now, forty million album sales down the line, it's 'In the Lobby with . . .'

Well, with quite a few people actually: the Korean promoter and his assistant Kee-Lee, who was so gorgeous I could hardly bear to look at her, various record company people, and a Japanese law student called Nori: Def Leppard's number-one fan in the world (he sees almost every gig) whose hair – this will prove significant later – was as long and black as Kee-Lee's. The only people not there were the band. They'd gone to bed a long time ago but, keeping a discreet distance, a group of fans was still hanging round in case the Leppards returned for a last-drink encore. It was not likely. Guitarist Phil Collen had already sunk enough to hospitalise most people. My God, did he pack it down him! Orange juice, ginseng juice, kiwi juice, melon juice, *water* juice. Anyone without his iron constitution would have OD'd on the vitamin rush.

Billy Joel famously remarked that a typical day in the life of a heavy-metal musician consisted of a round of golf and an AA meeting. Make that kick-boxing in Phil's case but this lust for the healthy life (in his late thirties now, he quit drinking nine years ago) represents one of two archetypal destinies for the long-haul rocker. The other is flat on your back with a lungful of puke, the route taken by guitarist Steve Clark, who died of a drugs and pills cocktail in 1980. He was replaced by Viv Campbell who, on the basis of tonight's performance, was still a full-on head-banger (two beers: *before* dinner).

I was tired from the flight but, back in my room, I couldn't sleep. With the AC on it was too cold, with it off it was too hot. I did a couple of lines of cable porno but there wasn't anything going down. I switched to a music channel and there were the boys doing a number from their new album *Slang*: a scaled-down record, bassist Rick Savage (Sav) would explain the next morning, less lavish, less bombastic than the canonical *Adrenalize* and *Hysteria* but still – to my ears – pretty lavastic. There are some hip sarangi samples courtesy of Ram Narayan but world embellishments like this emphasise the core sound's essential inadaptability, its inherent resistance to dilution or development. I thought about noting down that thought but by now I was too frazzled by tiredness to do anything but toss and turn the TV off and on. What was stopping me sleeping was the pillow: a bouncy, rubbery thing. I threw it on the floor, tore a sheet off the spare bed and tried to bundle that up under my head, but it wasn't thick enough, so I scrunched up the eiderdown but that was too *thick* so I got all the towels from the bathroom but they were too hard, and so I threw them off as well. I may not have been trashing my hotel room but I was certainly putting the towels and linen through their paces. It was five in the morning. I phoned reception but they had trouble understanding, so I put on my pyjama jacket and marched down to the lobby.

'I can't sleep,' I said to the night receptionist. 'I'm a journalist, here on a very important assignment, and I can't sleep because the pillows are too hard. I need a nice soft pillow, a soft fluffy one. This is meant to be a luxury hotel,' I yelled, 'and you haven't even got a nice fluffy pillow. Every single guest in this jumped-up refugee camp is tossing and turning, bending their pillows into shape, trying in vain to get a few minutes' sleep, but they can't, they can't, because you haven't got a decent fluffy PILLOW!' With that I turned on my heel and strode back to my room.

The next day I was totally exhausted. The band were in great shape, splitting up into various permutations for interviews with Korean journalists. In 1984 Rick Allen, the drummer, crashed his car and severed his left arm at the shoulder. A TV crew were asking him about being disabled, about how he'd single-handedly got back into playing the drums. 'Well, I prefer to say physically challenged,' he said and it was nice to hear one of these, oft-derided PC expressions come into its own. The crew kept asking Rick about his arm and I was very happy to eaves-drop because, obviously, I wanted to ask Rick about his arm but was reluctant to do so because that's all anybody asks Rick about, his arm. 'All the information I have for playing the drums is in my head,' he was saying. 'It's a question of channelling that knowledge in a different way. What I could do with my left hand I now do with my foot and so on. I see myself as whole, as having all my faculties. It's frustrating but then I get over my frustration and find a new way to do it.' The interview came to an end a few moments later, which was a shame because I was hoping they might also have asked him about something else I didn't feel up to asking myself, namely the article I'd read in a magazine which claimed that, a few days previously, the police had been called to a hotel room where he'd been trying to strangle his wife.

After lunch we reconvened in the lobby, ready for the sound-check at the Gymnasium. This promised to be a big moment for all of us: *it involved leaving the hotel*, and afforded the opportunity to confirm my suspicion that we were not in Seoul at all. We had sat in a plane for twelve hours but for all I knew we had spent that time circling Heathrow before being taken to an Asian theme hotel on the outskirts of Hounslow. And even if we were *physically* in South Korea we could have been anywhere. On the plane, appropriately enough, I'd been reading *Non-Places: Introduction to an Anthropology of Supermodernity*, in which Marc Augé argues that more and more people spend more and more of their lives in non-places: international hotels (if you're lucky, refugee camps if you're not), planes, transit lounges, motorways. From this I extrapolated that rockers like the Leppards were not so much outriders as *residents* of super-modernity: they spent their lives in these non-places. They had houses scattered over several continents but these were just relics of earlier, archaic modes of habitation: the rock star's true home is actually a hotel lobby, a dressing room, a stadium, which, irrespective of whether it's in Seoul or Hounslow, is actually nowhere.

There was a massive security presence in the lobby: men in black suits with ear pieces, talking into their lapels, looking into the middle distance (the lobby was easily big enough to accommodate this kind of scrutiny). Rick assumed that a high-ranking politician had turned up at the hotel but no, the security was for us. Not, I suspect, to protect us from assault but to cushion us from the shock of stepping outside the hotel. For a few stunned moments we were out in the fresh (i.e. foul-smelling) air, then we were sealed in the bus, wading through traffic.

Ah, the traffic! If the greatness of a city is measured by the sprawling extent of its tower blocks, by its pollution, by its commitment to a policy of unrelieved congestion, then this place – wherever it was – could hold its own with the best of them. The ten-minute drive to the Olympic Gymnasium took about two days. The sheer immobility of the experience was thrilling, moving (paradoxically), almost religious.

The sightseeing segment of the day completed, we milled around in the dressing room: the usual crowd: lighting people, road crew, the lovely Kee-Lee (if I could just run my hands through that lovely shiny hair, I thought, brush it back over her ear and kiss her throat, I would die a happy man) and Nori. I forgot to mention earlier that Nori, the number-one Def Leppard fan, lacks a hand. Now this could be a coincidence, of course, but it was interesting that the number-one fan of a band famous for having a one-handed drummer should himself be one-handed. What happened? Did he cut it off and, so to speak, hand it to Rick as a token of his undying devotion?

Before I had a chance to find out, the Seoul wing of the Def Leppard fan club was shown into the dressing room. They came bearing gifts and had their photos taken with the band, who received them, as always, with exemplary mildly flirty friendliness. As the show was drawing near all talk began to focus more seriously on the real business of the evening: getting back to the hotel and watching the football. So many of us had said that the game *might* be shown on Star Channel that this had now become an established fact.

Thirty minutes before show-time we hangers-on left the dressing room so that the band could move into their private pre-show preparations. Just before kick-off (musically, speaking) I too moved into my final preparations, cramming toilet tissue into my ears while 9,000 fans prepared to pay their ecstatic devotions. The band hit the stage in a surge of light and volume. That's the problem with rock shows like this: nothing that happens subsequently can quite live up to those opening moments when all the power suddenly erupts and you are, emphatically, no longer waiting for something to begin.

Pretty soon, though, you are waiting for it to end. The pace varies, of course, and the big songs, those with the auto-ovational choruses – 'Rock of Ages', 'Rocket', 'Let's Get Rocked' – come at the end, but the climax is recognizable as such, less because of some gathering pressure and momentum than because, by simple sequential determinism, it is followed by the encore. And while the band's sound is, ostensibly, juggernaut-heavy, epic, there is – or so it seemed to my tissue-insulated ears – a hint of blandness about much of their material. And this, I suspect, is what accounts for their phenomenal success.

Everyone knows Def Leppard are one of the biggest rock acts in the world but any non-devotees I asked had trouble summing up what was special about their music. In this respect *Slang* turns out to be an instructive title. According to J.E. Lighter in the *Historical Dictionary of American Slang*, 'the proportion of slang actually created by identifiable individuals is minute'; slang, what's more, 'maintains a currency independent of its creator, the individual writer and speaker.' Def Leppard's music, to translate this back into musical terms, has relatively little to do with the people who bring it into being:

it's rock-generic – and far from limiting the product's appeal, this guarantees its longevity, its ongoing marketability.

Backstage, the crew swapped stories of technical catastrophes narrowly averted. Joe thought he had sung badly, but the audience had been great. Years ago the band would have been keen to go out and get loaded, but now the important thing was to get back for the football.

Except the football wasn't on so we all hung out in the hotel's Skylight Lounge with its moonlit view over the non-specific city. The Lepps had a couple of juices and went to bed, leaving we hangers-on with nothing to hang on to except our bottles. Once the band had gone to bed, though, everyone else could move up a few notches in the glamour hierarchy. The road crew told us about their exploits in the fleshpots of Manila. I bragged about all the non-places I had been. We ordered more drinks. There was talk of going to a disco. I was place-lagged, confused from snorting hard rock with one nostril and French theory with the other – and this, I think, is what accounts for the unfortunate incident that followed. Kee-Lee was sitting with her back to me. I studied her shadow-black hair and then moved my face towards that mane of dark hair, which smelled like no one in the world had ever smoked a cigarette. In a friendly, well-the-gig's-over-and-it's-our-last-night-in-town way, I touched her hair, stroked it, ran my fingers through it, tilted her head towards me, revealing a pair of outraged eyes.

'Jesus!' I said. 'I'm sorry, Nori . . .'

1996

The Ghost and the
Darkness: Safari Notes

Amboseli National Game Reserve has a reputation as one of
Kenya's most tourist-infested national parks – minibuses drawn
up around a leopard like chairs round a camp-fire – but the part
of it around Tortilis Camp is as empty as the sky, the acid sky.
Actually there *are* a couple of clouds, each the size of Britain, but
they occupy only a tiny segment of the continent of blue overhead. Plenty of game on view: giraffe, buffalo, antelope, impala,
big-arsed zebra in skin-tight stripes. Technically the impala are
bad hurdlers: instead of skimming over obstacles – fallen
branches, bushes – they leap as high as possible, transforming
their forward momentum into sudden vertiginous flourishes: a
lovely way to demonstrate the limits of efficiency, of an over-
pragmatic view of evolution.

Every time we see some wildlife, Stefano – who runs
Tortilis – stops and turns off the engine – but the brief silence
is immediately broken by a cacophony of whirs, clicks, beeps
and flashes as we let fly with a volley of telephotos, wide-
angles and zooms. A leopard once jumped into a minibus full
of tourists, apparently, and who can blame him? Probably
wanted to take some pictures of his own. Leave nothing but
footprints, take nothing but photos: that's the conventional
eco wisdom these days, but the time might well come when we

look back on this heyday of photographic safari as we do on the era of mass slaughter of wildlife. In some as-yet-undiscovered way all this clicking is probably eating away at some ozone or other. I begin to think that the native's proverbial fear of being photographed is not as ludicrous as we think. Personally, I think that the world will exist only as long as some part of it remains unphotographed. When that last blade of grass has been photographed the evolutionary project will be complete and the world will cease to exist. This is the way the world ends: not with a bang, not with a whimper, but with a click and whir.

Some elephants are cooling off in the muddy edges of a marsh. They look sad, bowed down by all the remembering they allegedly do. They can live until sixty-five, apparently, but they look much older, as if they've been trudging and munching away for millennia. No wonder they look tired. Their skin is geological. It's great seeing them up close like this but how much greater it would be if we didn't know it was an *elephant* we were looking at. What would we make of this huge thing if we didn't know what it was we were seeing?

One particular bull moves towards us. Then moves closer still. Stef tells us to be still. All the whirring and clicking has stopped. We're all petrified. For long minutes the elephant, which we refer to as a bull, looks as if he's about to go ape.

We drive up a hill to watch the sun set. For the last ten minutes I've not really been taking any notice of the scenery. I've been thinking of beer. Cold beer. Glasses of it. By the time we get to the top of the hill my thirst-lust is so acute that I hallucinate an African dressed in a bow tie, dispensing refreshments from a little table. Then I realise it's not a mirage: it's for real: one of the little treats Stef lays on for his guests. Also there, gazing into the sunset, is a Maasai, dressed in red schuka: a vision of Africa as eternal as Kilimanjaro. Now I *know* that's a cliché, just as I know that the scene has been arranged for us, for the tourists, but it is a supremely effective – not to say elemental – contrivance.

Early the following evening, near Ol Donyo Wuas, we stop at a Maasai village for a quick peer. We peer at them, they stare at us and it is difficult to tell who is the more astonished. They are decked out in incredible jewellery, some have their ears tied in knots. They would look out of place everywhere but in the most extreme situations: here in the bush, or at a night-club in one of the world's great capitals. I have a stupid thought: they look exactly like the Maasai in Angela Fisher's *Africa Adorned*: coffee-table proof of the authenticity of my experience.

As we drive from the village I find myself thinking what a great little planet this is! And while we're on this euphoric note, what a great species we are, we *Homo sapiens*! There are the Maasai, radically different from us, and yet essentially the same: they laugh, we laugh. Is there a tribe on earth for whom laughing and smiling are signs of hostility? It's inconceivable. The best we have been able to come up with are cultures where laughing is frowned upon. Speaking of laughing, I am becoming aware of a member of our group, Angela, her lovely laugh. She is always laughing or wiping away tears of laughter. A confusion of response ensues: because she laughs a lot I begin to think I would like to sleep with her. She would probably find the idea laughable.

On the way back to camp our guide, Richard Bonham, Kenya's own Crocodile Dundee, tells us that two factions of the Maasai, the Kaputai and Kasongo, have had three big set-tos in the last ten years. Such conflicts seem absurd to us but, back at the camp, we run into a pair of old ruling-class English women. The place rings with their voices, with that vile accent of entitlement. Immediately I feel pure hatred: class hatred that has been learnt, acquired, but which feels like instinct. As befits a tribal hatred like this, I don't see them as individuals (I avoid being introduced) but as concentrated essence of their class, their tribe. We are natural enemies; my tribe would happily kill their tribe even though, God knows, I left my own tribe years ago, and now belong to no tribe. They are old now, seventy or eighty, I should think, and the rest of my party is charmed by their spunkiness in setting out on such an adventure. I would like to kill them. I begin to get the first inkling that this is to be a safari into Englishness.

Everyone we meet in the bush is like Othello: they woo us with tales of hair-breadth escapes – from lions, elephants, leopards, crocs, hippos, rhinos. People wake up and see a lion staring at them from the end of the bed; they get up for a pee and find a cobra hissing in front of the toilet. What lends these tales credibility are the stories of escapes that didn't happen: deaths at the hands – paws? – of lions, leopards, rhino. I say they woo us but we are desperate to *be* wooed. I spend the whole dinner, for example, coaxing atrocious yarns from Stef, stories of a leopard shredding a man's face, a rhino tearing off a woman's arm.

Owing to a shortage of beds I am going to be spending the night up the road in Bonham's guest room, and so, after dinner, we hurtle off in his jeep. Suddenly he veers off the road and stops. By road I mean track; by room, I see, Richard meant *tent*. There is a bathroom out the zipped-up back of the tent, notionally protected from the outside world by a low wall. Then Bonner is gone and I am alone, overwhelmed by the remoteness of my situation. Ol Donyo Wuas is a three-and-a-half-hour drive from Nairobi; Bono's place is eight miles from Ol Donyo Wuas; my tent is an unspecified distance from his place. I get into bed but, with my head still full of Stef's wildlife assaults, am too petrified to sleep. A migrating wind batters the tent. All around is hissing, hooting, rustling, scratching, snorting, barking. Just as

I think I might drift off a new noise starts. Christ knows what is out there. I don't sleep at all, not a wink. As soon as it is light I unzip the tent: an amazing view which immediately dissolves all my tiredness: savannah stretching away into the distance, as far as the eye can, as far as Kilimanjaro: unclouded, indifferent, blue. Kilimanjaro: the supreme example of place-name as photo.

At Harare airport the attitude of the immigration officials is at once diligent and relaxed: in the middle of an exhaustive check of my passport the guy decides it's time to go to the lavatory, and disappears for five minutes.

Africa is a great destination if you don't want to carry your own bags. I have problems with this, however. It probably dates back to 1982 when my then girlfriend went berserk because I had my shoes shined in Morocco. 'They want money, not scruples,' I yelled, but just as a child who has been scolded for some offence can never commit it again without some misgiving, I can't let other people do anything I feel I should do myself. Besides, I like carrying my (not very heavy) rucksack, I like hoisting it on to my shoulder one-handed – it *has* to be one-handed – and striding into the bush – well, into the luxury of Imba Matombo, a pseudo-ethnic executive retreat in the suburbs of Harare. Why don't I mind people cleaning my hotel room, then? Because I always make sure I'm not around when it's being done.

From Victoria Falls airport we cross over the Zambezi, from Zimbabwe into Zambia. For lunch. From the bridge separating the two countries you can do a bunjee jump into the Zambezi gorge. We watch a white South African do a jump. In his fifties and lacking an arm he seems the incarnation of Afrikaner stubbornness (it seems quite possible that he lost his limb on the Great Trek). Even if the rope broke you get the impression he would, so to speak, bounce back. The instructor starts the countdown – 5, 4, 3 – but before he has a chance to go any further the guy hurls himself off – backwards.

We opt for the more sedate, scarcely less spectacular option of lunch on Livingstone Island, right on the lip of the Falls. Frankly, the Victoria Falls piss on those at Niagara. It's all on too huge a scale to make sense. I lie at the edge and look over. A double rainbow down there in the churning mist-smoke. There was a time, a few years back, when I would have taken my impressions away with me and researched a paper on 'Africa and the Sublime'. Now I content myself with watching Angela in her swimming costume, bathing in a pool a couple of feet from the edge of the Falls. *She* looks sublime, but the people who have the best view are those across the Zambezi on the other side of the gorge, in Zimbabwe; to them it must look incredible that women are bathing maybe three feet from the edge of the apocalypse. Actually it's quite safe: the water flows to the edge at the speed of a brook. There's no danger of falling. Except for Angela. I'm falling for her.

It's gone five by the time we begin the drive from Tongabezi camp back to the Zimbabwe border. On either side of the road are dark green trees and even greener grass. The sky is also greenish with the rain that fell in the afternoon and the rain that will fall in the evening. It is a good road to drive along but I wish I was walking like everyone else: boys in shorts, a smartly dressed postman on a bike (even cycling seems to be a form of walking), women carrying pots on their heads.

In *Imperium* Ryszard Kapuściński writes how, throughout the undeveloped world, you come across people sitting, doing nothing, waiting: a special kind of waiting, devoid of expectation. But, watching people walk along this road, it seems to me that walking – specifically that lovely, undaunted African walk – is also a form of waiting. You move your feet and wait for them to bring you to where you want to be. Everything waits: the animals wait (for it to cool down enough to leave the lakes, for it to get dark, for prey to come along), even the landscape waits. What for? Somehow: itself.

Today's the day: white water rafting. A great mass of us – seventy? – sign a Faustian waiver: in return for the buzz of shooting the rapids we relinquish all rights and responsibilities. We travel to the national park in a convoy of buses and begin a perilous descent to the river, reminiscent of the opening shots of *Aguirre: the Wrath of God* with the conquistadors going down some mighty cliff face in South America. It's such a huge operation – kayaks to fish out people from the water, a helicopter circling in the event of serious injury, lots of equipment and men to carry it – I feel we could invade Normandy with all the resources at our disposal.

Our guide is called Tetrex, a magnificently muscled man who has ridden the river thousands of times, far more often than anyone else. He looks like he's in his mid-thirties but is actually fifty-one: hence his nickname: Old Man River. As we clamber into the boats I have a premonition that if there is one person on this expedition who is going to be injured it will be me. We drift downstream amid much calling and chanting to allay fear and whip up *esprit de tribe* (one crew keeps doing 'Uggy, uggy, uggy!', which is so inappropriate I feel like lodging a complaint). Tetrex tells us how to fling ourselves on top of each other to stop the boat flipping over. We glide down the river. The sun comes and goes. We hit the first rapid – a grade four – and it's over before we know it. Actually it's a bit disappointing: a great surge and splash of water and then we're drifting calmly again. One of the other boats flips on this first rapid and several more get turned over on the second. We flip – more appositely, are flushed out – on the third rapid, The Devil's Toilet Bowl.

Difficult to say what happens. One moment we're crashing into the water, the next the boat's coming over on top of us. I cling on. We yank the boat back face up again and clamber aboard. Before I had been frightened of flipping: now I want it to happen again. What actually happens is that at the next rapid Brian is catapulted out from the back of the boat. Suddenly he's not there any more. We see him face down, rushing ahead of us in the water. A kayak picks him up and he is hoisted on to another raft. By the time he clambers back on our boat he has got his breath back but is pretty shaken up by all the river he has swallowed, by what he is already referring to as his 'near-death experience'. We have a choice at the next rapid: an exciting, difficult one or a tame, easy one. I want to go for the former but am outvoted. I immediately request a transfer to another boat and take my place alongside the intrepid, one-armed – and in this context, somewhat disadvantaged – Afrikaner. We opt for the difficult route and make it through unscathed – which is more than can be said for a lot of the other boats: people are spilling out all over the place. The river is awash with them. We pick up one sorry-looking guy – blue lips, exhausted, coughing and spluttering – who thanks us over and over for saving his life.

It starts raining as our great armada heads to the lunch-time docking area. The atmosphere is rave-like (that great shared friendliness). The perfect vacation package, it seems to me, would be white water rafting in the morning and Evian water raving in the evening. I'm surprised no one's come up with it.

Those of us who are doing only half a day's rafting clamber up a steep path to the top of the gorge. At the top a guy is serving beers and Coke from a cooler, opening them African-style, using one bottle to flip the cap off another. He does it so fast that opening the bottle scarcely interrupts its passage from the cooler to your hand. It's immediately obvious to me that this is one of the great skills of the world; anyone who could open bottles like that in England would have women queuing up to sleep with him. I ask how it's done. It looks simple but it turns out – like so many things in this easy-seeming world – to be impossible. I try ten times and have to stop because my hand hurts badly, especially the thumb joint which is meant to serve as a fulcrum. Still, I'm very happy sitting here with my African brothers with their long thin arms and long thin legs, their giraffe-like limbs that are as long and thin as mine.

Most of the twenty people who are doing half a day's rafting have made their way back. One guy has hurt the ligaments in his knee because a Swedish woman in the front of the boat fell awkwardly on him. Another woman smashed her leg on a rock and has been carried up on a stretcher. The path up the cliff is incredibly steep, but four Africans lashed her to the stretcher and carried it up. The woman who hurt her leg is in pretty bad shape: the rafting was awful, she said, but the most terrifying thing was being carried up the cliff! She can't walk but her main emotion is relief that her leg, though hurt, is not broken. My main emotion is also relief – that it's her with the fucked-up leg, not me.

Back in Zimbabwe, we spend the night at Matetsi, a private game reserve about thirty miles from the Falls. 'A spiritual kind of experience', according to one entry in the visitors' book but, at three hundred and fifty bucks person per night (sharing), a fairly material one too. Another visitor 'watched a buffalo being struck by lightning and killed instantly during a thunderstorm late afternoon. One flash and it was all over.'

I say yes every time I'm offered a beer, not because I want to drink it but so I can practise opening the bottle. By the end of the evening my hand feels like it's had a car door slammed on it and I still have not succeeded in opening a single bottle.

Because the camp is open – no fence to keep out animals – you have to be escorted to and from your room by a guard. I'm escorted by Lovemore. Just as I am about to go into my room it occurs to me that Lovemore has to make the return trip on his own and should therefore be escorted back by me. I have a vision of the two of us escorting each other back and forth for the rest of eternity.

Some confusion about our tickets from Victoria Falls to Lake Kariba: on our itinerary it says 12:00, on the actual ticket it says 15:00. At the airport we find that the flight is actually at five. Not that it matters: it's been cancelled anyway. Shearwater – the company that owns Kipling's, the lodge on Lake Kariba where we are staying – arranges to send a plane to pick us up.

I spent my twenties labouring – more accurately, idling – under the misconception that women liked intellectuals. In Africa I am confronted with an elemental truth: they prefer rangers and pilots. Take Steve, for example, who is flying us to Kipling's. He gestures above the roar of the engine to ask if anyone would like a Coke. I yell 'yes'. He reaches into a bag and opens the bottle, African-style, *while flying a plane*. Angela practically comes in her seat.

We fly over toadstool huts, bird-claw rivers, then over Lake Kariba itself, the milky flatness of the water broken, here and there, by the protruding branches of dead mopane trees. We land and take a boat across to the camp, which is right on the edge of the lake. It looks like Mosquito Village, Camp Malaria! As soon as I turn on the light in my open-fronted chalet it immediately fills up with every conceivable kind of bug. I head for the bar but lose my way in the tangle of paths and quickly become terrified. Earlier in the day a python had been seen sleeping in a tree near the bar but it had since disappeared, no one knew where. The noise of crickets and other things is tidal, surging. I keep thinking of a python drooping out of a tree and coiling itself around me. I call out nervously. I hear Angela squealing – spooked by bugs – and, communicating like this in the international language of distress, I seek refuge in her room. The others are going to call for her, she says, so I should stay in her room while she showers.

My initial reaction is one of relief to be out of the bug-infested, python-draped night, but this soon turns to elation. I can't believe my luck! By a fluke combination of mirrors I can see Angela in the shower! It is a near-life experience. Then there's a knock at the door – it's Steve, alerted by all the screaming and yelling, offering to escort me to the bar. I don't know him well enough to suggest that we both stay and watch Angela in the shower and so, sulkily, I leave with him.

At dinner Steve sits at one end of the table. Immediately three women take the places nearest to him, their eyes shiny with longing. Instead of wine I keep ordering beer to practise my opening skills even though my hand is, by now, pretty well useless. I would be hard pressed to open a milk bottle with it.

It is the last night of our trip, the last chance for anyone to sleep with anyone else. I end up back in my room on my own, naturally, fantasising that Angela and I spent the night together in the tent at Richard Bonham's, Tarzan-style, in the bush, miles from anyone, miles away from pilots. Then this fantasy dissolves into stark reality: women are more attracted to twenty-nine-year-old pilots than they are to scrawny thirty-eight-year-old writers. In *Green Hills of Africa*, his safari book, Hemingway mentions that, at camp one night, drunk, he realised he was 'getting the evening braggies'. I am getting the opposite: the evening pities. Can it really be that I am almost forty, will actually *be* forty next year? Is it physically possible? Have I already had my period of greatest sexual confidence? Can I have passed through that phase without being aware that it was happening?

In my head, I am the great white hunter of women, bagging trophies left and right. In reality my hand hurts so much I can't even whack off. Instead of stalking my prey I am tracking myself in a futile safari of sexual regret. Still, as Hemingway said of bragging 'when you could not be understood', it is 'better than nothing'.

In the morning we visit a local school and a baby rhino which makes cute purring sounds. By now, though, our entire party is more interested in opening bottles than anything else in the whole of Africa. That bitch Angela has succeeded in opening a bottle on her own. For my part I am leaving a trail of partly opened bottles in my wake: the perfect metaphor for my entire existence. I've spent my life partially opening bottles, opening them just enough to take the fizz out, just enough to make everything go flat.

Two planes are going back to Victoria Falls. Steve says he can take three passengers in his plane. The women volunteer, to a man, so to speak. They take a boat to the plane. I watch them curve away, waving. Resigned to being the eunuch in the harem I find now that I don't even have my harem. There is only one safari, I think to myself as the plane takes off into the African sky, and it remains the same irrespective of where it takes place: the wretched safari of the self.

1997

The Wrong Stuff

I'm in the cockpit of a MiG-29 fighter: a two-seater version with a maximum airspeed of 1,320 mph or Mach 2.3. Right now, to be frank, we're going at 10 mph, about twice the speed of feet. We taxi out on to the runway and stop. The engines shriek. The plane strains at the leash of its power. Then we're hurtling forward and I'm forced back into the ejector seat by the suddenness of the acceleration. The runway is three miles long but in less than 300 metres we're up and banking hard to the right, afterburners blazing, pulling gs. From the ground it sounds like we're ripping the sky apart. Up here, now that we're airborne, it's library-quiet. We circle the airbase and then punch straight through the clouds. Except for the scars of old vapour trails the sky is deserted. It has that special kind of blue you never see from the ground, even on the clearest day: an empty, limitless blue, a nothing blue . . .

This is the climactic flight of three days at the Zhukovsky airbase, forty kilometres south-east of Moscow. For the last fifty years the Flight Research Institute here has been the centre of the Russian aviation and test-flight programme. Until a few years ago it was top secret. Now, with the collapse of the Soviet Union and the end of the Cold War, you can come here and fly

supersonic, state-of-the-art military aircraft like this. If you've got the money.

Our stay begins with tests at the Institute's Medical Centre. Blood pressure. Eyes. Ears. Heart. Whether these tests serve any crucial medical function, I'm not sure; their effect, though, is to up the ante, to make us feel we're being put through our paces, tested to see if we've got what it takes to survive what the Liability Release terms 'an inherently dangerous adventure'. There are eight of us and we all pass the examination.

Then it's out to the airbase proper where the stairs are lined with photos of medal-bedecked test pilots, all in the glum aesthetic of official Soviet portraits. Not just unsmiling, but heroically, defiantly, miserable.

The briefing room is a surprisingly homely place with flock wallpaper and phones that ring in a variety of colours. One of the pilots explains what we will be doing in our first flights, in the L-39, a two-seater, fully aerobatic Czech trainer. Not for the last time we address the question of nausea. Before leaving for Moscow, a friend who had done aerobatics told me that I would spend half my time trying not to be sick and the other half cleaning vomit from the cockpit. After each manoeuvre, the pilot reassures us, we will ask if you are OK. If you feel bad we make period of level flying until you feel better. OK?

The briefing over, we troop off to get kitted up in our flying suits. This also takes place in what looks like a converted living room – the living room, it has to be said, of an aviation nut whose pride and joy is his collection of hi-tech aeronautical bric-à-brac. A nice elderly couple are in charge. He wears a black beret and has a grizzled Hero of the Soviet Union look about him; she is wearing red, fleecy slippers and has a kind, kitcheny way about her. First on is the g-suit: a pair of tight-fitting green leggings with an abundance of punk-style zips and a hose that attaches to an air supply in the aircraft. When the plane starts pulling gs the suit inflates, tightening round your legs, preventing blood from pouring from your brain to your feet – which is what it wants to do – and thereby preventing you from passing out. The elderly retainers get one of the zips of my g-suit caught. It won't come up, it won't come down. They're both tugging and pulling but it won't budge. I wriggle out of it like a snake and we start over. Re-zipped into another g-suit, I step into fire-retardant overalls. The outfit is finished off with accessories that are crucial to the whole enterprise (from the photo-opportunity, chick-appeal point of view): helmet and oxygen mask.

'Keep your helmet and oxygen mask with you at all times,' says Marina, our guide and interpreter. 'Now we go for ejection seat instruction.' Marina hurries everyone along while I pose for more photographs, standing with the helmet cradled in my arm, or crouched down with it between my feet like a football.

Marina comes rushing back:

'You're holding everyone up,' she says testily. I run out after her and scurry into the classroom where the ejection procedure for the L-39 is being demonstrated. In the unlikely event of having to eject, Marina translates, the pilot will tell you to 'Prepare to Eject'—

'Sorry Marina,' I interrupt. 'I've left my helmet back in the suiting-up place . . .'

Insignificant in themselves, little things like this – like the zip problem with the g-suit which wasn't my fault at all – are yet indications of some larger personality disorder. It's beginning to dawn on everyone in the group that I possess that mysterious combination of qualities that enables a man to fuck up in every imaginable circumstance: the wrong stuff.

Someone is despatched to retrieve my helmet. Marina resumes with more than a little impatience.

When the pilot tells you to 'Prepare to Eject' you reach down and grasp the two red cinch rings between your thighs. Don't bend forward. Sit back tight against the seat, head jammed back against the head rest. Make your body strong. Then:

'Eject! Eject! Eject!'

I enjoy the urgency of these words, the one word twice repeated. Split-seconds from destruction it might save time if the pilot simply said it once – 'Eject!' – but to announce it in triplicate like that really impresses on you that something very important and very extreme is about to happen. When the order comes – Eject! Eject! Eject! – you pull up the cinch rings, hard.

Your instinct is to lean forward for better leverage. Which is fatal because when the canopy flies off and you are blasted into the open air, the gs – up to 16 of them – will snap your spinal column.

Whatever happens you pass out, obviously. But hopefully you come round some time after the seat has separated and you are floating back to earth beneath a canopy in full bloom. The final piece of advice vouchsafed us is to land with your feet together.

Ejecting from the MiG-29 is altogether simpler. The pilot does it for you: he pulls the ring or hits the switch or pushes the button or yanks the lever – all this life-saving advice is washing over me: I'm wondering if there's going to be a chance for some photos in the ejector seat – that sends both of you hurtling out of the plane. All you have to do is sit tight. Any questions?

As a matter of fact I do have a question, if question is a euphemism for worry. I have a lot of worries, all converging on this deepening conviction that I'm one hundred per cent, pure fuck-up, wrong stuff incarnate. For a start I'm very tall, six three, and, as I see it, it's going to be impossible to clear the cockpit without taking my legs off at the knees. If the 16 gs don't break my back, if the parachute opens and I regain consciousness and everything goes like clockwork, then I am still going to hit the ground on two bloody stumps. In the circumstances I rather doubt I'll have the presence of mind to keep them together.

I suppose it doesn't really matter. The chances of having to eject are minimal . . . but, knees apart, so to speak, a side of me *wants* to eject. Flying in a high-performance military jet is one thing but ejecting from it . . . The first time I'd seen a MiG-29 was on television, during the Paris airshow in 1989. A bird-strike when the plane was at low altitude took out the starboard engine. The plane buried itself in the earth but the pilot survived what *World Air Power Journal* coolly termed 'an

out-of-the-envelope ejection'. There isn't time to dwell on this.
We're hurrying back to the minibus, heading for the runway. An
old Alice Cooper number is coursing through my head. For
the amusement of my companions I sing it aloud: 'I wanna be
ej*ec*ted . . .' Marina isn't amused. She is even less amused when
I tell her – and I can hardly believe this has happened – that I've
left my helmet in the ejector seat classroom. I'm so busy trying
not to fuck up that I'm fucking up every couple of minutes. At
this rate I'll be lucky to have my helmet with me in the plane –
which is where the *real* spunk-machine photos are going to
happen.

The pilot for my L-39 flight is Vladmir, who turns up in a Top
Gun baseball cap and an impressive assortment of cuts,
scratches, and bruises. Two stories circulate about how he came
by these. One version has it that someone tried to mug him in
Red Square two nights previously ('*tried* to mug him', note.)
The other, that a girlfriend had flown into a jealous rage ('*a* girlfriend', note). Vladmir has calm, cloudless eyes and a very
relaxed way about him. Since this is my first flight, he explains,
we will take it very gently, very easily . . .

'Ah no,' I interrupt (I'm always interrupting: another sign of
the wrong stuff). 'You see this is going to be my only flight in the
L-39, so I want to experience as much as I can, pull some serious
gs, push the outside of the envelope.' A little self-conscious
about using this phrase to a real test pilot I pause and add a qualifying, 'As it were.'

'We'll see,' says Vladmir, as though the only outside of the
envelope experience I'm good for is sending a postcard home
saying, 'Dear Mum, I fucked up.'

I climb the ladder to the plane, pause for a couple of pictures,
clamber into the cockpit. The ground crew connect my g-suit,
radio link and oxygen mask so that I am umbilically linked to
the plane's life-support circuitry. More photographs. I wish I

hadn't worn my glasses. I'm strapped in tight to the seat and then tighter still. A switch to the left converts the air supply to pure oxygen. This comes in handy if you start feeling sick: like stepping outside to get a breath of fresh air. The canopy comes down and is sealed. Vladmir asks if I'm ready, which I am except . . . Well, it's too late to mention it now but during the helmet-fitting session I'd had real trouble disconnecting my oxygen mask. Not wanting to hold everyone up I'd gone on to the ejector seat instruction session before I'd got the hang of it. Now if I do need to throw up, it occurs to me, I'm going to vomit straight into my oxygen mask. This is bad but it is not a worst-case scenario. That involves ejecting while drowning in my own puke and having my legs ripped off at the knees before my spine is snapped by 16 gs.

We're off. One moment we're accelerating along the runway, the next we're banking sharply, and the fields beyond the airfield are a hundred metres below. If a normal passenger aircraft is like a bus then this feels like a motorbike, with everything happening not just all around you but *to* you. We skirt the airfield and follow the foil flatness of a river. Seen from the air, it occurs to me, fields are the same the world over. So are cities. In fact, seen from the air, the world is pretty much the same the world over. Now we're clinging to a wall of cloud and vaulting into the aerobatic zone.

First, says Vladmir, we will try a roll. The sky slides away to the right and the land comes looming over us. Strapped tight against the seat, I experience the roll only visually, as if it's not the plane but the earth and sky that have swirled round each other.

'Now you try,' says Vladmir. There is nothing to it. Push the stick to the left and keep pushing till there is nothing but fields and then sky again. The plane responds instantly, as fast as thought. Next a loop: the sky expands until there is nothing but sky, sky, sky and the earth plunging up to meet it, filling the cockpit and vanishing again. Vladmir asks if I'm OK. We do a Split-S, an Emmelman, a 4-point roll – whatever they are. Sky and land speed, fall and bend into each other. As for gs, the main sense of them is an added weight on the chest and a slight panicky feeling followed instantly by the tightening of the g-suit which is designed to stop you feeling gs. It's not until you try a simple manoeuvre, like raising your arms or feet, that you feel the doubled, tripled or quadrupled weight of gravity tugging your limbs down.

After each manoeuvre Vladmir asks if I'm OK. Yes, I say, surprised to find that I am, that I'm neither fucking up nor throwing up. 'OK, now we try the tail slide.' Vladmir takes the plane up at a steep angle, very slow, lets it stall and slip back to earth before blazing ahead again. It feels eerie. The noise of the engines is minimal inside the cockpit but in the brief and utter silence of the stall you are suddenly lost, bereft, powerless.

The whole flight feels like it's taken just five minutes but we've been up for half an hour. We surf the edges of clouds, roar low over the airstrip – upside down, I should add – and then come into land.

The ground crew disconnect everything and we climb down to the tarmac that isn't actually tarmac. Vladmir announces that we pulled 5.5 gs. Hot dog! And I hadn't felt nauseous once. Oh, I strut over to the boys, some of whom had pulled a mere 3 gs. Three? Three was nothing, barely worth mentioning. You pull more gs than that on a double-decker bus going round Piccadilly Circus in heavy traffic, I say. And I'll tell you something else, I feel like saying to Marina, you see what's cradled in the crook of my arm? My helmet and oxygen mask – I haven't left them in the plane, I haven't fucked up because I've got it: the one hundred per cent, pure adrenalin, stamped and franked airmail envelope, high-octane, *right* stuff.

After this interlude of exhilaration I realise I'm not feeling quite right, as if the stuffing is in the process of being tugged out of me. Not sick exactly. More like the aftermath of someone else's hangover. By the time we get to the base cafeteria I feel like my stomach and head are in the process of changing places. My head has a stomach ache and my stomach has a headache: not a hangover, an *overhang*.

'What's up, g-man?' says Bill, an American journalist. 'Lost your appetite?'

I spend the rest of the afternoon at the hotel, crashed out on my bed. Even one g, the normal experience of gravity, seems to place an intolerable strain on the upright human body. I sleep for a couple of hours and wake to find that I'm OK, miraculously restored to normal. The phone rings. It's Bill.

'Hey, g-man . . .'

'Hey, that sounds like the top Moscow fighter jock who pulled all of half a g?'

'How's it going hot dog?'

'I've been pulling a few zs. What about you? Did you sleep? Over.'

'Negative. You ready to pull some bs?'

'Affirmative. Over.'

'Roger and out.'

With variations, this forms the basis of our conversation for the rest of our stay in Russia. An entire grammar is generated from two verbs ('pushing' and 'pulling'), a single noun ('envelope') and an abundance of acronyms.

Next morning the weather is not good. There's a thick shelf of cloud from 1,000 metres up to 5,000 metres. After that there is another 4,000 metres of mist. It isn't until you get above 9,000 metres that you have anything that clearly lives up to the word sky. Not a good day for flying. In fact not a good day for anything: a sitting-in-your-hotel-room-playing-cards kind of day. Or a going-fifteen-miles-up-in-a-MiG-25 kind of day . . .

Bob, chief financial officer with a real estate firm in Connecticut, had traded in one of his flights in the L-39 (and forked out an extra five thousand bucks) for a spin in the MiG-25. It's a remarkable plane, the Fox-bat, as we call it in the fighter jock world. Designed to intercept a high altitude American bomber that was never built, the MiG-25 was, from the outset, a plane without a mission: a counter to a non-existent threat. As a dogfighter, says Bill, it's a dog. Aside from the fact that it goes very high very fast its true role is to push the outside of the superfluousness envelope.

Bob's flight plan involves climbing to 10,000 feet. Then the after-burners will kick in and he will soar towards a ceiling of 75,000 feet at Mach 2.4.

This means he has to wear a pressure suit, a green outfit that is alive with hoses and tubes. He gradually disappears beneath layers of protective technology and with each layer his passivity increases. Long before they seal the jar of his well-being with an astronaut helmet he has abandoned any claims to being an active participant in his own life. By the time he's ready to go, he looks like nothing else so much as a life-size Action Man. All this preparation has its effect though.

'How's the dryness in the throat coming along Bob?' asks Bill as we drive out to the runway.

'Pretty good,' says Bob, drily. His nervousness is relieved some-what when the pilot rocks up wearing a standard-issue helmet. You don't really need the astronaut's helmet, it turns out, but wearing one is good for the punter's ego. Still, for a flight in a superfluous plane, why not take along a superfluous helmet?

Superfluous or not, the MiG-25 is an awesome piece of machinery: two massive engines strapped to a long silver tube. Bob's seat is way out in the nose of the aircraft, in front of the pilot. From where he is sitting you cannot see any part of the plane except the nose, not even the wings. He will be suspended in this little pressurised cocoon fifteen miles above the earth.

The engines are turned on. A roar like you've never heard before. It starts loud and then, for a full five minutes, gets louder and higher and louder and higher. When it moves forward and turns towards the runway a wash of kerosene heat ripples over us.

Then it's gone, disappearing into the clouds. We sit in the minibus and wait. It's freezing. In terms of pulling *k*s (kicks), this is on a par with sitting in a layby on a wet day in Cumbria.

After half an hour Bob, the rocket man, returns: triumphant, a little dazed. What had it been like? Fun. And? He'd hit 2.4 Mach at 45 degree bank and had continued like that, spiralling upwards. Did he have any sense of speed? Not really. Fifteen miles up you can see the curvature of the earth but all Bob had seen was the curvature of the clouds. The sky was black above and blue below, like they'd said in the brochure. Was it worth the money? He'd have paid double. Why had he done it?

'I wanted to be able to say I'd flown Mach two and been fifteen miles up.'

Now this, it seems to me, is the crux of the matter. You experience thirty minutes of raw sensation and then what? You can tell people you've done it. Apart from that, it's over with. You've got nothing to show for it. You've done something pretty far-out but – and this is not the case when you've climbed a mountain or survived a parachute jump – you've achieved nothing. Now that we are all together again, back on *terra firma*, there is nothing to choose between us. In a sense, Bob might as well not have made his flight.

The truth is, though, that if I had an infinite amount of money I would spend it on one thing after another like this. So what if it costs five grand? Or ten? If I had been up in the Fox-bat for half an hour I would have been happy while it lasted. When I got down I might have returned to my life of loneliness and boredom, but if I had the money I'd go up again and again until it no longer made me happy and then I'd take off and do something else that made me happy.

If I had the money. Obviously they're not cheap, these flying holidays. The basic package – three flights in an L-39, one in a MiG-29, including hotel, excluding flight to Moscow – is about thirteen thousand dollars. (All things considered – administrative costs, pilots, ground crew, people taking you to and from the airbase, fuel by the ton, wear and tear on the planes: the engines only have a finite life in them – I'm surprised it's not a lot more expensive.) And plenty of people *do* have this kind of money. In the eight months since it started, in October 1993, over 120 people have flown courtesy of MiGs Etc. On our course, Andy, an ex-marine, is head of a company that makes fourth generation computer software, Jim is a lawyer specialising in something or other, Michael, a German, makes packaging for supermarkets . . . These are the kinds of positions you start losing interest in a third of the way through the job descriptions.

Still, from the point of view of the Flight Research Institute, their money comes in very handy. It may be one of the great centres of military aviation but the airbase, like the rest of Moscow, has a worn-out look to it. Around the perimeter are the hulks of planes plundered for spares. Now that the state is no longer pumping money into military aviation, the flying tourists provide a source of much-needed income.

The whole enterprise is underwritten by a massive irony, of course: in America you cannot fly state-of-the-art military jets however much you're willing to pay. But here, in the ex-Soviet Union, in desperate-for-cash Russia, everything is for sale. If you really want to push the outside of the expenditure envelope, 'The Ultimate Flight Programme' offers twenty flights, climaxing with 'a no-holds-barred simulated dogfight' between two punters in the planes of their choice. Cost? Fifty thousand bucks. Each. Shell out enough and you can probably arrange to strafe the runway, bomb the control tower and buzz the Kremlin. The only limit on what you can experience is how much you can spend. If we are at the end of history then this is what it feels like, this is what it costs. For a long time I believed that money could not buy you happiness but it is only now, as I clamber into the cockpit of the MiG-29, that I realise just how true this is. Money can't buy you happiness because money *is* happiness. We taxi out on to the runway and stop. The engines shriek. The plane strains at the leash of its power, poised to become fully itself once more.

1994

Point Break

Freefall: the air screaming past, the earth surging upwards. Less a sense of falling than of flying, of accelerating suspension. A streak of cloud below and then gone. Struggling to hold the freefall position, reaching for the ripcord and waiting before looking up to check that the canopy has blossomed overhead . . .

All of this was happening at the Parachute Club at Sibson Airfield near Peterborough, part of the Accelerated Freefall (AFF) course they run there. We were in the bar watching – what else? – *Drop Zone*, waiting for the weather to clear. The windsock was stretched out horizontal, holding its own. Clouds were coming in at tree-top level – except there were no trees and so the clouds perched on the horizontal airfield buildings. Corrugated iron banged and rattled in the wind.

After *Drop Zone* we watched a parachuting video and then, when I had become bored with that, I listened to the other jumpers swap parachuting stories or flicked through parachuting magazines. I liked the letters to the editor, especially the sign-offs, the many variants of the fraternal 'Blue skies and soft landings'.

I was quite happy with the grey skies that prevented my jumping but I was very worried about the idea of hard landings. Ten days ago I'd been on the brink of cancelling because I was worried about my right knee which, as far as I can tell, has got everything wrong with it: ligaments, cartilage, tendons, bone – you name it. In parachuting jargon my knee was undergoing a major malfunction, a total, a streamer. I called Kevin McCarthy, my instructor-to-be, to say that I was worried: I'd heard that a parachute landing was like jumping off a twelve-foot wall and wondered if my knee was up to it. How bad *were* the landings? With the parachutes we use, if you get it right, said Kevin, it's like stepping off a kerb. And if you get it wrong? Then it's like stepping off a table. Reassured, I said I'd be there in three days and hurried out to buy a serious knee support.

Then something strange happened. The morning before I was due to start the freefall course I woke up with my lower back paralysed. I couldn't stand up straight, could hardly walk, couldn't even bend down to get my knee support on. I called to cancel because although my knees were fine, now my back had gone. What happened? Kevin asked. I didn't know. The only thing I could think was that I had sat in a draught at a dinner party the night before. In the argot of *Point Break*, I was looking for the ultimate ride, but I had started by coming up with the ultimate lame excuse.

A week later I was fully mobile again in the sense that I was only severely incapacitated by my knee. I called Kevin to say I was raring to go and the next day I headed for the airbase. It's the obvious place to have a parachute course. Driving from central England the sky gets perceptibly bigger as you head east. Everywhere else in England the sky feels hemmed in. East Anglia is the only place where birds get a chance to stretch their wings. Elsewhere you get little shires of cumulus, here you get great prairies of cloud.

The first day was all instruction, all training. Kevin took me through what would happen on my first jump: exit the aircraft at about 12,000 feet with two instructors grabbing hold of you. Get into the freefall position: back arched, head, arms and legs stretched back. Check the altimeter, tell your instructors in turn that you're OK and then go through the motions of pulling your ripcord. Repeat twice. Keep checking the altimeter and continue dropping until you get to 5,500 feet, whereupon you pull the ripcord, the parachute opens and you guide yourself to the drop zone.

We went through the routine over and over, dirt-diving in the hangar. Say it out loud: 'Look' (for your ripcord), 'Reach' (your right hand down and your left hand over your head so that you maintain a stable position), 'Pull', 'Count' ('one thousand, two thousand, three thousand, four thousand'), 'Look up', 'Check the canopy'.

Once the canopy is open there is then the (to my mind) tricky business of recognising the drop zone, steering yourself towards it (taking into account windspeed and direction), avoiding power lines, houses and roads and landing safely. Assuming the canopy *does* open, that is. If it doesn't, if you've got a streamer (which I was certain I would have) then you have to cut away the main 'chute (a two-stage, right-hand manoeuvre) and pull the reserve. I kept practising this in the hangar, suspended on a pulley about twenty feet from the floor, and I kept getting it wrong.

I was more confident about the written test but I made a mess of that too. I got the most rudimentary questions wrong but it was the last one that really gave me pause. 'Are you satisfied with the instructions you have received and do you feel ready to make your first AAF skydive?' Yes, I did feel satisfied with the instruction, but no I didn't feel confident about doing the jump. And if I didn't feel confident maybe that was because the instruction had been defective in some ways – why else was I getting so many things wrong? I mulled the question over, pencil in hand. In a life riddled with self-doubt I have always been confident of one thing: I am extremely clever – so *why* was I having such trouble absorbing things? Why did I have this block? Because I didn't *want* to learn. I wanted to fail this little exam, wanted Kevin to take me aside and say, 'Hey, you're a stand-up guy, you've tried your best but you're just not cut out to be a skydiver. Try macramé.' Like that I could have exited with dignity of a sort. I could have done what I always seek to do in life: avoid responsibility for my actions and blame someone else. Instead, he said sleep on it. I couldn't even get that right. I lay awake on it.

Did I feel ready to do the jump? I certainly didn't feel competent to deal with an emergency, but then, I reasoned, I didn't feel competent to deal with any aspect of my life so it would have been very strange if I had felt competent to deal with this. In training Kevin said the moves had to be done automatically, robotically, because when we were doing it for real we were going to be in what he called 'a stress situation'. Now it so happens that I am no stranger to stress situations. I am in a stress situation for most of my waking hours and recently I had been in what might be called an accelerated stress situation. I had bought a kitchen from Ikea and had tried to assemble and fit it myself. After three days of solid head-fuck and no progress made I gave up, abandoned it, left it in pieces. No sooner had I thought of that than I thought of my tabla classes, which I had started two weeks ago and had abandoned after just one lesson because I couldn't get the hang of that either. I gave up on everything. I was always worrying about my knee and my back but they were camouflage ailments: my real problem was my personality: I was a chronic giver up. In fact, if we are being utterly frank, for the last several months my greatest desire had been to give up living. All day long, behind the beat of my pulse, I heard another beat: *I don't want to live, I don't want to live.* At least three or four times a day I would think of killing myself. But now, on the brink of my first parachute jump, I found I had even given up on the idea of giving up. Faced with the statistically remote danger of death by freefall, I wanted very much to live.

The last thing I wanted to do was to die – but I was also aware that my doubts about surviving the skydive were nourished by the same pervasive sense of worthlessness, of my being, in both the colloquial and literal sense *hopeless*, that had driven me into suicidal depression in the first place . . .

I drove back to the airbase the next day, tired from lack of sleep but feeling calmer. The weather was perfect in the sense that it was absolutely terrible: wind, cloud, even a little drizzle. Perhaps this is why, as we rehearsed the jump again (the jump which, in view of the weather conditions, looked increasingly theoretical), I made far fewer mistakes, performed the moves much more smoothly. A couple of times in the course of the morning the sky cleared and the wind dropped enough for experienced skydivers to do a jump. Only one person did a first-time jump that morning and she was blind. Yes, really. She was doing a tandem jump with one of the instructors. After that the weather closed in again and everyone stopped jumping. We watched some more parachuting videos and hung out. It's nice, the parachuting fraternity, the way that gatherings of people sharing a similar passion always are: you probably get the same feeling among the dog-owners at Crufts. I wasn't quite a part of it but I wasn't excluded from it either. Someone asked if I wanted to play *Risk* and from then on I was in my element. The game went on for hours. Some people started playing volleyball outside. I conquered Asia, advanced into eastern Europe and then began a long retreat which also went on for ages. When I saw I couldn't win I gave up and went to play volleyball. It was turning into an idyllic afternoon, a kind of youth club for people of all ages. The sun started shining. If they'd had a Ping-Pong table I'd have been in paradise. As I got caught up in the volleyball I completely forgot that I was here to do a parachute jump. I didn't even think about my Ikea kitchen. I didn't have a care in the world.

The windsock began to detumesce. Kevin said it looked like we might be able to jump. I got kitted up, surreptitiously put on my knee support, helmet and goggles. Practised the routine again. One plane load of jumpers went up. Then the gap in the sky closed. It was six-thirty. I went off and played volleyball again, exactly as before, except this time I kept my jump suit and knee support on.

The windsock sagged, dangled, so to speak, around its own ankles at about the 5 mph mark. The tannoy declared that the best weather of the week was on its way in. The evening sky began blazing blue. Will your magazine want pictures? Kevin asked. Yes, I said. Definitely. We went over to the plane, practised the exit a couple of times, and took off.

We circled upwards. As we passed through the last rags of cloud I checked my altimeter: 5,500 feet, the height at which I would pull the ripcord. Christ! We got up to 8,000 feet. Kevin gave me the thumbs up. 10,000 feet. I thought of the Nike slogan. '*Just Do It*'. It really was as simple as that. So I did, I just did it: I held out my hands and crossed my forearms back and forth over each other in the universal gesture of abandonment, the gesture the referee makes to a boxer to show the fight is over.

'I'm not going to do it,' I yelled above the engine.

'You're sure?'

'Yes.'

'Is it something you want to talk about.'

'Oh no.'

It was as easy as that. It was as simple as saying 'no' when asked if you wanted to dance. 'So what happened?' friends asked later. 'You lost your nerve?' But it wasn't that at all. I had no nerve to lose. There was no battle between desire and dread: I just didn't have the slightest inclination to jump. On the edge of the vast ballroom of the sky I decided to sit this one out. I was quite happy where I was, in the plane, thank you very much.

The other jumpers – including the photograph[er who] been poised to take my picture – leapt out of the plan[e to] watch. This surprised me because it was precisely my love of watching parachuting that had led me to embark on this farce in the first place. *Point Break* is my favourite film; I even admire *Drop Zone*; I love being in a hotel room watching parachute stunts on satellite TV. But, I realised now, not only did I not want to freefall, I only liked *watching* it on film.

The jumpers were on the ground already, folding away their chutes, by the time the plane landed. I didn't burn with shame like 'the youth' in *The Red Badge of Courage* and there was no sense of being shunned – but I was now emphatically not one of them. This was a community of people united by their love of an activity that I had decided absolutely that I didn't want to take part in, and in so doing I felt as if I had tacitly insulted them. In my sense of not belonging I even detected a glow of specialness which is, I suspect, the trace of vanity that nourishes failures and outcasts the world over. I could have hung around but there was nothing to stay for so I left.

The sun was setting as I drove home. In terms of the dramatic psychology of film I should have had a feeling that I had been forced to confront or recognise some hitherto undisclosed truth about myself, but real life almost never has this allegorical undertow. All I had discovered was that I didn't want to skydive. If my life had reached a turning-point then I had responded by failing to turn. For some reason I kept thinking of my Ikea kitchen lying in torn flat packs and mis-assembled pieces: I was going to have to confront the problem of that kitchen when I got home.

The sky shrank as I headed away from East Anglia and back into the heart of England. I drove home, through the darkening country, safely, thinking about my Ikea kitchen.

1995

Cherry Street

I met Don Cherry only once – that is, I accosted him as he passed by the Sidewalk Café in the East Village and told him how much I loved his music – but his death touched me as deeply as if he were . . . I was going to say 'a personal friend' but that's not quite right. When he died I felt not just a sense of loss but, for several days, as if I had lost my way. Not a friend, then, but something much rarer: a *guide*.

Most reference books still categorise him as a 'jazz musician' or 'trumpeter' but, by the mid-60s, he was already moving ahead of any kind of limiting description. He was a musician and traveller, able to play half a dozen instruments, in any number of contexts. Whereas Paul Simon exploited the energy and diversity of the world's musical styles to bolster his own career, Cherry absorbed other musics by putting himself at the service of the cultures of which they were part. If it is true that we can learn only from our equals, then Cherry learned so much because he found musical equals all over the world. Wynton Marsalis's grumble – that Cherry had 'never bothered to learn to play his instrument' – is both accurate and wide of the mark: it wasn't the *notes* that mattered to Cherry it was the experience of making music, any kind of music. It wasn't what he knew that was important, it was what he had the potential to discover. One of the first albums he played on was Ornette Coleman's *Change of the Century* and Cherry never stopped changing, never stopped learning.

I saw him play on many occasions, in many different formats, in many cities. The last time was in September 1994 at the New Morning in Paris. He was wearing his hair in lovely palm tree dreads and couldn't play the trumpet at all. It was too much for him, he was too thin and weak. No sooner had he picked up one of his other instruments – melodica, wood flute, doussn'gouni, bits and pieces of percussion – than he put it down again and tried somethin' else. He could still play some Monkish piano, could sing a little, but mostly he shuffled around doing his nimbly bewildered dance. He had passed beyond all musical categories years ago and now he had passed to the other side of the mirror: he didn't play music, he *was* music.

There was an irritating woman in the audience who kept shouting and climbing onstage, trying to dance but succeeding only in making a nuisance of herself. Security tried to bundle her offstage but that only added to the rumpus. The situation threatened to turn ugly. Everyone was getting tense. Except Cherry, who leant into the microphone and said, smiling, '*Elle est un grand esprit, non?*' Whereupon she sat down, quietly.

He was born in Oklahoma City in 1936 and he died on 19 October, 1995. It doesn't matter where. He could have died anywhere because he was at home everywhere in the world. Since his death I have always put a picture of him above my desk, wherever that desk happened to be: a way of making myself at home in the world. Which makes him, I suppose, a guiding *spirit*.

In 1997 I was living in Rome, where, if there was nothing else to do, I buzzed around the blazing city on a Vespa. One August night I came across a performance by a group of African drummers in Piazza Santa Cecilia. The drummers were decked out in red, green and gold and there were dancers, too. I was sublimely happy; I had the feeling that I was leading absolutely the life of my dreams. I felt utterly at home in myself. After listening to the music for a while I went to look at the various art objects – donated, apparently, to raise funds for some Afro-European art initiative – that had been arranged in the middle of the piazza. The centrepiece of the whole display was a shrine to Don Cherry.

Later that year I spent two months in North Carolina, working in the Gedney archive at Duke University. At weekends, while my colleagues – who thought of me as a jazz fan – went to each other's houses for dinner or went to the movies, I pursued my latest musical enthusiasm: psychedelic trance. The scene was incredibly dispersed: one weekend there would be a party in Raleigh, the next in Greensboro, then in Charlotte . . . I almost never drive in England but in North Carolina I loved getting in my car and following the directions on the flyer to wherever the party was being held. I always went alone and I never felt lonely.

One Sunday afternoon there was a free festival in downtown Winston Salem. They had set up the sound-system in the Corpering Plaza in front of immaculate, sky-reflecting office blocks. Police cars cruised by frequently, adding to the impression created by the incongruous combination of corporate setting and thumping music, that there is something inherently subversive about dancing to repetitive beats. It was a hot afternoon in November and even though it wasn't much of a festival – a couple of dozen teenagers in phat pants and snowboard T-shirts – there was nowhere else in the world I wanted to be. My whole life had been worthwhile because it had led to this moment, to my *being* here now, engulfed by music.

Standing with my back to the BB & T building, I looked past the DJ desk and out at the older American cityscape of billboards, clapboard houses, water towers, freeway and railroad. A huge sign on the freeway gave directions: straight on, Interstate 40 West; next right, heading our way, Cherry St . . .

1998

Acknowledgements

The first thing I ever published was a 150 word 'review' – if you can call it that – of Milan Kundera's *The Farewell Party* for *City Limits*. That was a massive break for me. I wouldn't go so far as to say that, from then on, I never looked back but, since then, I have usually had something to look forward to, even if it was only a jiffy bag full of books. I would like to thank Vron Ware who – after a certain amount of subterfuge on my part – commissioned that piece, and the many editors since then who have asked for or published pieces, especially those who were unfazed by the fact that the reason I wanted to write about X or Y was, precisely, because I knew next to nothing about X or Y and fancied finding out. Various sized thank yous, then, to Malcom Imrie, Harriet Gilbert, Sally Townsend, Boyd Tonkin, Natasha Walter, Greg Williams, Rosie Boycott, Tim Hulse, Roger Alton, John Mulholland, Richard Gott, James Wood, John Walsh, Andrew Anthony, Tim Adams, Jane Ferguson, Claire Armitstead, Giles Foden, Stephen Moss, Karen Wright and Phil Hilton.

In what has become a very pleasing routine, I would like to thank Alexandra Pringle, Richard Beswick and Antonia Hodgson for their invaluable help in the preparation of this book.

It is no accident that one name – John Berger's – crops up more than any other in this book. At first he was an influence, then a mentor, now – best of all – a friend.

Versions of most of the pieces in this book first appeared in the following publications:

'Jacques Henri Lartigue', 'Henri Cartier-Bresson', 'W. Eugene Smith', 'Robert Doisneau', 'Comics in a Man's Life', 'Nils Petter Molvær', the third part of 'Albert Camus', 'Artificial Stupidity': the *Observer*.

'Ecce Homo', 'Violets of Pride', 'Andres Serrano', 'Pierre Bonnard', 'The Life of Roland Barthes', 'The Life of Graham Greene', the second part of 'Albert Camus', 'Michael Ondaatje', 'Cormac McCarthy', 'Pounding Print', 'Muhammad Ali', 'The Absent Woman: Janet Malcolm', 'Def Leppard and the Anthropology of Supermodernity', 'Cherry Street': the *Guardian*.

'Robert Capa', 'Louis Althusser', 'Jayne Anne Phillips', 'Martin Amis', 'Nusrat Fateh Ali Khan', 'Fred-Perry: Jameson and Anderson': the *Independent*.

'Atkinson Grimshaw', 'Edvard Munch', 'Egon Schiele', 'Milan Kundera', 'Unpacking My Library', 'John Carey', 'Parting Shots': *New Statesman* or *New Statesman/Society*.

'Richard Misrach', 'The Airfix Generation', 'Action Man', the first part of 'Albert Camus', 'Oradour-sur-Glane', 'The Wrong Stuff', 'Point Break': *Esquire*.

'If I Die in a Combat Zone', 'Leaf Reed Land-er', 'The Life of Paul Gauguin': *Modern Painters*.

'Richard Ford': *London Review of Books*.

'Jay McInerney': *The New York Times Book Review*.

'The Guidebook': *Emergency*.

'Rabih Abou-Khalil' is made up of liner notes written for *The Sultan's Picnic* and *Arabian Waltz*.

'Blues for Vincent' was first published in *Give Me Shelter*, compiled by Michael Rosen (The Bodley Head).

'My Favorite Things' was first published in *Lives of the Great Songs*, edited by Tim De Lisle (Pavilion).

'William Gedney' was first published in *What Was True: The Photographs and Notebooks of William Gedney*, edited by Margaret Sartor, co-edited by Geoff Dyer (Norton).

Index of Names

Note: figures in **bold** indicate the main subjects of the essays.

Aarset, Eivind, 292
Abou-Khalil, Rabih, **282–90**
Acker, Kathy, 259
Action Man, **149–55**
Adams, Ansel, 108
Adams, Neal, 164, 167, 168
Adonis, 282, 285
Adorno, Theodor, 157, 258, 263, 314
Akabusi, Kriss, 12, 14
Ali, Muhammad, 18–19, 241, 247–50
Ali, Rashied, 274, 275, 276
Allen, Rick, 321–2
Althusser, Louis, 4, **195–8**
Amis, Kingsley, 207
Amis, Martin, 1, 3, 157, **237–240**
Anderson, Perry, 197, **260–5**
Andrews, Julie, 271–2, 277
Antonioni, Michelangelo, 284
Anwar, Gabrielle, 296
Arbus, Diane, 30, 80–1, 85
Arendt, Hannah, 181–2, 184
Arnold, Matthew, 177
Assis, Machado de, 157
Atget, Eugène, 37, 78–9

Auden, W.H., 58, 86, 252, 315, 316
Auerbach, Erich, 156–7
Augé, Marc, 322
Austen, Jane, 223
Ayler, Albert, 9, 250

Bachelard, Gaston, 157, 259
Baker, Nicholson, 158, 160, 216, 232
Balanescu Quartet, 286, 287
Balzac, Honoré de, 87
Banks, Russell, 159
Bao Ninh, 5
Barthes, Roland, 4, 36, 46, 58, 157, 160, **189–94**, 206, 240, 257, 258
Bataille, Georges, 259
Baudrillard, Jean, 264
Beckett, Samuel, 43–4
Bell, Clive, 251
Bellamy, Peter, 82
Bellini, Gentile, 17
Bellocq, E.J., 74–5
Benedict, Pinckney, 244–6
Benesch, Otto, 137
Benjamin, Walter, 4, 77, 158–60, 257
Bennett, Arnold, 251, 255

Berger, John, 2–3, 4, 31, 50, 121,
    124, 157, 191, 240, 263
Berman, Marshall, 134–5
Bernhard, Thomas, 5
Bird, Jon, 257–8
Blanchot, Maurice, 260
Bloom, Harold, 245
Blythe, Arthur, 283
Bonnard, Marthe, 129–31
Bonnard, Pierre, 34, 38, **129–31**
Bourke-White, Margeret, 62
Braque, Georges, 35, 37
Brassaï, 71–2
Breton, André, 32, 35
Brinnin, Malcom, 31
Broch, Hermann, 206
Brookner, Anita 223, 253
Burrell, Leroy, 12
Burroughs, William, 259
Burrows, Larry, 54, 56, 57, 58–60

Cage, Nicholas, 165n
Calasso, Roberto, 165
Calder, Angus, 46
Callas, Maria, 278, 295, 296
Calsoum, Om, 278
Calvet, Louis-Jean, 189–94
Calvino, Italo, 69, 71, 203
Campbell, Viv, 320
Camus, Albert, 34, 65, 159, **171–88**
Canady, John, 77
Capa, Robert, **39–51**, 53, 54, 55, 57,
    313–14
Capote, Truman, 31
Carey, John, **251–6**
Carey, Peter, 129, 158
Cartier-Bresson, Henri, 29, **31–8**, 54,
    63
Carver, Raymond, 43, 243
Castan, Sam, 56, 58
Castro, Fidel, 249
Chandler, Raymond, 237

Chapelle, Dicky, 58, 59
Cheever, John, 96, 212
Cherry, Don, 291–2, **359–61**
Cholitz, General Dietrich von,
    47–8
Cioran, E.M., 248
Clark, Steve, 320
Claxton, William, 65
Coleman, Ornette, 250, 271, 274,
    360
Coleridge, Samuel Taylor, 77
Collen, Phil, 320
Coltrane, Alice, 274, 275
Coltrane, John, 9, 250, **271–7**, 291
Conrad, Joseph, 241
Constable, John, 141
Cooper, Alice, 343
Cooper, James Fenimore, 218
Costello, Elvis, 277
Cowper, William, 259
Cram, Steve, 13
Curtis, Edward, 103

Dali, Salvador, 168
Davis, Francis, 273
Davis, Miles, 292
Davis, Steve, 272
Dean, Roger, 168
De Beauvoir, Simone, 173
De Gaulle, Charles, 45, 46
Def Leppard, **319–25**
DeLillo, Don, 5, 108, 166, 264n
De Niro, Robert, 238
De Quincey, Thomas, 29
Dickens, Charles, 117
Dickmann, Otto, 306
Didion, Joan, 266
Doisneau, Robert, **65–8**
Dolphy, Eric, 273, 288
Dostoyevsky, Fyodor, 18, 241, 244
Duchamp, Marcel, 35
Dundee, Angelo, 249

Duong Cong Thien, 56
Dylan, Bob, 111, 271

Eagleton, Terry, 258
Early, Gerald, 248
Eco, Umberto, 260
Eicher, Manfred, 292
Eliot, T.S., 30, 99, 251, 252, 267
Ellington, Duke, 285, 289
Elliott, Joe, 319, 325
Ellison, Robert J., 53–4
Eribon, Didier, 190
Eubanks, Chris, 13

Faas, Horst, 52
Fairbrother, Nan, 75
Falkenhayn, General Erich von, 310
Faulkner, William, 218, 226, 231,
   243, 246
Fielding, Henry, 88–9, 224
Fisher, Angela, 328
Fitzgerald, F. Scott, 29–30, 236
Flaubert, Gustave, 36
Ford, Richard, 13, **211–18**
Foreman, George, 247, 250
Forster, E.M., 255
Fortune, Sonny, 283
Foucault, Michel, 160, 190, 195,
   258, 260
Fowles, John, 166
Franco, Francisco, 301–2, 303
Frank, Robert, 54
Frazier, Joe, 18–19, 241, 249
Freud, Sigmund, 168, 197
Friedlander, Lee, **69–73**, 74, 94
Friedrich, Caspar David, 117
Fuentes, Carlos, 31, 35
Fukuyama, F., 262
Fuller, Peter, 261

Gabriel, Peter, 279
Galtier-Boissière, Jean, 47

Garcia, Andy, 296
Garrison, Jimmy, 272, 273, 274
Gauguin, Paul, **119–28**, 132, 135
Gedney, William, **74–94**, 361
Giacometti, Alberto, 34
Giotto, 17
Gissing, George, 251
Glover, Dorothy, 200
Godard, Michel, 284, 287–8, 289
Goldberg, Vicki, 29
Goldin, Nan, 34, **95–9**
Goncourt brothers, 96
Greene, Graham, **199–202**, 252, 255
Grey, Zane, 231
Grimshaw, Atkinson, **115–18**
Gurney, Ivor, 20, 24, 25
Gurtu, Trilok, 291
Guy, Francis, 79

Haden, Charlie, 271, 274
Hamilton, Ian, 268
Hammerstein, Oscar, 271
Harrison, Tony, 256
Hastings, Max, 306, 310
Haynes, Roy, 273
Hazlitt, William, 4, 241
Heller, Reinhold, 134
Hemingway, Ernest, 96, 212, 226,
   231, 241–3, 246, 336, 337
Hemphill, Julius, 274
Hendrix, Jimi, 56, 271
Heppenstall, Rayner, 255
Herrigel, Eugen, 37
Hine, Lewis, 78
Hitler, Adolf, 253–4
Hofmann, Michael, 35
Holbein, Hans, 18
Hopper, Edward, 68
Horne, Alistair, 159
Huet, Henri, 55, 56, 58, 59, 60
Hughes, Jim, 63
Hughes, Robert, 130

Hughes, Ted, 267–9
Huxley, Aldous, 4

Inshaw, David, 116
Isaac, Jeffrey C., 181–2, 183–4

Jacobs, Jane, 80
Jahan, Pierre, 52–3
Jamal, Ahmad, 277
Jameson, Fredric, 249, **260–5**
Jarrett, Keith, 271
Jennings, Humphrey, 64
Joel, Billy, 320
Johnson, Ben, 13
Johnson, Douglas, 198
Jones, Elvin, 272, 273, 274, 275, 291
Jones, Thom, 243–4, 245
Jordan, Ronny, 277
Joyce, James, 70, 140, 218, 241, 255
Joyner-Kersee, Jackie, 13

Kafka, Franz, 203
Kapuściński, Ryszard, 5, 331
Kelman, James, 223
Kerouac, Jack, 286
Kertész, André, 49–50
Kesey, Ken, 83, 165–6
Khaiat, Nabil, 287–8
Khan, Mubarik Ali, 279
Khan, Nusrat Fateh Ali, **278–81**
Khan, Ustad Fateh Ali, 279
King, Martin Luther, Jr, 250
Kirby, Jack, 168
Kirk, Roland, 283
Klimt, Gustav, 136, 137, 139
Koenig, General, 47
Krabbe, Katrin, 12
Kristeva, Julia, 191
Kundera, Milan, 136, **203–7**

Lake, Steve, 275
Lange, Dorothea, 86

Larkin, Philip, 67, 153, 191, 192, 195, 272
Lartigue, Jacques Henri, **27–30**
Lawrence, D.H., 22, 24, 35, 97, 125, 128, 157, 162, 166, 176, 223, 252–3
Leary, Timothy, 83
Leclerc, General Philippe, 45–6
Lee, Ang, 165n
Leopardi, Giacomo, 240
Leopold, Rudolf, 139
Leroy, Catherine, 54, 57
Levitt, Helen, 33, 72
Levy, Howard, 284, 285
Lewis, Carl, 12
Lewis, Wyndham, 254
Lhote, André, 32
Lighter, J.E., 324
Lottman, Herbert, 159, 186
Lowell, Robert, 38
Lyotard, Jean-François, 262

McCarthy, Cormac, **223–31**
McCullin, Don, 57
McGuigan, Barry, 14, 15, 16–17
McInerney, Jay, **232–6**
Mailer, Norman, 71, 124, 241, 247–9
Malcolm, Janet, **266–9**
Malcolm X, 248, 250
Mani, T.A.S., 294
Mann, Sargy, 131
Mapplethorpe, Robert, 96
Mariano, Charlie, 283, 284, 294
Marsalis, Wynton, 359
Masefield, John, 313–14
Massey, Gerald, 120
Masson, Jeffrey, 266
Matisse, Henri, 34
Melville, Herman, 241
Messager, Madeleine (Bibi), 29–30
Messina, Antonella da, 14, 16
Michaels, Anne, 5

Michelangelo, Buonarroti, 168
Miller, Henry, 79
Miller, James, 190
Millett, Kate, 125
Mine, Hiromichi, 58
Misrach, Richard, **105–13**
Moeller, Susan, 55, 56, 57
Moerenhout, Jacques-Antoine, 120
Molster, Morten, 292
Molvær, Nils Petter, **291–3**
Monet, Claude, 130
Monk, Thelonious, 275, 277, 287
Montier, Jean-Pierre, 37
Mueller, Cookie, 96
Muhammad, Elijah, 248
Muir, Edwin, 253
Munch, Edvard, **132–5**
Murray, David, 9

Narayan, Ram, 320
Newhall, Beaumont, 31
Nietzsche, Friedrich, 4, 160, 201, 253, 254, 258, 280, 296
Ninh, Bao, *see* Bao Ninh
Nusrat Fateh Ali Khan *see* Khan, Nusrat Fateh Ali

Oates, Joyce Carol, 241
O'Brien, Conor Cruise, 182–3
Olson, Charles, 262
Ondaatje, Michael, **219–22**
Orwell, George, 202, 253, 255
Osborne, John, 176
Osinski, Christine, 93
O'Sullivan, Timothy, 107–8
Owen, Johnny, 13
Owen, Wilfred, 24, 53, 250

Pacheco, Ferdie, 19
Page, Tim, 56, 57
Parker, Charlie, 286
Pepper, Art, 296

Peraud, Jean, 53
Pétain, Henri Philippe Omer, 47
Pettigrew, Antonio, 12
Philby, Kim, 200
Phillips, Jayne Anne, **208–10**
Picasso, Pablo, 127, 302
Pinckney, Darryl, 95
Pissarro, Camille, 123
Plath, Sylvia, 197, 267–9
Plummer, Christopher, 272
Pollock, Griselda, 258
Pope, Alexander, 259
Pound, Ezra, 34
Powell, Bud, 167
Pozzo, Andrea, 168–9
Priestley, J.B., 253
Proust, Marcel, 29

Ramamani, 294–6
Ray, Man, 78
Reese, Everette Dixie, 52, 53
Regan, Edward K., 40
Renoir, Jean, 33
Ricks, Christopher, 260
Rilke, Rainer Maria, 276–7
Rodger, George, 33, 54
Rodgers, Richard, 271
Roessler, Arthur, 137
Rollins, Sonny, 9, 271
Rose, Jacqueline, 268–9
Rumi, 280

Sabri brothers, 279
Said, Edward, 124, 182–4
Salgado, Sebastião, 34
Sanders, Pharoah, 250, 274, 275, 276
Sandle, Michael, 257
Sante, Luc, 95, 96, 98
Saroyan, William, 41
Sartre, Jean-Paul, 34, 173, 184
Sassoon, Siegfried, 44
Savage, Rick, 320

Sawada, Kyoichi, 54
Schiele, Egon, **136–40**
Schiele, Gerti, 137
Schoendoerffer, Pierre, 56
Schweitzer, Albert, 62
Self, Will, 238
Serrano, Andres, **100–4**
Seymour, David, 33
Shankar, Lakshmi, 295, 296
Shepp, Archie, 273–4, 276
Sherry, Norman, 199–202
Sissons, Peter, 314
Simon, Paul, 282, 359
Smith, Barry, 167
Smith, Chris, 14, 15, 16–18
Smith, Patti, 96
Smith, W. Eugene, 54, **61–4**
Sotelo, Leopoldo Calvo, 302
Steinberg, Saul, 31
Steiner, George, 93, 254
Steranko, Jim, 167, 168
Stevens, Jay, 82–3
Stevens, Wallace, 33
Stevenson, Anne, 267
Stieglitz, Alfred, 35, 37, 64, 87
Stoker, Bram, 116
Stone, Dana, 53, 54–5
Strand, Paul, 33
Sturrock, John, 3
Sully, Francois, 60
Swallow, Steve, 284
Sweetman, David, 119–28
Szarkowski, John, 27

Talese, Gay, 249
Taylor, D.J., 238
Taylor, Graham, 206
Tennyson, Alfred, Lord, 197, 260
Thompson, E.P., 198
Thompson, Hunter, 249
Threadgill, Henry, 283
Toft, Albert, 155

Tolstoy, Leo, 241
Toynbee, Arnold, 262
Travolta, John, 165n
Tuohy, William, 56, 57
Turgenev, Ivan, 241
Tyner, McCoy, 272, 273, 274, 275, 291
Tyson, Mike, 241–2

Updike, John, 214, 224

Van Gogh, Theo, 7–8, 122
Van Gogh, Vincent, 7–8, 123

Wadud, Abdul, 274
Walston, Catherine, 100
Watkins, Carleton, 107
Watson, Paul, 54
Webster, Ben, 9
Wells, H.G., 251
Welty, Eudora, 34
Werkstatte, Wiener, 137
Wertenbaker, Charles, 46
Westerbeck, Colin, 28, 54
Wheeler, Kenny, 293
Whitford, Frank, 138
Whitman, Walt, 79, 90
Wilde, Oscar, 23
Williams, Raymond, 4, 24, 121, 157, 160, 176, 251, 256
Winogrand, Garry, 54
Wolfe, Tom, 249
Woo, John, 165n
Woolf, Virginia, 251, 252
Wordsworth, William, 243
Workman, Reggie, 273
Wright, Wilbur, 28
Wrightson, Berni, 167

Yeats, William Butler, 251
Yourcenar, Marguerite, 30, 77

Zadkine, Ossip, 7–8